Getting Started
as a Freelance Writer

GETTING STARTED
as a
FREELANCE WRITER

Revised and Expanded Edition

Robert W. Bly

SENTIENT PUBLICATIONS

First Sentient Publications edition 2008
Copyright © 2008 by Robert W. Bly

Cover design by Kim Johansen
Book design by Timm Bryson

Library of Congress Cataloging-in-Publication Data

Bly, Robert W.
  Getting started as a freelance writer / Robert W. Bly. -- Rev. and expanded.
      p. cm.
  Includes bibliographical references.
  ISBN 978-1-59181-069-8 (alk. paper)
1. Freelance journalism. 2. Authorship. I. Title.

PN4784.F76B59 2008
808'.02--dc22

                                    2007052670

Printed in the United States of America

10 9 8 7 6 5 4 3 2

SENTIENT PUBLICATIONS, LLC
1113 Spruce Street
Boulder, CO 80302
www.sentientpublications.com

Contents

· · · · · · · · · · · · · · ·

To my godfather, Phil Rosen—in loving memory

*To be a writer is to be a shuttlecock
in a badminton game, one racquet of which
is naïve optimism and the other a cynical despair.*

—John Jerome, *The Writing Trade*

ACKNOWLEDGMENTS

I'd like to thank Connie Shaw, my editor, for making this book much better than it was when the manuscript first crossed her desk, and for her unending patience in waiting for it to get there ... and to my agent, Bob Diforio, for finding a home for it in the first place.

Additional thanks go to Veronica Yates, for her research and writing assistance on chapter 14 and to Victoria Rosendahl for the same help on chapter 16. In addition, chapter 15 reprints, with permission, columns written by Harlan Ellison.

I'd also like to thanks Fred Gleeck and Joel Christopher for getting me started in what is probably the most lucrative money-making opportunity for freelance writers today: writing and selling simple information online (covered in chapter 12).

INTRODUCTION

·························

Kurt Vonnegut, Jr. once described writing as "making idiosyncratic arrangements in horizontal lines, with ink on bleached and flattened wood pulp, of 26 phonetic symbols, 10 numbers, and about 8 punctuation marks." This book shows how anyone with the desire—and the willingness to work at it—can get published and make a comfortable living by making and selling these arrangements to clients, editors, and publishers.

Even a writer with average abilities and modest ambitions can get published and make $800 to $1,000 a week or more as a freelance writer. Most of a writer's success comes with persistence and practice. You have to be a good writer, but you don't have to be great. Other skills, which are easily learned and are discussed later in this book, can take even an average writer to the top levels of success in the field.

Whether you're an advertising copywriter, corporate speechwriter, novelist, short story writer, playwright, freelance magazine writer, critic, screenwriter, new media enthusiast, blogger, newsletter publisher, or poet, others in your profession have gotten their words into print or on the screen ... and now, you can too.

Getting Started as a Freelance Writer covers the gamut of freelance writing tasks. You learn to start, run, and build a freelance writing business doing whatever type of writing you prefer. There are, however, a few things you need to know to take the first steps, avoid common mistakes, and jump-start your writing career so you get published—and get paid—sooner.

In this book, I will show you how, by following my simple guidelines, you can get started in freelance writing and reach your goals—literary and financial—faster.

You'll discover where the work is, and how to get assignments, negotiate fees and contracts, turn out acceptable manuscripts, get paid, build your business, and get published. We'll explore the different types of freelance writing, what is required to tackle each assignment, typical pay scales and deadlines, and pitfalls to avoid.

In addition, *Getting Started as a Freelance Writer* helps writers at every stage of their career—from wannabe and novice to seasoned professional. Beginners learn how to launch a freelance writing business and become profitable immediately. Old pros can sharpen their sales and business skills while expanding into new markets.

One thing that makes this book different from the other "how to become a freelance writer" books on the market is the experience and financial success of the author. I have been comfortably supporting myself and my family as a freelance writer for nearly a quarter of a century, and became a self-made multi-millionaire while still in my 30s. Today my income from freelance writing is well over $600,000 a year.

Another difference is the method I've used to reach this income level. It isn't luck: I've never written a best seller or a blockbuster movie. The methods I have used can be consistently replicated by other writers to achieve a six-figure annual income, even if fame and the best-seller list elude your grasp, as they have mine (but I hope your luck is better than mine!).

A third difference is that I have explored a large variety of writing opportunities and can tell you about them firsthand. These include annual reports, sales brochures, essays, newspaper and magazine articles, book reviews, columns, nonfiction books, public relations materials, humor, e-books, audio programs, and advertising copy.

The bottom line: You can make your dream of becoming a published writer—and getting paid for your writing—come true. Not once, but again and again and again.

Whoever and whatever you are now, you can add *author* and *writer* to your list of credentials—and your business card. You can have your writing read by thousands, maybe even millions, of people—people who will be educated, inspired, motivated, aided, moved, and entertained by your words. You may even make a tremendous difference in some of their lives.

You can become a little bit famous—and maybe a little bit rich. As a direct result of becoming a writer, I have met celebrities, shaken hands with presidents, appeared on TV and radio, been profiled in major newspapers and magazines, given speeches at huge business conferences, earned many millions of dollars from my writing, and improved people's lives.

Plus, I've been able to do all this working for myself. I'm my own boss. I set my own schedule—get up when I want and quit work when I feel like it. I do what I want to do, when I want to do it, and I am never bored. And oh yes, I don't wear a suit and tie, my dry-cleaning bill is close to zero, and there's no commute.

I work alone in my office: We have a virtual office, and my assistants live and work in their own homes, in another town about eight miles south. And, having earned $672,282 last year from my writing, I can well afford to pay assistants to do tasks I find boring or distasteful—from negotiating fees and deadlines with clients, to bookkeeping and billing.

If I am interested in a subject, chances are I can get someone to pay me to write about it, most of the time—even if I'm not an expert on the topic. No college degree or special credentials are required.

Sound good to you? Then let's get started!

Do You Really Want to Be a Writer?

Writing almost killed you, and the hard part was making it look easy.
—Roger Angell, writing about E.B. White in *The New Yorker*

May Sarton once said that many people want to have written a book, but very few actually want to do the work of writing one. This chapter can help you assess whether you have the skill, talent, aptitude, temperament, and desire to become a freelance writer—and whether you should be a full-time freelancer, moonlighter, part-timer, occasional contributor, or simply a hobbyist who writes solely for the pleasure and artistic satisfaction.

We will also look at the pros and cons of the freelance writing life, as well as the truth behind some popular myths (e.g., "Writers in Hollywood spend their days rubbing elbows with movie stars" and "You have to have a literary agent who lives in New York City to get your book published").

What is a successful writer? The first step in achieving success in writing or any other endeavor is to come up with a satisfactory definition of what success means to you. You must create a personal definition of success that makes sense for you and fits your personality, ambitions, dreams, goals, and lifestyle. If you let others impose their definition of success on you, you are unlikely to meet it, and despair and unhappiness will be the result.

My personal definition of success (which will likely not be the same as yours) is the following: *to do what I want to do, when I want to do it, with people I like and want to work with, and to avoid doing the things I don't want to do, and get paid well for it*—sometimes very, very well.

I'm happy as a writer because writing allows me to fulfill all those requirements. Writing, reading, and thinking are the only three things I love to do (at least for long stretches of time), and as I'm a freelance writer, they are virtually the whole of my job.

One of my major goals in life is to avoid boredom, for the simple reason that I hate to be bored (a pet peeve I find that many writers have in common). When I worked on the marketing communications staff of a Fortune 500 corporation, I spent less than 10 percent of my time actually writing, though I had naively thought I was taking a job as a writer. Most of my time was spent in meetings, doing paperwork, and performing project management and administrative tasks, and I disliked all of that busy-work intensely.

I thought that by quitting to become a full-time freelance writer I would escape all that, and I was largely right. As my income grew, I had the cash flow to outsource everything I found undesirable about being self-employed—bookkeeping, tax preparation, filing, photocopying, routine Internet research, scheduling, negotiating contracts, and selling my work—to various vendors. That gave me what I value most in a career: freedom from doing things that bore me.

My writing income enables me to carry over this outsourcing of the undesirable to other tasks at home. I don't mow the lawn, rake leaves, shovel snow, or do handyman repairs around the house; instead, I hire others to do these things for me.

A few years ago, I was asked to give a talk to a convention of college seniors. Perhaps a thousand students were in the audience. I stepped up to the lectern and asked, "How many of you want to be successful?" Virtually all the students in the audience raised their hands. I then asked, "How many of you can tell me what success is?" Not a single person out of the thousand volunteered to give an answer. I said, "If you don't know what success is, how can you possibly become successful?"

You get the point. Danielle Steel and Stephen King are multimillionaires from their writing, but you may not have to duplicate their sales or wealth to find success and happiness in your own writing career.

Would I like to become a published novelist or a best-selling writer? Yes. Do I consider these achievements as necessary to my being successful as a writer? No. Your definition of success may be different.

TEN SECRETS OF SUCCESS

My good friend Roger Parker, who writes great books on desktop publishing and web design, recently asked me to come up with "10 success secrets" and talk about them in a tele-seminar, which I did.

Here's my list of what I think it takes to be successful:

1. Define what success means to you. Then pursue success as you define it—not as others do. For me, it's doing what I want, and avoiding the things I don't want to do. For you, it may be getting your novel published or becoming a radio talk show host.

2. Love what you do for a living. Noel Coward said, "Work is more fun than fun." Time never moves more slowly during the day than when you are working at a job you loathe.

3. Find the intersection of your passions and the needs of the market. What do you like that also interests other people, and that they are willing to pay for? Therein lies your writing career.

4. Become the best you can be at what you do. Work tirelessly to increase your skill and knowledge. It's been said many times that there are only two ways to improve your writing: write and read. So do both. Write every day. Read all the time, and read widely. Also, take writing classes. Attend writing conventions.

5. Specialize. Master and dominate a niche of the market, rather than attempt to be a jack of all trades. Constantly add to your storehouse of knowledge and experience in the specialized fields you write about, whether it's cats, crafts, cooking, or computers.

6. Be the consummate craftsman. Always do your best on every job.

Never give work short shrift because you agreed to short money. Once you tell the client you are taking the job, she expects and deserves nothing less than your best effort.

7. Be the client's ally and partner, not her adversary. The angry writer who is constantly screaming at agents and editors is a cliché. Embrace the positive attitude of prolific author Isaac Asimov, who said, "I love my publishers!"

8. Do not undercharge. Charge what you are worth. But don't overcharge; don't make it difficult for clients to hire you.

9. When in doubt, get the money up front. A retainer check for half the fee is the quickest way to separate serious clients from time-wasting prospects.

10. Don't waste time with things that may be pleasant or entertaining, but do not help you achieve your goals. Value your time as the precious, limited resource it is.

THE SARTON SYNDROME

I think May Sarton is right on the money: A lot of people find the idea of being a published author appealing. But whether they are willing to do what it takes to achieve that goal is another story.

How about you?

There is a huge difference between wanting to be a writer and actually wanting to *write*.

You and I have images—stereotypes—stored in our minds of what we imagine writers and their lives to be like. These images can include:

- The macho writer—Ernest Hemingway

- The "literary lion"—Norman Mailer

- The fashionably misanthropic writer—Fran Leibowitz

- The gritty urban realist—Richard Price

- The best-selling writer of popular commercial novels—John Grisham

- The spellbinding master storyteller—Stephen King

- The outlaw—Hunter Thompson

- The recluse—J.D. Salinger

- The angry young man—Harlan Ellison

- The romance queen—Danielle Steel

- The prolific nose-to-the-grindstone writer—Isaac Asimov

- The tough guy gumshoe—Mickey Spillane

- The cowboy—Zane Grey

- The hip urban Gen-Xer—Bret Easton Ellis, Tama Janowitz

- The serious new generation of artist—Michael Chabon, Jonathan Franzen

- The studious intellectual—Joyce Carol Oates, Joan Didion, Barbara Ehrenreich

- The dandy—Tom Wolfe

- The military man—Tom Clancy

Do you ever find yourself wishing you were one of these people ... or other writers you admire?

Do you spend any significant time daydreaming about any of these scenarios and scenes?

- You are living in a loft in Greenwich Village or the Upper West Side of Manhattan—and not the suburban split-level that is your current residence.

- You are holding a handsome, glossy hardcover book—your first published novel.

- You are hobnobbing with literary agents and editors ... you spend part of the day emailing and chatting on the phone with other famous writers ... evenings you attend fabulous book parties for authors who are your peers and colleagues.

- You pick up the Sunday *Times*, and your book is given a glowing review on the front cover of *The New York Times Book Review*.

- The phone rings. It's Oprah's people. They want your novel as the next book club selection ... and can you fly out to Chicago tomorrow to tape a show with her?

- You are being interviewed on *The Tonight Show* about your latest book. In response to Leno's question, you say something witty. The guest sitting next to you laughs and looks at you admiringly. It is (depending on your gender and sexual orientation) either George Clooney or Jessica Alba.

- You get your latest royalty statement. Once again, your books have outsold the Harry Potter series. Inside is your royalty check for $1.4 million.

- Your agent calls. Stephen Spielberg wants to make your book into a movie ... but he'll do it only if you agree to write the script.

- You take up pipe smoking and people actually think you look distinguished, not silly.

Although you may think I am reaching too high to make a point, it is images like these that instill in thousands of people the desire to be a best-selling author. But these daydreams, pleasant though they may be, are the worst reasons to want to become a writer ... and if they are the sole reasons you want to become a writer, I urge you to consider another profession or avocation, like dentistry or playing the piano.

The fact is that writing is seldom glamorous, often difficult, and financially rewarding to only a minority of practitioners. As Robert Benson writes in his book *The Game* (Penguin Putnam, 2001):

> Most of us [writers] spend most of our days seldom seeing or talking to other people beyond those who live in the same house that we do. Most of us stay in our houses or our studios most all day and avoid the telephone and the radio. We can go days or weeks without leaving our houses or our neighborhoods except to run a few errands.

Many of us have days that are made up of little routines that we practice to get ourselves into the places and the frames of mind where we are supposed to be in to try to make sentences. We get up at certain times, we try to show up at our writing at certain times, we work a certain number of hours or pages per day, and then we try our best to forget about the work so that we can be human beings to the people that we live with.

With the possible, and highly likely exception that what we do very often has less material value to anyone else on earth than does the work that other people do, our lives are pretty much like everyone else's, only without the commute, the insurance benefits, or the steady paycheck.

William Zinsser, author of *On Writing Well* (HarperCollins, 2001), agrees with Benson's assessment, stating, "Professional writers are solitary drudges who seldom see other writers."

The common denominator among people who are writers is that they like to write. This is not true in other professions. Many investment bankers, for instance, don't love helping companies buy other companies; they go into investment banking because they see it as a way to make a lot of money. And how many dentists just can't get enough of bad teeth and saliva?

Writing, on the other hand, is a field in which the average practitioner does not make much money (of course, there are many exceptions). And so money is not the primary motivator to go into writing; you should become a writer because you love to write.

I'd go so far as to say that if you don't love to write, don't be a writer; and certainly do not become a writer if you don't at least like to write. If you're going to spend all day doing distasteful work, or work that doesn't move you or thrill you or stimulate you or excite you, there are plenty of other jobs you can do—investment banker, orthodontist, middle manager, Dunkin' Donuts franchise owner—that can at least pay you handsomely while you do them.

The happiest writers love to write. They have an all-consuming passion for writing and reading and the written word. Ray Bradbury, author of *The Martian Chronicles* and other classic science fiction novels, captures this passion eloquently:

> The act of writing is, for me, like a fever—something I must do. And it seems I always have some new fever developing, some new love to follow and bring to life.
>
> I've never doubted myself; I've always been so completely devoted to libraries and books and authors that I couldn't stop to consider for a moment that I was being foolish. I only knew that writing was in itself the only way to live.

Harlan Ellison, author of numerous novels and short stories, explains it this way:

> I think I came out of the womb writing. The first thing I ever sold was when I was 10 years old. A five-part serial to the *Cleveland News* young people's column. And before that I was doing my own little newspaper in the neighborhood. I've always written. I never decided to be a writer, I was just ... There's a scene of a film called *The Red Shoes*, where Moira Shearer, who was a brilliant ballerina, is talking to the ballet entrepreneur. A Balanchine kind of figure. And he says to her, "Why must you dance?" She wants to join his company, and she thinks about it a moment and then she says to him, "Why must you breathe?" And he says, "I must!" And she smiles and walks away. I didn't choose to be a writer. That's what I am—I'm a writer.

Isaac Asimov is my role model for a productive writer who just loves writing more than anything else. In his autobiography *I, Asimov* (Doubleday, 1994), he wrote:

> I would rather write than do anything else. In fact, some wise guy, knowing of my penchant for gallantry to young women, asked me during a question-and-answer session once, "If you had to choose between writing and women,

Dr. Asimov, which would you choose?'"

I answered instantly, "Well, I can type for 12 hours without getting tired."

People say to me sometimes, "How disciplined you must be to get to work at the typewriter every day."

I answer, "I'm not disciplined at all. If I were, I could make myself turn away from the typewriter now and then, but I'm such a lazy slob I can never manage it."

It's true. It doesn't take discipline for someone like Bing Crosby or Bob Hope to play golf all day long. It doesn't take discipline for Joe-Six-Pak to snooze in his chair while watching television. And it doesn't take discipline for me to write.

And I am unseducible. The fact that it is a perfect day outside makes no impact on me. I have no desire to go out and get some healthful sunshine. In fact, a perfect day fills me with the nameless dread (usually fulfilled) that Robyn will come to me, clapping her little hands in excitement, and say, "Let's take a walk in the park. I want to go to the zoo."

Of course, I go, because I love her, but I tell you I leave my heart behind, stuck in the typewriter keys.

So you will understand when I tell you that my favorite kind of day (provided I don't have an unbreakable appointment that is going to force me out into it) is a cold, dreary, gusty, sleety day, when I can sit at my typewriter or word processor in peace and security.

John Steinbeck said that when you write, you have to act as if what you are writing is the most important thing in the world, even though you know it is not. Most successful writers I know have a compulsion to write, regardless of whether they think their work makes any real difference to the world. In his poem "Night Letter to the Reader," Billy Collins says, "I am wondering if you are even listening and why I bother to tell you these things that will never make a difference ... But this is all I want to do."

So the first requisite or issue to consider in your writing career is: Do you want to do the work? Do you want to spend your time writing? Or are you, as May Sarton suspects, more enamored with the thought of being a published author than with the act of writing itself? To be happy and successful as a writer, the latter should be much more important to you than the former. Not that we can ignore the issue of publishing, though; it is also central to being a freelance writer.

THE QUESTION OF TALENT

Okay. You like to write. But are you any good at it? Good enough to get published or even make a living at it?

One of the questions I am asked most frequently by beginning writers is, "How do I know whether I am a good enough writer to become a successful freelancer?" What I've found is this: If you are reading this book and you have the burning desire to become a freelance writer, you are probably good enough. Almost universally, people don't desire to become freelance writers unless they can already write. Exceptions? Of course. But not many.

Here's a more rigorous test: How do you rate yourself as a freelance writer—excellent, good, fair, poor, or terrible? If you rated yourself fair or higher, you can probably make a decent living doing some kind of enjoyable freelance writing work, even if you never write the next great American novel.

Some skills require a lot of education and training before you can do them at any reasonable level of competence; two that come to mind are surgery and playing the violin. There are other skills that most people can do at an adequate level with little or no formal training; these include taking photographs and writing. But even though you can gain a modicum of competence in these disciplines easily, becoming a master photographer or writer is probably about as difficult as becoming a master of the violin. All take long years of practice.

Practically speaking, this means you will be able to write at an acceptable level of competence soon, if you do not already. And that level of writing skill will be enough to launch your freelance writing career.

A friend of mine, best-selling author and multimillionaire entrepreneur Michael Masterson, says that it takes 1,000 hours of practice to become competent at virtually any skill, including writing. So if you write 4 hours a day, 5 days a week, you will have practiced writing for 1,000 hours within 1 year.

After you reach a level of competence upon completing your 1,000 hours of practice, you will then spend many decades, if not the remainder of your life, honing your skills and slowly becoming a better and better writer. This process of improvement continues until you retire or die; you will never reach a point where you can say, "I am now the best writer I can possibly be, and no further improvement is humanly possible."

Further improvement is always possible for every writer—there are no exceptions. As writer Lou Redmond says, "We never write as well as we want to; we only write as well as we can."

There are three ways to improve your writing skill:

- *Become a voracious reader.* Read everything you can get your hands on—fiction and nonfiction, books and articles, plays and poems. Read all the time. Read a mix of popular books and highbrow; light reading and serious literature. Read classic books, but also best sellers.

- *Write as much as you can,* as often as you can, as well as you can. If you travel, always carry a pad and pen or your laptop—or at least a book. Don't waste time when you could be reading or writing instead.

- *Take courses* on specific writing styles, media, and formats you want to master. A good course will at least teach you the formats and rules of that particular genre or medium; a great course will do that and also make you a better writer.

THE PUBLISHING CONUNDRUM

Writing is odd in that it is one of the only arts or crafts in which practitioners do not feel validated unless they attain exposure at a professional level.

If you take piano lessons, your goal is to be able to play the piano at a reasonable level of competence. You are satisfied when you can sit down at a keyboard and play some of your favorite melodies. You don't want or expect to become a concert pianist or put out your own CD.

But almost all amateur writers are not content merely to write and produce material, good though it may be. Their goal almost universally is to get published in a magazine or other medium; and secondarily, to get paid for their work.

Getting published and getting paid are not necessarily synonymous: Many venues for your work pay only in author's copies or not at all. So you have to decide what's important to you: getting published, getting paid, or both.

Even if you desire to get published and get paid, starting out writing for low-pay/no-pay outlets is a path you may want to pursue. There are several benefits, especially if you are a beginner with little or no published writing to your credit, in writing for little or no pay:

- You gain immediate clips and credentials. In cover letters, you can provide editors with a list of publications in which your writing has appeared, and you can enclose copies of some of the articles.

- You improve your skills in venues that are not critical to your career long-term. If you make mistakes—miss a deadline, hand in an article that the editor hates, get your facts wrong, or publish a crappy column—no one else will know about it.

- The no-pay/low-pay publications are generally easier to break into than high-paying markets, so your chances of acceptance are greater. Keep at it, and you will get published.

- Successful publication in the no-pay/low-pay markets can pave the way for breaking into bigger, better, and higher-paying markets.

Here's the interesting thing: When you send someone your clippings, those clippings don't say "got paid $500 for this article" or "wrote this one for free." The recipient of your clippings has no idea, for the most part, of whether you got paid for the piece and if so, how much.

Therefore, although you might tend to dismiss writing for free, don't. For many writers, it's the easiest and best way to get started.

What are these no-pay/low-pay venues I am referring to?

- Local town newspapers—known as "penny savers," these are usually published weekly and distributed at no charge. Their help-wanted sections often advertise "reporters wanted," as they always need writers to cover local stories—everything from the library bake sale to a town meeting about approving zoning changes.

- Trade journals—magazines written for people in specific industries ranging from hog farming to semiconductor fabrication.

- "Little" literary magazines—*Writer's Market* lists numerous magazines that publish poems and stories, and pay nothing (or give you a few free copies of the magazine in which your story is published) to contributors.

- Local and regional publishers of books and magazines.

MONEY AND THE WORKING WRITER

So far, we've established that you:

- Love to write—or at least like to write. If you hate to write, freelance writing is not a good career choice for you.

- You are a competent writer, rating yourself excellent, good, or at least fair at writing. You are not illiterate. Or if you are not a competent writer, you are willing to do the work and put in the thousand hours of practice it takes to become a good writer.

- You want to get your writing published, to see your byline in print. And getting paid would be nice, too.

Now one final consideration: How much money do you need or want to make from your freelance writing? The amount of money you want to earn determines whether writing is merely an avocation or your vocation.

Many writers, perhaps the luckier (smarter?) ones, do not intend to rely on the money they make from writing to make a living. For them, writing is an avocation, a hobby, a pleasurable extracurricular activity. These writers typically seek out obscure or low-paying markets where the competition is less than in major markets, so their chance of getting published increases. Of course, the markets are read by fewer readers and pay little or nothing for articles, but the "writing is an avocation" writers are more interested in the self-satisfaction of seeing their words in print and are less concerned with how they are compensated.

Why is pay so unimportant to writers who are not full-time freelancers? Some writers in this group are retired and have the freedom to pursue their interests. Others have income from other sources—a 9- to-5 job, a trust fund, a spouse, a parent—and do not have to put bread on the table.

The second group of freelance writers is burdened with the financial restriction of having to earn enough from their writing to pay the mortgage and the grocery bills. They do not have a spouse or parent to support them; they have left the 9-to-5 world to pursue full-time freelancing.

Why do we (I am a member of this group) give up the safety and security of our 9-to-5 jobs for the uncertainty and risk of freelance writing? For the simple reason that 9-to-5 jobs make us feel like indentured slaves and bore us to tears. We want to do only one thing—write—and nothing else will do for us.

If you, like me, absolutely cannot abide working in an office or factory doing a job you don't care about for one more day, and want to write more than you want to do anything else on the planet, then you may be blessed (doomed?) to pursue a career as a full-time freelance writer—writing as a vocation.

The main difference between those of us who write for a living and those of us who write just for the fun of it is the "living" part—the need to earn enough money from your writing to live on. Having these financial constraints puts those of us who write for a living in a totally different world from those who write just because they want to.

In his book *On Writing Well* (HarperCollins, 2001), William Zinsser paints an accurate picture of these different writing worlds:

> A school in Connecticut once held "a day devoted to the arts," and I was asked if I would come and talk about writing as a vocation. When I arrived I found that a second speaker had been invited—Dr. Brock (as I'll call him), a surgeon who had recently begun to write and had sold some stories to magazines. He was going to talk about writing as an avocation.
>
> "What do you do on days when it isn't going well?" Dr. Brock was asked. He said he just stopped writing and

put the work aside for a day when it would go better. I then said that the professional writer must establish a daily schedule and stick to it. I said that writing is a craft, not an art, and that the man who runs away from his craft because he lacks inspiration is fooling himself. He is also going broke.

"What if you're feeling depressed or unhappy?" a student asked. "Won't that affect your writing?"

Probably it will. Dr. Brock replied. Go fishing. Take a walk. Probably it won't. I said. If your job is to write every day, you learn to do it like any other job.

And in his book *Portrait of an Artist, as an Old Man* (Simon & Schuster, 2000), *Catch 22* author Joseph Heller paints this picture of a writer, most likely semi-autobiographical in nature:

> His travels through the literary hall of fame of America had steered him into a mortuary of a museum with the failed lives and careers of suffering heroes who were only human. These were not the heroes of the ancient Greeks and Trojans like Achilles, Hector, Zeus, and Hera. These were only driven human beings of high intentions who wished to be writers and who, in most other respects, seemed more than normally touchy, neurotic, mixed up, and unhappy.

"I believe all writers fall into two categories: writers who simply want to write and those who want to make money doing it," writes Kelly James-Enger in her book *Six-Figure Freelancing* (Random House, 2005). "If you want to make money as a freelancer, stop thinking of yourself as a writer first. Instead, consider yourself a self-employed businessperson—whose business happens to be writing. That means you're no longer writing purely for satisfaction. Now you're writing for money. That simple fact is a major mind-set change for most freelancers."

Most writers don't make much money. But Kelly and I are exceptions to the rule, and you can be one, too—if that's what you want.

And not only can writing make you wealthy (or at least financially secure), but there's also new evidence that it can keep you healthy, too. In a 2002 study at Ben-Gurion University, people who wrote about stressful events made fewer visits to health clinics over the next 15 months. And researchers at Chicago Medical School found that when cancer patients without family support wrote about their illness for 20 minutes a day, they reported less stress for up to 6 months.

Plus, as a writer you have to do an enormous amount of reading, interviewing, and research for your writing. So literally, by following the plan I outline for you here, you can become healthy, wealthy, and wise!

In this book, I give you a road map for achieving your ultimate goal: leaving the 9-to-5 world forever, becoming a full-time freelance writer, and earning enough money from your writing to live in the style to which you either have become accustomed or aspire.

2

Things You Need to Know
and Do Before You Start

I never had any choice but to be a writer.

—Tennessee Williams

There's a famous quotation, attributed to various sources: "God is in the details." And a friend, writer and speaker Paul Karasik, has said that "success comes from doing the small things in business exceedingly well."

I was tempted to leave this chapter out of the book, because when we talk about mundane matters like incorporation, accounts receivable, estimated quarterly tax payments, software, or setting up a home office, the eyes naturally glaze over. But you ignore these important details at your peril.

Learn from my expensive experience, and you don't have to lose the thousands of dollars I did by being a sloppy businessperson.

I have no patience for paperwork, filling out forms, keeping receipts, and any of a hundred other details of running a small business, writing or otherwise. This lack of attention has cost me tens of thousands of dollars in lost income and money wasted over the years. And slowly, I am beginning to learn my lesson. Don't make my mistakes; learn these lessons now and avoid my expensive experience.

This chapter covers a wide range of miscellaneous but practical matters, including: personal finance; logos, letterheads, and business cards; recommended computer systems and Internet connections; how to do online research; reference books you should own; organizations and societies worth joining; publications, books, and other resources for writers; setting up and organizing your home office; zoning; incorporation; and more.

MONEY

Americans are terrible savers. The savings rate of the average U.S. citizen today is zero percent, meaning the average American spends as much money as he makes. For a freelance writer, this undisciplined approach to financial planning is the road to financial disaster. Although you can make good money writing, most writers don't. So you have to be careful with your money, save what you earn, and avoid extravagant spending.

The best piece of financial advice for freelance writers I ever heard comes from Florida freelance writer David Kohn, who says, "Live below your means." Train yourself to enjoy the feeling of affluence and power that comes from having money, rather than depend on material possessions for these feelings.

Material possessions weigh you down and trap you. For instance, if you own $50,000 worth of fine jewelry, you have to pay an annual added insurance premium on your homeowner's policy to protect it. Material possessions drain your wealth rather than add to it. The only exceptions are appreciating assets, like fine art, coins, and real estate. Depreciating assets, like plasma TVs and BMWs, rob you of wealth and financial security.

Money, on the other hand, frees you. When you have plenty of money in the bank, you don't panic if your writing hits a dry spell and you don't sell anything for a while. Wealth also allows you to pick and choose your writing projects, rather than feel you have to take everything that comes along just to pay the rent.

Before you take the plunge and become a full-time freelance writer, I advise you to have enough money saved in the bank so that you could live off these savings for 6 to 12 months if you have to. I doubt you'll actually make zero income your first 6 to 12 months of freelancing, but you'll feel less pressured knowing you could survive if that happened.

Can you start full-time freelancing with a nest egg of less than six months of living expenses? Yes, if you have another source of income: a trust fund, a small business, investment real estate, other investments, a working spouse, or even your parents.

Throughout my career, I never worried about retirement, because I figured I can write forever, and writing is so much fun, who wants to retire? So with my writing income, I won't need to live off a pension and savings like most retirees, because I'll always have money coming in.

But things change. What if you or I wake up one day and decide we're tired of writing? Unlikely. But it could happen. And as you get older, you start to think it would be nice to have options—just in case. So you should get serious about money and saving.

LOGOS, LETTERHEAD, AND BUSINESS CARDS

It sounds like a small matter, but I advise you to get your envelopes, letterhead, and business cards designed and printed before you plunge into freelancing full time or even part time.

I recommend doing the same for all the accoutrements of freelance writing. Buy a desk, set up your home office, get the right PC and software, sign up for a high-speed Internet connection, buy reference books and file cabinets and files—in short, set up everything you'll need as a full-time freelancer before you quit your day job.

When you finally make the decision to quit your 9-to-5 job and risk the perils of freelance writing, it may come at a point of maximum burnout with your job—and therefore, you may want to get up and running quickly.

If you have to do and buy everything on day one, you can quickly become overwhelmed and pressured. On the other hand, if your home office is all set up, and you can just sit down at the desk, turn on the PC, and write, you'll be able to concentrate on getting and completing assignments.

Print 500 letterhead, envelopes, and business cards at a shot, but not more than that. Reason: You may want to change them sooner than you think—for instance, add a new website, email address, or logo design—and you don't want to be stuck with a large inventory of the old stationery.

RECOMMENDED COMPUTER SYSTEMS AND INTERNET CONNECTIONS

The standard for freelance writers is an IBM PC compatible with a high-speed Internet connection. You can get by with 56 Kbps dial-up, but I recommend broadband—either a cable modem or DSL.

You will be spending a lot of time on the Internet: sending and receiving emails, browsing websites, and mailing copy to editors and clients as attached files. In the good old days, clients would send you a thick envelope of background information for a writing project by mail or Federal Express. Today, those same clients send you an email with half a dozen or more attached files in Word, PDF, and PowerPoint. You don't want to waste your time cleaning your monitor while you wait for those files to download, which is what will happen with a slow connection.

Therefore, the speed of your Internet connection directly affects your productivity. A fast connection enables you to quickly download large numbers of big files. Once you download files of source material, you want to be able to print them quickly, staple them, and file them.

I have a high-speed HP LaserJet 4si printer, a large unit that's ultra-reliable, prints 19 pages a minute in black, and holds up to 1,000 sheets of paper at a time. The speed of printing is important: Again, your time is valuable, and you don't want to waste it waiting for your document to print. My first computer—in 1982—a Kaypro, had a daisy wheel printer that took more than a minute of agonizingly slow printing to produce a single page!

I know you can send a fax from your PC, but I've always preferred a standard fax machine with its own dedicated phone line. It's simple, convenient, and easy.

Also on your shopping list for equipping your office should be a copier. Yes, my fax machine can make copies. But for anything more than a page or two, it's faster and easier to use a dedicated copier.

You also need an optical scanner. We use an HP Scanjet 7400C scanner with OmniPage Pro optical character recognition (OCR) software. Many times, you will have printed source material available in hard copy but not electronic format, and will want to use sections of that text, provided you have permission, in something you are writing. Retyping that text is an enormous waste of your time. So you want to be able to scan the hard copy and convert it into a digital file. Proofread whatever you scan carefully, as the scanning process is error-prone, and the worse the quality of the hard copy text, the more errors you will find.

FILING

In back of my desk is a bank of metal filing cabinets with high drawers that hold hanging Pendaflex files. Pendaflex files are easier to manage than manila file folders, which tend to fall and slide in the drawer.

Careful, vigilant filing of source and reference material is critical for the working freelance writer. I've had this happen on more than one occasion: An editor or client calls to ask you to verify a fact and provide the original source document. You go to your file for that project ... and you can't find the document. After hours of searching, if you're lucky, you find the document in a nearby file.

This is yet another huge time waster for the freelance writer, and it needn't be. Take the time to carefully organize your project and reference files. Be sure to file documents in the file where you're most likely to look for them when you need them.

You may have noticed that much of my advice on setting up and running your office centers around technology, techniques, and tasks designed to prevent you from wasting time. There's good reason for this: As a professional freelance writer, you'll be under constant deadlines, with your desk full of work that needs to be produced.

It's tough enough meeting all those deadlines with quality work under normal circumstances. But when you're in a crunch, you simply can't afford to waste hours searching for lost papers or waiting endlessly for a manuscript to pop out of the printer, or to download and print needed source files. So it's worth investing extra time and money up front now, to ensure that your office runs as efficiently as possible later on.

Have an accurate filing system for electronic documents stored on your hard drive, too. On every file, I type the file name in the upper left corner of the first page of the document, e.g., "Filename:BOCGaseslaserbrochurewelding1."

I always print out the documents and store a hard copy in the Pendaflex file for that project. If I forget what I named the Word file, I can always find the file name on the hard copy, and therefore, quickly find the file on my PC by searching the file name.

My file naming methodology is client name, topic, type of document, and draft number. Therefore, "BOCGaseslaserbrochure1" means the first draft of a brochure on laser welding written for BOC Gases.

Word allows you to create branched subdirectories. This is a useful tool for organizing your files on hard disk, as long as you keep your branching scheme simple.

Increasingly, writing clients today send you source documents as electronic files sent via email. I print these files out and store them in a Pendaflex file for the job. But now, I also create a subdirectory with the client or project name, and store the electronic versions on that subdirectory.

Reason: these documents often contain text, tables, and graphics I want to use in my draft. As long as I have the original source documents on my PC, it's easy for me to cut and paste the material I need into my document using the Word cut and paste feature. If the client owns the copyright to the source document, there may be text within it that can be used as is in the material you are writing for them. Why waste time re-typing it when you can cut and paste it from their source document to yours?

How to Do Online Research

Using a search engine like Google or Yahoo is a pretty simple matter, and you will gain proficiency as you practice. I don't think there's anything I can add here to help, except that I'm a big fan of outsourcing your research rather than wasting time doing it yourself.

If you handle corporate work, you no doubt command an hourly rate of $50 or more. At that point, it makes sense for you to farm out your Internet research to freelancers, so you can concentrate on writing and marketing. The best way to find people to do online research for you is to ask around. You will quickly connect with a retiree, student, or homemaker who wants to earn extra cash. And you will be surprised: Depending on your part of the country, you can hire fairly intelligent, literate people to do your online research for you at rates between $10 and $25 an hour.

Email is another online research tool. When you are working on a writing project, you can search the web and find the websites of experts in the subject you are writing about. You can usually send an email to the expert right from the website. Explain who you are and what you are doing, and ask if they would mind answering a simple question or two. Then type the questions, limiting them to three if the expert has not previously agreed to field questions from you.

You will again be surprised to find that many experts will answer your questions, some in quite a bit of detail, without payment or without any real proof that you are a real writer working on a real assignment. And because you are emailing, their answers come back to you the instant they send them.

Best of all, those answers are already written out, eliminating the need for you to tape record an interview and then transcribe it. I literally cut and paste the expert's answer into my Word document, then edit it for style and space. Of course, I also save a hard copy of the email.

REFERENCE BOOKS YOU SHOULD OWN

Although the Internet is a great research tool, most writers maintain a modest library of reference books.

The advantage of having hard copy reference books is that they are immediately at hand, and you know they will be there when you need them. By comparison, the article you accessed on the Internet for your last article may no longer be at the same URL when you go back to consult it again.

Most of my reference books fall into three categories: (a) books on writing, (b) books on advertising and marketing, and (c) books on the subjects I write about most frequently, such as energy and biotechnology.

Mark up your books. When you find a relevant passage, highlight or underline it, and note the page number on the title page or elsewhere in the front of the book. That way, you can quickly find the material when you go back to the book.

ORGANIZATIONS AND SOCIETIES WORTH JOINING

Appendix D provides a partial list of professional organizations for writers. Others may be found in various writers' magazines.

Most writers' and other professional organizations have reasonably priced annual membership dues. So if you're not sure whether an organization is for you, you can either attend one or two meetings as a guest, or simply join for one year. Then, if it is not worthwhile, don't come back or renew.

If you find an organization whose members are potential clients for your freelance writing services, it's probably a smart move to join. Reason: Most organizations give their members access to the membership list, either on mailing labels or disk, or as a print directory. For marketing purposes alone, those lists usually more than pay back the cost of the membership.

PUBLICATIONS

Despite the fact that, since the advent of the Internet, information is instantly available online, I urge you to subscribe to several magazines.

First, get one or two writers' magazines, such as *Writer's Digest* and *The Writer*. Beginners will gain useful advice and ideas, while old pros will also learn some new tricks as well as receive inspiration. I specialize in writing direct marketing copy, so I also get *DM News*, *Direct*, and *Target Marketing*.

Second, get a couple of news magazines that can keep you up to date on what's going on in the world around you. I recommend *The Week*, *BusinessWeek*, *Newsweek*, *Time*, and *Forbes*.

Third, subscribe to magazines in the fields about which you write. I write about science and technology, so I subscribe to *New Scientist* and *Science News*. I also write about investments and personal finance, so I get *Kiplinger's Personal Finance* and *Investor's Business Daily*.

You should also get into the habit of reading the newspaper. You probably get a free weekly "penny saver," a local town paper, and you may want to spend a few minutes with that, seeing what's important to people on a local level. You should also read a daily newspaper several times a week, if not every day.

Why read magazines and newspapers when you have the Internet? Several reasons.

First, when you go on the Internet, your search engine takes you directly to the information you need, bypassing other content. With magazines, on the other hand, a collection of content is delivered to you. You are not searching for specific information. So you are exposed to a wide range of news and knowledge you would not otherwise read.

Second, when you read magazines and newspapers, it's easy to tear articles out of the publications and file them for reference as source material for various writing projects.

Here's an interesting phenomenon: When you take on an assignment to write about a particular topic, you will suddenly see numerous articles that are perfect research material for the assignment almost daily in the periodicals you read.

It's not that the topic is suddenly getting in the news because you are writing about it. The reason is that your mind, focusing on the topic because of the assignment, is on special alert to notice and pick out anything it can find about that topic. And often you will find great source material in your periodicals that you either don't find or don't notice on your web searches.

WEBSITES FOR WRITERS

Appendix B lists a selection of writing websites that you may find useful. You can also search on Google for *writing* and *freelance writing* to find additional sites.

This advice may seem contrary to common sense, but avoid spending an inordinate amount of time on websites, forums, discussion groups, blogs, and other online venues frequented by freelance writers. Many writers become addicted to these online activities, which unfortunately pay them nothing and waste time they could be using to write.

SETTING UP YOUR HOME OFFICE

Should you work at home or rent an office?

More than 90 percent of the freelance writers I know work at home. I am in the 10 percent minority that rent an outside office.

Economics dictate that most freelance writers should stick to a home office. Rented offices cost money, and most beginning freelancers just don't make enough to justify the expense.

And for many people, working at home is the ultimate lifestyle—no commuting, no office politics, no dressing up in a suit and tie. But despite these benefits, a lot of at-home professionals (including writers) eventually consider getting an outside office.

Here are some of the most common reasons why:

- *A change of scene.* After 7 years of staring out the same bedroom window at the same tree 5 or 6 days a week, 50 weeks a year, I wanted a change. But there was no other room in my house I could use.

- *Separating your work from your personal life.* A home office makes that difficult. Clients call during dinner; you get faxes at 9 at night. An outside office affords you more privacy and a place to leave your worries when you come home.

- *No kids.* When my son Alex was born, his crying made it difficult to conduct business over the telephone—his bedroom was next to my office/bedroom. When he became a toddler, he wanted to play with me constantly during the day.

- *There are too many distractions at home.* Children aren't the only distraction. If shopping, housework, lawn care, TV, dogs, and the refrigerator beckon too frequently, an outside office will eliminate these distractions. My productivity doubled when I moved to an outside office.

- *Outgrowing your space.* After my 10th year as a freelancer, I had almost 10 times as many papers in my files as I had in my first year in business. I had a lot more equipment, too.

- *Clients visit.* Meeting clients in a rented office doesn't disrupt your home life and keeps the presence of pets, children, and friends from creating an unprofessional setting.

- *Hiring a staff.* Hiring a full- or part-time secretary or researcher requires another workspace. Your home office may be too cramped. And your spouse and children may object to the invasion of privacy.

- *Neighbors complain.* This rarely happens, but the fact is that most home-based businesses are run in offices not zoned for business. An outside office in a business district eliminates this concern and protects you from neighbors who want to keep the neighborhood free of commercial enterprises.

Five key factors to consider when you evaluate office space are size, location, luxury, type of office setup, and cost.

Take the minimum-size space that will meet your needs. Don't overpay for a larger-than-necessary office to accommodate future growth. If you end up needing a bigger office later, you can always move.

As for location, you want a nice, safe neighborhood, but it probably isn't necessary to be in the heart of the local business center. Offices in suburbs and rural areas are much less expensive than office space in major cities. An office close to your home will also minimize commuting.

You also don't need a fancy office. One with good lighting, and adequate heat and electric outlets should suffice. For me, an office with a window and a good view is also important.

Some of the best deals can be found with converted houses and other small office buildings owned by local landlord/entrepreneurs. Oftentimes these owners are least able to afford prolonged vacancies and will negotiate terms with you to get you as a tenant.

If you need support services such as typing, faxing, and photocopying, consider renting space in a small office suite shared by self-employed professionals. Large office buildings are often too costly, but recent high vacancy rates in some areas of the country have made owners of such buildings more flexible.

Rent the office only if you can comfortably afford the monthly payments. Aim for rent payments of less than 5 percent (and certainly no more than 10 percent) of your annual income.

Don't hesitate to be a fussy buyer and negotiate a lower rental than is advertised or initially proposed for the office you want. Most landlords require a security deposit equal to the first month's rent plus the first month's rent in advance. If they ask you to sign a lease, show it to your lawyer first.

ZONING

Most people running freelance writing businesses out of their homes do not bother to inquire about whether they need to be zoned for business.

I can't give you legal advice, since I am not an attorney. So you may want to ask your attorney about zoning and other legal requirements for your home-based freelance writing business.

INCORPORATION

Incorporation is another issue best discussed with your attorney or CPA, or both, to determine which business structure is best for you.

On the advice of my accountant, I operate as a limited liability corporation (LLC). This form of incorporation seems to offer significant tax advantages to self-employed professionals. But there is also more paperwork than for a sole proprietorship, which you must either process yourself or (my preference) pay your CPA to handle for you.

TAXES

My best advice is: Don't prepare your own tax returns. Hire a CPA or other tax preparer to do your taxes for you.

Here's why: The tax laws are complex and constantly evolving, so only a tax professional can even begin to keep up. The tax professional amortizes the cost and time invested in learning new tax laws over dozens or hundreds of clients served. As an individual taxpayer preparing only one person's tax returns (yours), it doesn't pay you to attempt a similar mastery of tax law.

When you use a professional tax preparer, you benefit from his or her more extensive knowledge of tax law, resulting in larger refunds and lower tax payments.

It would likely take you two to five times as many hours to figure out your taxes as the professional. So you actually save both time and money paying for tax preparation rather than doing it yourself. You also free yourself to do more writing assignments, thus increasing your earnings.

The major difference between a freelancer and a full-time employee regarding taxes is that the full-time employee has taxes deducted from every paycheck. But when you are paid as a freelancer by clients, no money toward your tax payments is withheld. To make up for this, the government requires you to make a quarterly estimated tax payment to the federal and state tax authorities every three months. The quarterly tax payment is based on the amount of money you estimate you will earn that year.

If you end up making less money than you estimated, you get a tax refund on April 15. Likewise, if you make more money than you anticipated, you owe the government more money. Ask your accountant to calculate your quarterly tax payments based on last year's earnings; there is a penalty if you do not make quarterly payments sufficiently large to cover what you can expect to earn based on the previous year's income.

3

THE SELF-CONFIDENT WRITER

Nothing can save you except writing.

—Charles Bukowski

A trait I consistently see in novices approaching me for advice is lack of confidence in themselves and their writing ability.

In this chapter, I share with you my two most powerful techniques for building confidence in yourself and your writing abilities: (a) gaining experience part time as a moonlighter before going freelance full time, and (b) becoming a specialist in one or more types of writing or subject areas.

DOES MOONLIGHTING BECOME YOU?

If you're not ready to take the plunge into full-time freelancing, moonlighting is an attractive alternative. Moonlighting enables you to write and earn extra income without the financial insecurity of full-time self-employment. But be warned: In addition to its many rewards, moonlighting has its own share of problems and pitfalls.

Moonlighting allows you to practice being a freelance writer before you make the decision to leave your day job and pursue freelancing full time. It's a risk-free way to decide whether freelance writing is the right career for you.

When you moonlight, you get the rewards of full-time freelancing without the risks. Your moonlighting activities bring in extra income, bylines, and clips of published articles. Because you're not dependent on freelance writing for economic survival, you can pick and choose your assignments, fret less over rejections, and enjoy the luxury of writing without the unrelenting pressure to earn a living from it.

There are disadvantages, of course. If you already have a full-time job, you may not be free to attend client meetings, do research, or interview subjects during normal business hours. When you come home exhausted from a hard day at the office, and it's a choice between putting in an hour or two at the word processor versus watching *Lost* or *American Idol*, TV frequently wins out.

Okay. Let's say you'd still like to try moonlighting. Here are some of the key considerations.

CAN YOU MOONLIGHT?

One question that comes to mind as you think about moonlighting is, "Will I get in trouble with my employer if I work on the side?"

The answer depends on your individual situation.

First, discreetly check your employment contract or company policy manual. Don't ask your manager whether it's okay to moonlight. Don't tell the personnel department you're interested in freelancing on the side.

If your contract or employee manual expressly prohibits moonlighting, you could risk being fired by doing so. If your company doesn't forbid moonlighting, but does discourage it, then you have a decision to make: Are you willing to risk moonlighting and being discovered if it could result in a reprimand or be harmful to your career?

Analyze the corporate culture of your firm. Perhaps you work at a company where management doesn't care what you do in your spare time, as long as you maintain good performance on the job. If that's the case— go for it.

If you feel your boss would be likely to approve of your moonlighting, then by all means mention it and ask for his or her permission. That way, if someone else in the company objects, you have already cleared it with your immediate superior.

If you feel your boss would disapprove of your moonlighting, but would not take action against you, then go ahead and do it. But don't tell him or her. Again, be discreet.

That brings us to another question: Can you conduct your moonlighting activities discreetly? For instance, you can probably moonlight as a ghostwriter with no one ever being wiser. But if you're writing cover stories for national magazines, sooner or later your moonlighting will be discovered by others in your firm.

There are several other factors that determine whether it's feasible for you to moonlight:

- Do you have enough personal freedom on the job and flexibility in your work schedule to occasionally conduct freelance activities, such as interviewing subjects or meeting with publishers, during normal business hours?

- Can you take an occasional personal day or vacation day and use it to conduct freelance activities? For example, my former boss at Westinghouse uses most of his five weeks of vacation to do freelance work for his outside corporate clients.

- Do you have the time and energy to handle moonlighting assignments during evenings and weekends ... and are you willing to give up your free time to do so? (You may say "yes" now. But many quickly tire of moonlighting when they see others relaxing and having fun evenings and weekends while they work away.)

- Can you find clients, editors, and publishers willing to work with you on a moonlighting basis? Generally, this isn't a problem. Some will, some won't. Fortunately, there is more than enough business out there to keep you busy.

- Are you ethically comfortable with the idea of moonlighting? Or do you feel that you are somehow cheating your daytime employer? Many companies frown on moonlighting because they believe it tires people out and makes them less productive in their 9-to-5 endeavors. Do you agree?

- Can you withstand the stress and pressure of having two jobs?

MOONLIGHTING PROBLEMS AND
HOW TO HANDLE THEM

That last question—can you hold down two jobs—addresses one of the biggest problems faced by moonlighters. I've heard several clients of mine complain, "I've hired moonlighters, but when they got busy in their regular jobs, they neglected my work and didn't return my phone calls."

When your full-time work interferes with your moonlighting, it's easy to fall behind on your moonlighting projects. But your writing clients will expect you to meet your deadlines the same as their full-time freelancers do.

The best way to make sure you meet your freelance writing deadlines is to not take on too much work. I recommend that moonlighters handle only one assignment at a time. Also avoid projects with too-tight deadlines. Full-time freelancers may need to take on many rush jobs at once to keep the cash flowing and pay the rent. As a moonlighter, you don't have that pressure, because your day job pays the bills.

Another special problem, especially for freelancers handling corporate and advertising assignments, is whether to let clients know you are a moonlighter. When you're seeking an assignment, there's no need to highlight the fact that you're moonlighting. If the client wants you to perform services at times that would be inconvenient because of your regular job, suggest that meetings or conferences take place after 5 p.m. or during the lunch hour.

If a client asks whether you're a moonlighter, explain your situation this way: "Yes, in addition to handling writing assignments for numerous clients and publications, I also have a staff job as a senior writer for XYZ Company." Don't use the term *moonlighter*, which has a negative connotation for some. And don't apologize. Treat your full-time job (especially if it's a writing job) as a credential that shows you're the best, rather than as a drawback.

Another difficulty for moonlighters is the inability to accept phone calls from your freelance clients during normal business hours. If the calls are infrequent, and your company has no objection, you can make a few phone calls from the office during business hours.

Otherwise, give clients your home telephone number and install a phone answering machine to take their calls while you are at work. A remote feature available on answering machines lets you collect your messages while you're at work. Then you can get back to clients during a break or lunch.

A more difficult stumbling block is not being free during the day to make sales calls, attend editorial conferences, meet with agents and publishers, interview subjects, visit distant locations, or do other writing-related activities that require travel or personal contact.

One solution to this problem is to take your vacation time by the day or half-day for these tasks. This approach is difficult for those with little vacation; it's easier for people who get three or more weeks per year.

If your employer is flexible about hours, perhaps you can arrange to have some time off during the day, which you can make up on evenings or weekends.

OVERCOMING GUILT

You may feel guilty about pursuing freelance writing on a part-time basis. You may feel you're cheating your employer by not devoting your exclusive attention to your regular job, or by sneaking out now and then to attend to some freelance writing matters.

Similarly, if you're married or are in a relationship, you may feel you're being selfish when you sit alone to write rather than spend leisure time with your partner. Parents especially feel a strain when their writing and their children compete for attention.

This is an issue you must resolve in your own mind; I can't do it for you. It may help, however, for you to set a schedule and clearly allocate time for writing versus other pursuits.

Bill Greene, a promotions writer for ABC-TV, moonlighted as a suspense novelist. He lived close to the office, so commuting time was minimal. When he got home, he wrote in his study for two hours until dinner was ready, then spent the rest of the time with his family or just relaxing. Having a set schedule and amount of time for moonlighting, and not exceeding that limit, helps separate work from personal life and prevents guilt feelings.

Conflict with your day job may not be as easily resolved. When I moonlighted, I felt terribly guilty about using the company phone (though most other employees made far more personal calls than I did), rushing out of the office at 5 p.m. to get home and write, taking an occasional long lunch to do an interview, and not devoting myself 100 percent to the company and its business.

I was never able to resolve this guilt. That's why I quit my job and began freelancing full time.

You have to do what works for you, and this is something that all employed people, not just moonlighters, must cope with. Moonlighters aren't the only employees who occasionally use the office copier for personal copying, for instance; many do. Is this acceptable? Your behavior must conform to the personal code of ethics that makes you comfortable.

Best Projects for Moonlighters

Your personal interests, energy, and ambition will dictate the types of writing projects you tackle as a moonlighter. But there are certain assignments that are better "second jobs" than others.

The rule of thumb: The less contact the assignment requires with other people, the better. The rationale for this rule is simple: The responsibilities of a full-time job or raising a family make it difficult for moonlighters to attend to writing-related tasks during everyone else's regular business hours. I discussed ways to minimize this concern earlier, but the best approach is to avoid the situation as often as possible.

If you're a magazine article writer, look to how-to, service, informational, confession, humor, personal observation, and other articles that can be written from firsthand knowledge or library research. These articles don't require interviewing subjects, most of whom are available only during daytime hours.

Interviews, profiles, celebrity bios, investigative journalism, and other types of articles requiring extensive interviewing, travel, and research are difficult to handle when you're a moonlighter tied to a desk job from 9 to 5.

The same goes with books. How-to, reference, humor, popular science, history, children's, business, computer, and fiction books are easier for the moonlighter to do than biography, current affairs, investigative journalism, exposé, social issues, and similar research-intensive books that may require a full-time effort.

If you're freelancing for business and corporate clients, the best projects are ads, brochures, sales letters, direct mail packages, audiovisual scripts, and other short copy assignments. These projects can be handled primarily by mail and phone, with perhaps only one or two meetings with the client.

On the other hand, annual reports, company newsletters, executive speeches, computer manuals, and other lengthier assignments requiring a lot of interviewing, meetings, and back-and-forth contact are more difficult.

MOONLIGHTING FUNDAMENTALS

The only real difference between a moonlighting writer and a full-time writer is the number of hours each must devote to other tasks. Once the moonlighter sits down to write, he or she operates in essentially the same manner as the full-time writer. The rules for dealing with publishers and agents, clients and sources, accountants and tax collectors don't change according to the number of hours you log at your PC.

If there is a difference, it's that moonlighters need much less work than full-time writers to keep busy or pay the bills. Moonlighting novelists may have the luxury of polishing a book longer before turning to its sequel. Article writers may push aside a few lukewarm ideas in favor of topics that truly excite them.

Many moonlighters do no marketing or selling at all and are busy just from the requests that come in over the transom. Perhaps you get occasional requests to handle moonlighting projects from people who know you are a writer. If you accept such assignments, and inform these people that you are actively seeking more freelance projects, you may get all the work you can handle just from referrals and word of mouth.

If your company deals with website designers printers, ad agencies, graphic arts studios, public relations agencies, trade publications, and other such vendors, these vendors could be potential clients for you—or, if you feel there would be a conflict, you can at least ask them to recommend you for writing assignments to others they know who might need a freelance writer.

If your full-time job dictates you keep your moonlighting activities quiet, make sure a vendor will keep your request for work or referrals confidential. Other traditional methods to generate assignments—query letters to magazine editors, book proposals to agents and publishers, sales letters to potential corporate clients—are not subject to public scrutiny and thus are ideal for moonlighters.

Avoid marketing techniques such as print advertising, networking, and telephone selling. These make your moonlighting activities extremely visible and may get you into trouble.

And never reply to a blind help-wanted ad in the hopes of getting freelance work from the advertiser. Once I replied to an ad that read "Ad Agency Needs Freelance Writer for Special Assignments." It turned out to be the ad agency that handled all the advertising for the company for whom I worked as advertising manager.

MOONLIGHTING MONEY

How much extra money can you make as a moonlighter? It depends on how well you are paid and how much you can do.

If you want to write a book, be aware that the average advance for a first nonfiction book or novel ranges from $5,000 to about $100,000. And it can easily take a year of moonlighting to complete the book. So your earnings for that year would be equal to the advance. Future sales may result in additional income from royalties, but don't count on it: The majority of books don't earn back their advance.

How about article writing? Say you get $600 per article and can moonlight two articles a month—that's an extra $1,200 per month in your pocket. (But article payments can begin as low as $50, depending on where you sell your writing.)

Freelancing for ad agencies, corporations, PR firms, and other corporate clients will bring a somewhat higher rate of return. Let's say you write audiovisual scripts and get $3,000 per script. If you do one a month, that translates into earnings of $36,000 a year—enough to considerably improve your lifestyle.

MAKING THE TRANSITION FROM MOONLIGHTING TO FULL-TIME FREELANCER

If moonlighting allows you to practice being a freelancer before making the break to full-time writing, when do you make that transition?

There's no ideal time. I'd say do it when you have enough money in the bank to live for one year, have three or four steady clients (magazine editors, corporate clients, or book publishers), and feel you could earn enough to live on if you devoted yourself to freelancing full time.

Of course, you might choose to never leave your day job. Just because Tom Clancy quit the insurance business after *The Hunt for Red October* insured his future does not mean the moonlighter must eventually become a full-time freelancer. Poet William Carlos Williams never quit being a New Jersey physician, for instance.

People moonlight as writers for all sorts of reasons. Maybe you are looking to sock away some extra income for a child's college education, or find the cash to add a room to your house, or satisfy the itch to see your name in print, or publicize a cause that's important to you, or ... well, any reason is a good enough one.

Once you couple that ambition with the energy it takes to go back to work at your keyboard after you come home from the office, you'll have all that is necessary to be a successful moonlighter.

SPECIALIST VERSUS GENERALIST

I often get asked by writers who are interested in earning a six-figure income from freelancing, "Should I be a specialist or a generalist?"

The short answer: Be a specialist. Reason: Specialists are more in demand, and they can charge more than generalists. You have a better chance of being paid top dollar—and reaching the $100,000-a-year mark—as a specialist.

"Write what you know" is age-old advice for writers. When you are a specialist, you gain the confidence that comes from always writing about what you know ... and avoid the fear and uncertainty that comes from delving into new topics in which you are not an expert or which you may not understand well.

With so many writers to choose from, clients and editors are more likely to call you if they can pigeonhole you into a specialty; you increase your chances of getting called for assignments when you specialize. Need a writer who knows fashion? Call Diane. Want someone who can quickly pull together an article on a complex new computer technology? That's what Steve does best.

"Clients want to pigeonhole you," says Ilise Benun, a self-promotion consultant. "Although you hate it, let them do it. In fact, help them. Give them a box to put you in, and a label to put on your box. There's plenty of time later to tell them more about your full range of services."

What can you specialize in? Many writers specialize by topic. Jerry Baker is "America's Master Gardener." Tom Hopkins is the guy who writes about selling. Robert Fulgham is the touchy feely guy. Timothy Ferris, science.

Fiction writers specialize in genre. Raymond Feist does fantasy; Danielle Steel, romance; Stephen King, horror.

Writers who handle commercial assignments often specialize by format. My friend Cameron Foot writes annual reports and speeches almost exclusively. Katie Muldoon specializes in catalog copywriting.

Still others specialize by industry. David Woods, a colleague in New Hampshire, writes marketing materials exclusively for construction companies. Roscoe Barnes specializes in fund-raising.

And others specialize by medium. My friend Nick Usborne, once a direct mail writer like me, now specializes in writing online direct marketing almost exclusively.

Why do publishers, editors, and clients prefer specialists to generalists?

Say you are launching a new breakfast cereal, and have put your life savings into the venture, along with funds from a lot of anxious investors. You are introducing the product with a TV commercial to air during the Super Bowl at a cost of $1 million. You are looking for a writer to handle the job. Dave has 20 years' experience on Madison Avenue. He has a reel full of absolutely fabulous TV commercials written for dozens of major packaged goods clients, including Post and Kellogg's. Six have won Clios, the ad industry's highest award.

John is also a good writer, but his portfolio contains mostly sales brochures and magazine ads for consumer electronics and industrial equipment. There's one script for a TV commercial he wrote for a local bank, but he doesn't have it on video because it hasn't run yet.

You like both of their writing. Who do you pick?

That's easy. All else being equal, you go with Dave because of his expertise doing TV commercials for major national brands. Why? Because choosing Dave is the less risky proposition. John might handle the assignment brilliantly. But when the stakes are high, you want someone who's done it before.

Clients are willing to pay writers handsomely for their expertise. We can command top dollar, and we are more in demand. Our specialized knowledge and experience set us apart, add value to our writing services, and shift the supply and demand equation in our favor. So we have a constant flow of choice assignments coming our way.

Not only are specialists paid more than generalists, but we can also complete our assignments faster.

When you are a generalist, all the studying you do to get up to speed on gold mining is wasted when you never write about gold mining again and your next article is about raising prizewinning roses.

But if you specialize in mining and natural resources, your accumulation of knowledge and research is amortized over dozens or even hundreds of projects, not just one. You know about and have already bookmarked all the important websites on mining and natural resources. Because you write about this field all the time, you can afford to own the major reference books and subscribe to the key trade publications. Writers who are generalists can't.

You have a database or Rolodex of contacts and experts—key sources you can interview to get information for the article you are writing on mining and natural resources this week. Because you publish regularly in the field, these experts are more willing to talk to you than someone whose name they haven't seen in print. Therefore, you eliminate a lot of the "familiarization research" generalists conduct. You may in fact know more about the topic than the editor or client who hired you. So you can do the assignment better and in half the time it would take a generalist. If you can get twice the fee and each assignment takes half the time, you will make four times more money than the generalist.

Many writers have multiple specialties. *Writer's Digest* columnist Dan Poynter specializes in writing about self-publishing, parachuting, and being an expert witness. He says that three (or at most four) is the maximum number of specialties you can have; any more and you spread yourself too thin. Dan made the stretch, adding a fourth specialty—writing about taking care of aging cats—and he recently published his first book on that topic.

How do you establish and market yourself as a specialist? Here are a few suggestions:

- *Seek out repeat assignments.* When you find a specialty that appeals to you, actively campaign to get new assignments in the field, so you can build a large portfolio of samples in that niche. The best way to do this is with samples. If you want to write on health topics and just had a great article on stroke prevention published in a top magazine, make two dozen copies. Send them with query letters proposing new articles on health to other editors. Some will give you assignments, in part because you've enclosed a sample demonstrating your ability to write well on a health topic.

- *Network.* Join associations in your specialty field. Go to meetings. Network. A friend of mine, freelance writer Linda Ketchum, goes to conferences on nuclear medicine. She is not a doctor, but she is a writer specializing in that field.

- *Increase your visibility.* Write a regular column in your niche industry's leading trade publication. Even if the pay is low, the credibility you gain is priceless. Writing a book on the topic can also help establish you as an expert quickly.

- *Gain credentials.* See whether there is a degree, certification, or other credential you can gain with a reasonable expenditure of time, money, and effort. When I began doing a lot of work in high-tech marketing, I became a CNA (certified Novell administrator), which I did by taking one course. It cost $1,000, but it gave me an instant credential in the information technology (IT) world.

- *Prepare niche marketing tools.* Prepare versions of your one-page bio, letterhead, business card, sales letters, and other self-promotion materials tailored to each niche in which you specialize.

One other point: There's no reason why you can't be both a specialist and a generalist.

I specialize in two types of writing: direct mail and email marketing. But if someone asks me to write an annual report, I don't turn it down. Because I have no special expertise in annual report writing, I don't actively market myself in that area or seek assignments. I do actively seek assignments writing direct mail, my major specialty. Consequently, I write annual reports only occasionally. But I do write them. As a specialist, you can still function as a generalist in other areas when the request arises. Just don't actively market yourself as a generalist.

Your specialty clients won't mind that you take an occasional assignment outside your niche, but just the same, there's no need to advertise the fact. Build your reputation as an expert in your specialty, and clients and publishers will come to you rather than you having to go to them.

4

MONEY AND THE
FREELANCE WRITER

M y father once told me, "Money is not important." But I disagree. Money is very important.

Best-selling author and copywriter Ted Nicholas, writing in his *Direct Marketing Success Letter* (April 23, 1997, page 2), says, "The happiest possible life ideally rests on a balance between four elements: health, career, personal relationships, and money." I share Ted's view.

Without enough money, you cannot afford to feed your family, pay the rent, provide for your children's education, or enjoy the luxuries money can buy. You also doom yourself to a life of struggle and worry over money, and will never experience the freedom and relief that financial independence brings.

A few writers, like J.K. Rowling, get rich. The majority barely get by. I want to show how you can realistically achieve a middle level or better— that is, make a great living even if you never write a best-selling novel or a hit movie or TV series.

By that, I mean you can earn $50,000 to $100,000 a year or more as a freelance writer, with no other source of earned income. And you can become a self-made millionaire, even a multimillionaire, as I have.

Becoming a millionaire is no longer the rare thing it once was; we have more millionaires in the United States than ever before. But having a net worth of a million dollars or more still puts you in the top 7 percent of the American population in terms of wealth.

To earn six figures and become a millionaire, you have to change the way you think about writing and money.

And the first step is to…

STOP HAGGLING OVER NICKELS AND DIMES

I've read dozens of articles and letters to the editor in writer's magazines that go something like this: "The editor said the magazine only paid a nickel a word and no more. But I held my ground. Finally, he gave in and gave me the dime a word I asked for. I doubled my fee, just by asking for what I wanted! You can too!"

While these feats of negotiation undoubtedly excited and thrilled the writers that pulled them off, to me they're a big yawn. Why? Because these writers ended up with the same as they started—peanuts.

Say the article was 2,000 words long. The writer went from a nickel a word to a dime a word—an extra 5 cents a word. The increase in earnings for the article? A whopping $100. Yawn.

If you really want to make serious money as a freelance writer—and by serious, I mean $100,000 a year or more—the most difficult way to get there (if you get there at all) is to argue over nickels and dimes.

To become a six-figure freelancer, you have to get pay raises in the thousands of dollars per assignment—not in the hundreds. But how?

I think the common strategy of aggressively asking markets for more money is largely counterproductive. Take book publishing as an example. Let's say you are writing a nonfiction book on cats for a small press, and they offer you an advance of $2,000. They offer small advances because that's all they can afford based on the economics of their publishing company. You simply can't get a $100,000 or even a $10,000 advance out of them—they'll never pay it.

If you are a shrewd negotiator, and you hang tough, you might talk them up to $3,000 or even $4,000. But that's it. They're unlikely to do better than double the initial offer. So bottom line: You're still working for peanuts.

To get a big lift in fees and make really serious money, you have to do one or more of the following:

- Write about different subjects.

- Write in different formats.

- Write for different markets.

- Write for different clients.

Let's take a quick look at each option:

- *Write about different subjects.* Fact of the matter is, you're probably going to make more writing about sex, relationships, diet, exercise, investing, personal finance, and online marketing than you will writing about the Civil War, choreography, particle physics, or school administration. Exceptions? Of course.

- *Write in different formats.* Some of the lowest-paying formats: magazine articles, newspaper articles, articles for online publications, blogs, nonfiction books, poetry, plays. Some of the highest-paying formats: TV, movies, annual reports, advertising copywriting, speechwriting.

- *Write for different markets.* Some markets, either because of economics or tradition, place little value on writing and therefore pay writers poorly. Other markets, either because the writing generates an ROI (return on investment) for them, or because they value it and can afford it, pay fees near the top of the scale.

  An example of a poor-paying market is retailing. Copywriters who write circulars and newspaper inserts for retailers are at the bottom of the ad industry pay scale.

  Direct marketing, on the other hand, is one of the best-paying markets for advertising copywriters. Reason: Direct marketers see a direct return on their copywriting investment. If your sales letter generates a high response, it's money in the client's pocket.

- *Write for different clients.* Some of the worst-paying clients: nonprofits, local small businesses, individuals, self-employed professionals (e.g., doctors, lawyers, chiropractors), literary magazines, small independent book publishers, trade journals. Some of the best-paying clients: Fortune 500 corporations, Madison Avenue ad agencies, direct marketers, major-market consumer magazines with large circulations.

NEGOTIATING RULES

If you adjust your target—the type and topic of assignments you take, the clients you work for, the markets in which your work appears—you can quickly increase your writing income by as much as a thousand dollars a week or more. You'll also be happier, because you won't be in a constant battle with your clients over money. You'll be well compensated at the normal pay scales these assignments, clients, and markets pay.

Changing your target is what makes the greatest difference in your income. Having said that, there's still additional room to raise your pay even further, though usually by a smaller percentage, through negotiation.

Here are a few tips for talking your way into a higher fee:

- Realize what a given client or market can realistically pay. A publisher who offers an advance of $2,000 may be talked into $4,000. But $10,000 is almost as unlikely as $100,000—it's just not going to happen.

- It is better to have the publisher or client make you an offer than for you to quote a price first. In most instances, their offer will be higher than what you would have asked for, and you can simply accept it. If it's lower, you can always negotiate or pass on the deal.

- If the client won't make an offer and asks what you would charge, answer with a question: "Do you have a budget for this assignment?" If they say yes, then ask, "Would you mind sharing that budget with me?" About half of your clients will say what their budget is, and again, it's usually more than you would have asked for.

- If the client says they do not have a budget, then ask, "Do you have a dollar figure in mind of what you would like this to cost you?" Many who did not have a formal budget will answer this question with something like, "Oh, I don't want to pay more than $2,000 for this"— and usually their figure will be more than you would have asked for.

- When the client will not give you a clue as to what they want to pay, you have to give a cost estimate (I'll go into more about what and how to charge later). But if you are concerned that they will balk and you really want the job, try quoting a range—"between $3,000 and $5,000"—rather than a fixed number ("$4,725").

- The most powerful negotiating strategy is having the ability and willingness to say "no" and walk away from a bad deal. To be in a position where doing so is comfortable for you, you should constantly market and promote yourself so that you have much more potential new business coming in than you can possibly handle.

HOW TO SET AND GET THE FEES YOU DESERVE

One of the toughest questions beginning and experienced writers wrestle with is, "How much should I charge?"

The amount of money you charge and how you present this fee to your potential client plays a big role in determining whether you make the sale and get the project.

Charge too little, and you diminish your prestige and importance in the eyes of your client. You also diminish the perceived value of your services and dramatically reduce your own earnings. On the other hand, charge too much and you may price yourself out of the market, losing out on jobs to other writers who charge less.

Here are four factors to consider when you're determining what to charge the client:

Your status

Are you a beginner or an old pro? Are you well known in your field and highly recommended ... or are you still waiting to be discovered by the masses? Are you a novice, learning your craft as you go, or are you truly a master at what you do? And do you just think you're good ... or do you have the client list, testimonials, referrals, and track record to back up the big fees you want to charge?

Because of their status, experienced writers generally can command higher fees than beginners. But ability is even more important, so a highly talented novice is worth more to clients than a hack, no matter how long the hack has been working. Still, as a rule, those who are less experienced set their fee at the lower end of the scale; old pros, at the higher end.

But be careful about underpricing yourself. Beginners have a tendency to set their fees at the absolute bottom of the scale, reasoning that they do not have the experience or credentials to justify higher rates. I used this strategy myself when I started out because I felt most comfortable with it.

However, clients will probably take you more seriously if you put your fees in the range of medium to medium-high. I have found that the less a client pays for a job, the less he or she respects the work and the person who produced it.

The going rates for your type of writing

Unless you are the leading authority in your writing specialty, or the most in-demand freelancer in town, your rates will have to be somewhat reflective of what the standard rates are for the types of assignments you handle. And even if you are the leading authority, there's still an upper limit to what most clients can afford or are willing to pay you.

In some areas of writing, such as magazine writing, pricing is fairly standard. Magazine editors typically set standard article fees based on what they pay their other writers.

On the other hand, many writing assignments have no such standards, and the fees charged by writers vary widely. For example, in direct mail copywriting, fees for writing a mailing can range from $300 to $25,000 and sometimes higher!

The variation in fees in many writing specialties is tremendous. However, by talking with a few prospects, you can quickly get a sense of the upper and lower limits you can charge.

What the competition charges

Call some of your competitors and ask them what they are charging. Many will gladly tell you. If not, you still need to get this information, so it's acceptable to do so under cover. Call or have a friend call a few of your competitors. Describe a typical project and get a cost estimate. See if they have a published fee schedule or price list, and ask them to send a copy. Some writers post fees on their websites, so Google the key phrases "freelance copywriters," "freelance business writers," and "freelance writers" to see what some of your competitors are charging.

Finding out the competition's fees is a real help in closing sales. You learn just where to price yourself in relation to other writers handling similar projects.

You'll also benefit by asking your competitors to send you their brochures and other sales materials. By reviewing these materials, you can learn much about their sales and marketing approach.

Your current need for work

How much do you need the work and the income? In some situations, when cash flow is slow, you may feel financial pressure to get the work. At other times, you may not need the money but, psychologically, you need to close the deal to feel successful and good about yourself.

Your need to get the work should not really be a consideration in setting your fees. But, practically speaking, it is for most of us. Ideally, you should negotiate each project as if you don't really need or want the assignment. But when you're hungry or just starting out, this isn't always possible or even wise.

Sometimes, you need the ego boost that comes with landing a project or being busy with work. For the writer, "psychic" wages can sometimes be as important as the green, folding kind.

GETTING PAID

What's the secret to getting unpaid bills from clients and editors? Act fast.

Don't let past-due invoices continue to go unpaid. "As bills age, your chances of getting paid fade fast," writes Charlotte Lemoine in an article in *Channel Financial Magazine.*

Research from the Commercial Law League of America shows that 93.4 percent of delinquent debts a month old or less are collected. By comparison, only 57 percent of delinquent debts 6 months old are collected, and only 25 percent of delinquent debts a year old are paid.

Call all large-dollar accounts immediately after the account becomes 30 days old, advises Lemoine. Especially if your clients are large corporations and major publishers, your invoice could be tied up in the company's accounting system. Lemoine suggests finding an ally in the company who can help walk your bill through the system to get you paid.

To collect, be polite but persistent. Use a series of letters and phone calls to remind your clients the bill is past due and they should pay it now.

The first contact is a letter. In this first letter, never get angry or accuse the client of deliberately cheating you. Give them the benefit of the doubt. The first letter is written as a reminder and makes the assumption that the client meant to pay you but simply forgot. This prods him to pay without making him feel guilty. Your goal is not to put the client in a compromising position, or to prove that you are right and he is wrong, but simply to get the check he owes you.

Another way to get bills paid faster is to either give a small discount for prompt payment (e.g., "deduct $X if paid within 10 days") or charge the legal interest rate for overdue bills (e.g., "2 ½ percent service charge for bills 30 days or more past due").

Sometimes, even after the intensive collection effort, you still don't get paid. This means that the client either can't or doesn't intend to pay your bill.

Now is the time to write a strong letter saying that if you do not receive payment within two weeks, you will have no choice but to take legal action to collect the bill. This means court. Send this letter certified mail, return receipt requested, to prove that the client received it. If you don't hear back, wait the two weeks, then send a second letter stating the same thing.

If you still don't hear, hire a collection agency or attorney. Take the client to court. The more paperwork you have—a signed contract, a purchase order, correspondence, source materials, copies of any printed pieces the client produced using your copy—the better your chances of collection.

Here are some additional tips for making sure you get paid:

- *Get it in writing.* Get a contract, signed letter of agreement, or even a fax or email confirmation for every project in writing before you begin the work.

- *Get it up front.* Get a retainer up front, especially from new clients. A typical advance is one-third of the total fee. You bill the client for the second third after submitting your first draft. The final payment is billed upon completion.

- *Say what happens "if."* Written agreements should spell out what happens if the client cancels the project, delays the project, changes the

scope of work, or isn't satisfied. Spell out kill fees, cancellation policies, and billing procedures for these situations.

- *Photocopy the client's check.* Always make a photocopy of the first
check you receive from any client. This ensures that you have a record
of their business bank account, making it easier to collect any judg-
ment you obtain against them.

- *Accept credit cards.* Get merchant status with American Express, Visa,
MasterCard, and Discover. If a client's billing system makes it difficult to issue a retainer check, bill the advance payment to their credit
card. Or get their credit card information as a backup to the promise
of "we'll send you a check." The understanding is if you don't get the
check, you bill the credit card.

- *Do progress payments.* Get payments after major milestones. As has
been suggested, one-third, one-third, one-third is a popular arrangement. Book publishers typically pay half the advance up front, the balance upon manuscript acceptance. For smaller projects, I often get a
$1,000 retainer up front, and then bill the remainder upon completion.

- *Break big projects into several smaller projects.* Have a separate price
quote for each piece, even if you agree to a volume discount. This
way, if you don't get paid, you can conduct a separate collection effort
on each piece rather than the total amount. The dollar amounts for
each item are likely to be small enough to let you use small claims
court, which doesn't require an expensive attorney.

START SAVING TODAY

The classic story "The Richest Man in Babylon" and the more recent best-
selling financial advice book *The Wealthy Barber* both give essentially the
same advice: Pay yourself first.

That means, before you spend a dime this month, take at least 10 percent of the money you were paid by clients and publishers and put it away
in your savings account or another investment.

The remaining 90 percent (or lower) is the money you are free to
spend, whether it's for paying your rent or utility bill, groceries, eating

out, movies, or buying a new shirt.

Saving 10 percent or more of the money you are paid for your writing seems like a no-brainer, but most Americans do not achieve that rate of savings. Incredibly, the average savings rate for American families today is zero percent: The average American spends money as fast as she makes it! You can see why that equation makes it impossible to get rich.

Before you spend your paycheck, invest at least 10 percent of it. My habit is to invest in increments of $10,000: Once I have an extra $10,000 in my bank account, beyond the balance I need to maintain to pay bills and living expenses, I invest it, whether in a mutual fund, bond, or stock. I advise you to do the same.

Other than save at least 10 percent of the money you make from your writing, the most important piece of advice I can give to writers as far as investing and money is concerned is: Start early. In fact, start now. Don't wait.

No matter what your vocation, investing and saving should be everyone's "second career." The longer you wait to begin your second career as an investor and saver, the more difficult it will be to achieve your financial goals and retire in relative comfort and wealth.

Why is getting an early start so important? Compound interest. Investments earn annual returns ranging from 1 percent to 25 percent and sometimes much more. Naturally, the longer you hold an investment and it earns a return, the more its value increases. But thanks to compound interest, the increase in value is not merely linear—it's almost exponential. Therefore, when you start early, your investments will grow in value much more spectacularly than when someone gets a late start. In his book *Money Doesn't Grow on Trees* (Cumberland House), Mark Dutton and Breck Speed write, "Compound interest is the eighth wonder of the world."

For instance, Merrill Lynch says that a person who puts $2,000 a year in an IRA starting at age 18 will retire with more than double the savings of a person who starts only 10 years later, at age 28.

Wayne Kolb, my accountant, had an even more dramatic example in his *Tax Planning* newsletter. Let's say an 18-year-old invests $2,000 annually in an IRA through age 25, with an annual return average of 10 percent, and then stops. By age 65, his IRA will be worth more than $1 million! Not a bad return for a $16,000 investment.

By comparison, if a person waits until age 25 to start an IRA, as I did, he or she will need to invest $2,000 a year until retirement to have $1 million. Two thousand dollars a year for 40 years, from age 25 to 65, is $80,000—meaning the person who started his IRA 7 years later, at age 25 instead of 18, had to put in five times the investment of the person who started earlier.

But whatever your age when you read this, if you haven't started investing in earnest, the best advice I can give is: Do so now. Not in a week, but now. An example from Prudential Securities dramatizes this point: If you open an IRA at age 50, and contribute $2,000 a year earning 8 percent compounded monthly, at age 65 your IRA will be worth $54,300.

Had you opened the same IRA when you were 25, and put in the same amount of money annually earning the same rate of return, at age 65 your IRA would be worth more than half a million dollars—almost 10 times as much.

Be a saver. Invest. Americans are notoriously behind the rest of the world when it comes to accruing wealth. The average American family saves virtually none of their earnings each year, compared with nearly 10 percent in the United Kingdom and almost 13 percent in Sweden.

In addition to investing more, spend less. Lower your expenses. Do not throw money away. Combine abundance with thrift. When my net worth reached a million dollars in my late 30s, I was driving an 11-year-old Chevrolet Chevette, for which I had paid $6,500 in 1984.

Likewise, we lived in a modest three-bedroom colonial in a middle-class town. Could we have afforded a grander house in a snootier town back then? Yes, and eventually my wife won out and we made the move.

But I'd rather have money in the bank than a huge mortgage payment to make every month. Our old house wasn't showy, but it was comfortable, and we didn't need more.

I also advise freelance writers to avoid debt and buy only what you can pay cash for. There can be exceptions, such as your home and maybe your car, but that should be it. For instance, we now live in an 11-room house worth approximately $900,000. And since I own it free and clear, I am freed of the pressure to make a high monthly mortgage payment.

There's an old saying: "Money isn't everything in business; it isn't the sole factor defining success; but it is how people keep score." Throughout your life, you will often ask yourself, *Am I successful?* The search for a meaningful answer can be difficult and frustrating. Many of us spend our lives in search of that answer.

At least the money portion can be measured. Don't sacrifice your life for money. Don't put it so far ahead of the other elements of your life— family, friends, health, career, accomplishment, personal fulfillment— that these other elements go largely unfulfilled.

But do make the accumulation of wealth a priority in your life. When you have enough money that you can describe yourself as "comfortable," that's indeed how you feel: more secure; more content; less worried; proud of what you have accomplished; and more comfortable with who, what, and where you are in life. This I can attest to from personal experience.

RETIREMENT AND THE WRITER

Although you may be thinking, "I love writing; I will never retire," I advise you to save and plan financially so that by the time you are age 60, you have a net worth of at least a million dollars—the amount many financial advisors say is the minimum you need to retire, depending on your lifestyle.

When I was young, I was full of energy—for writing, for life, for intellectual pursuits—and I could never imagine retiring.

But things can change. In the stock market crash of 2000, I lost about half my portfolio—nearly $800,000—and it took years to recover. Also, your energy may not necessarily decline with age, but mine has.

Now almost 50, I am still going strong, at nearly the pace I worked at ten years ago—but I am beginning to have days when I think I may not want to for much longer. This may or may not happen to you, but if it does, you want to have the option of quitting work, laying back, and taking it easy—even if you never exercise that option.

For that reason, plan your financial life as if you are definitely going to retire. Arrange your finances so you will have sufficient wealth, at age 60, to stop working entirely, and live entirely off social security and your investments.

If you are a young writer, you may find this advice absurd. But do it anyway. Decades from now, when you look up, and your kids are grown and gone, and the world has changed, or you have changed, and you want to do something else with your life, you will thank me for giving you this advice today.

5

THE FREELANCE
WRITER'S BUSINESS PLAN
● ●

E very freelance writer should have a business plan. This business plan should fit on one side of a sheet of paper.

The planning process is simple: First, set a financial goal (e.g., "I want to earn $40,000 freelancing this year"). Next, create a plan that shows how to achieve that goal. The plan should show what you have to make per day, then identify what you can do each day to earn that dollar amount.

CREATING YOUR BUSINESS PLAN

I have never had a best seller, despite having written and published more than 70 books. Scriptwriting holds no appeal for me—I'm a print guy.

But I have consistently earned more than $100,000 a year for the last 20 years, and often as much as $500,000 to $700,000 a year by running my freelance writing business *as a business.*

I've done nothing else special. Everything I know about making a living as a freelance writer, I learned by trial and error. There isn't a mistake in the book I didn't make, not a technique I haven't tried.

Now you can learn from my "expensive experience" (as writer Dan Kennedy calls it), avoid my costly errors, and achieve financial security in a fraction of the time it took me. Believe me: If I can do it, anyone can.

How can you achieve a six-figure income as a freelance writer? If you treat your freelance writing as a home-based business and work at it steadily, providing writing services for clients who need them, you can build up a steady base of clients who give you repeat business and lucrative assignments.

According to the National Writers Union, freelance article writers who specialize in writing magazine articles typically sell 3,000 to 4,000 words a month, because of the tremendous amount of time spent looking for work—researching and pitching article ideas. At that rate of production, you can make $36,000 to $48,000 a year, provided you are paid $1 a word—a rate most markets no longer come close to. So the chances of you getting rich writing articles are slim, though a select few have done it or at least come close.

Therefore, you must pursue another type of writing, or at least supplement your fiction, scriptwriting, or article writing habit with it. I call it "commercial writing."

Commercial writing is any writing that helps a company sell or help sell a product or service, or helps an organization promote an idea or cause. We'll explore many of the commercial writing opportunities available to you soon. But here are a few of the most common:

- *Advertising copywriting*—magazine and newspaper ads, TV and radio commercials, for everything from software to shampoo.

- *Technical writing*—user manuals, online help, and other instructional materials for using hardware and software.

- *Online writing*—corporations and small businesses alike need tons of content for their company websites, not to mention their ezines (online newsletters).

- *Fund-raising*—letters to raise money for politicians, political parties, churches, museums, and a variety of other nonprofits.

- *Direct marketing*—direct mail, telemarketing scripts, and other copy to sell products and services by mail.

- *Public relations*—press releases, media kits, and articles for promoting a company, product, or cause in the media.

- *Corporate communications*—assignments can range from ghostwriting a speech for a Fortune 500 CEO to creating multimedia presentations for a company's annual sales meeting.

Some writers I know specialize in writing "marcom." Short for "marketing communications," marcom includes press releases, product sheets, sales brochures, trade ads, web pages, and other marketing materials for corporate clients. A good marcom writer can easily surpass the $100,000-a-year mark; at least two I know personally earn more than $200,000 a year.

Writers handling commercial assignments such as these can make good money, and they can do so with regularity, year after year. You are unlikely to become truly wealthy, but you are likely to become financially secure if you work hard at it, invest your earnings, and live conservatively, well below your means.

To pursue commercial writing, you need a business plan. Fortunately, it's simple, and looks something like this:

- *Set your annual income goal.* How much do you want to earn? Pick a specific number. Start with $100,000 a year.

- *Set your weekly and daily income goals.* If you want to make $100,000 a year and work 50 weeks a year, you must gross $2,000 a week from your writing. If you work 5 days a week, you must earn $400 a day.

- *Determine the writing service you will offer.* Can you find something to write that will earn you $400 a day? If you can—and believe me, you can—you are set to earn $100,000 a year as a freelance writer.

To earn this amount of money, you will have to pursue some type of commercial writing. The areas mentioned earlier in this article—advertising copywriting, technical writing, corporate communications, public relations, online—can all enable you to gross $100,000 a year.

The nice thing about it is that you can choose to write about subjects that interest you, for organizations that pay you extremely well. Another key advantage of commercial writing is that clients come to you with assignments they want written, rather than you having to pitch ideas to them. This eliminates the enormous amount of time the conventional freelance writer wastes in formulating ideas with no compensation.

I estimate that the average commercial assignment pays at least twice as much as the equivalent number of words for a similar editorial assignment on the same topic. Yet because your client is so cooperative, it takes half the time or less to write the copy. That makes commercial work at least four times more lucrative than editorial work.

Here's the best part: If you dream of writing the great American novel or an epic poem, you don't have to give up that dream. As a freelance commercial writer, you largely set your own schedule. After a hard day of writing direct mail packages, I often like to put in a pleasant hour or two writing a magazine article or working on one of my books.

Later in this book, I'll show you what types of projects you can write to earn $100,000 a year as a freelance commercial writer, how to find clients, how to get them to hire you, and how to excel so they come back to hire you for additional assignments again and again.

I started freelancing full time in 1982, and except for that year and the next, I have earned more than $100,000 a year as a freelance writer for 25 consecutive years. In 2005, I grossed more than $670,000. I tell you this not to brag, but to illustrate that making a six-figure income is a realistic goal for even an average freelance writer like me. I've never written a best seller, nor have I sold a script to the movies or TV. The following suggestions will help you achieve and exceed the $100,000-a-year mark.

Get serious about money

If money is not a concern, you can write whatever you want, whenever you want, as much or as little as you want, without regard to the fee you will be paid, how long it will take to write the piece, or the likelihood that you will sell the piece.

But if you want to consistently make $100,000 a year as a freelance writer, you need to avoid the poverty mentality that holds so many writers back from earning a high income. A doorman in New York City earns around $39,000 annually. If an unskilled laborer can make $39,000 just for opening a door, surely you can earn $50,000 to $100,000 for your skills.

Set daily revenue goals

To make $100,000 a year, you need to earn $2,000 a week for 50 weeks. For a 5-day workweek, that comes to $400 a day. Will people pay you $400 a day for writing-related work? Proofreading won't hit the mark, but ghostwriting books, annual reports, fund-raising letters, speeches, or ad copy probably can.

Do you have to make $400 each and every day? No. Some days you'll be writing queries or doing self-promotion and earn nothing. Other days you'll get into a writing groove, finish a $1,000 article in 6 hours, and still have time to write more queries. You're safe as long as your average revenue is $400 a day, or $2,000 a week, or about $9,000 a month.

Before he "retired" from commercial work to write nonfiction books, freelancer Robert Otterbourg specialized in annual reports, with an average price tag of $10,000 per project. By doing several of these jobs in a month or two, he was able to get way ahead of his income plan, leaving him time to write the career books that were his avocation and are now his full-time vocation.

Value your time

If you earn $100,000 a year and work 40 hours a week, your time is worth at least $50 an hour. You should base decisions about how you spend your time on that figure. If you spend an extra half-hour to go out of your way to save $10 in office supplies, it costs you $25 in lost productivity, and you are $15 in the red.

My time is worth at least $100 an hour. Therefore, virtually any service I can buy for under $100 an hour—including lawn services, handymen, and tax preparation—I outsource.

Of the two resources, time and money, time is the more valuable. You can always make more money. But time is a nonrenewable resource. Once it's gone, you can't get it back.

Be more productive

Develop habits that help you get more done in less time. The easiest is simply to get up and start work an hour earlier than you do now. That first hour will be your most productive, because you can work without interruptions before the business day starts.

Nancy Flynn, author of *The $100,000 Writer* (Adams Media), maximizes her productivity by avoiding in-person meetings unless they're absolutely necessary. "You can accomplish a tremendous amount—including establishing and maintaining successful business relationships—via telephone, email, and fax," she says.

Outsource tasks

I have not gone to the post office in 12 years. Why not? Because doing so is an absolute waste of time I could be using to write and make money.

The only thing you get paid to do is write, research, and think for your clients and publishers. All other activities are nonpaying and therefore should be farmed out to other people who can do them better and more cheaply than you can.

You don't need to hire a full-time secretary to outsource routine office work and administrative tasks. Plenty of bright high school and college students are eager to work with writers for the glory and glamour—and a relatively modest fee of $10 to $20 an hour or so.

Nix writer's block

Profitable writers write consistently, every day, whether the mood strikes us or not. The best way to maintain a steady output and avoid writer's block is to have many projects on various subjects and in different formats. This is the method I use, and it has never failed me. If I am writing a magazine ad and get stuck on the headline, I put it aside and switch to the direct mail package I'm writing for a software company. If I need more info from my software client to proceed with their sales letter, I can put that aside and work on an article or book.

Get paid more

Moving to higher-paying assignments accelerates your climb to the $100,000-a-year mark. It's much easier to meet your goal of $400 a day when you get $2,000 per project instead of $200.

When you consider the profitability of assignments, calculate your earnings per hour rather than per project or per word. If it takes you ten 8-hour days to do a $2,000 feature article for a glossy magazine, you make

$25 an hour. If an industrial manufacturer hires you to write simple news releases for the trade at $500 each, and you can do two per day, you make $125 an hour.

Multiple streams of income

The dentists' saying "The more you drill and fill, the more you bill" reflects that they are in essence hourly laborers, getting paid only for their time—just like writers. Writers basically have three options for escaping the limitations of "drill, fill, and bill":

- *Royalties.* When you write books or music, you get a royalty for each book or CD purchased. You make thousands of extra dollars a month from products on which you are paid a royalty—without doing any more work. Direct mail writer Dick Sanders, for instance, charges his clients a mailing fee per package mailed in addition to his flat fee for writing copy. If a publisher pays him 3 cents per package mailed, a mailing of 1 millon pieces earns him an additional $30,000 in mailing fees.

- *Sales.* You can create and sell your own information products, such as books, ebooks, subscription websites, newsletters, videos, audiocassettes, and special reports. Essentially, you package your expertise in different formats and sell it. This is the self-publishing option Dan Poynter discusses in his book *The Self-Publishing Manual* (Para Publishing) and in his "Self-Publishing" column in *Writer's Digest*. The greatest return on investment (ROI) for the freelance writer self-publishing his material is to sell it on the Internet, which we discuss in chapter 12.

- *Markups.* Some writers make money by buying products or services, marking them up, and reselling them to their clients. For example, a freelance corporate writer may supervise the printing of the brochure he wrote for his client. The printer bills the writer directly. The writer sends his own printing bill to the corporate client, with the actual cost marked up 20 percent to compensate him for his project management services. On a $20,000 print bill, your markup would be $4,000.

These strategies may enable you to make additional money, but they are not without pitfalls. What happens if you print 3,000 copies of your self-published book and sell only 100 copies? What happens when the corporate client declares bankruptcy, and you are stuck with a printer's bill for thousands of dollars of color printing?

Get repeat business

The most profitable assignments in freelance writing are repeat assignments from current clients. Why? Because you are familiar with the client and his organization, what you need to learn about him diminishes with each new assignment. You can charge the same price per job, or maybe even more if he likes you. And you can do the jobs much faster because of the knowledge you have accumulated.

How do you get lucrative repeat assignments?

- Give every writing job your best effort. The more satisfied the client, the more likely he is to give you another job.

- Provide excellent customer service. Don't be a prima donna. Clients avoid working with writers perceived as difficult or demanding.

- Ask the editor for another project. Often you won't get the work unless you ask.

May I share a secret with you? The year 2002 was the worst I'd had in some time. In the aftermath of September 11 and then the anthrax scare, my main business—writing direct mail—got hit hard. Despite that, I still grossed well over $300,000. The point? There is no bad time or good time for freelance writing. There is only now. And right now, you can make $100,000 a year as a freelance writer in today's market.

Tips for Working Moms and Dads Who Write at Home

Writer Carol Brzozowski offers the following advice for freelance writers who are also stay-at-home moms and dads:

- When you get up in the morning, stick a load of laundry in and keep the laundry factory up throughout the day.

- Dust off the slow cooker and prepare more meals with it. For most parents, the afternoon is crunch time, which comes with its accompanying fatigue (picking the kids up from school, schlepping to after-school activities, supervising homework). Having dinner ready in a slow cooker takes one more stressor out of the afternoon. Or make large batches of food and freeze some, so all you have to do on school nights is heat it up.

- Take 15-minute breaks in between the hours you work. This is good sense for your eyes. Use those breaks to conduct personal business such as paying bills, folding laundry, and loading and unloading the dishwasher. By day's end, you've accomplished a lot in both the work and household arenas.

- Enlist the children and your significant other in taking on more household chores.

- Look at the return on investment of your time for household projects. Hire somebody to do work such as housecleaning or lawn care that would free up your time to write more or spend more time with your family. For example, for what you make in one hour writing, you can have someone mow your lawn twice a month. By doing so, you gain two hours of time for your own use—and avoid an unnecessary and unproductive chore.

- Invest in a laptop if you don't have one. This gives you mobility to write in between volunteer obligations at the school, while waiting for the pediatrician on a child's sick day, and while waiting in the carpool line for dismissal. These times are also good for scheduling interviews on the cell phone.

- Many of us are most productive in either the morning or evening. Reserve your most important tasks for your productive time. You can multitask by supervising children's homework and doing more "mindless" freelance writing tasks while the children are home.

- Set a goal for a number of hours you must work to earn the money you need to support your family, yet which affords you the time you want to be involved in your children's lives. While you may have worked straight through when they were at home as babies or during the summer, expect that your work now will be more segmented.

For Carol, it means working in the morning through afternoon dismissal and then coming back to work after her children's bedtime if need be. Factor in volunteer time if desired. Sometimes she ends up working on a Saturday to catch up. Says Carol, "That's the price I pay … but the return for my investment is priceless to me."

6

Entry-Level Assignments to Get You Started

At the beginning of your writing career, the idea is to get practice and get published. This chapter identifies easy opportunities geared for beginners, and tells how to get these assignments and do them satisfactorily, so you will get clippings, more assignments (eventually with better pay), and referrals.

Local Newspapers

The easiest place to get published is as a reporter for your town newspaper. Check the help-wanted ads in your local weekly paper. Almost every week you'll find a "reporters wanted" ad.

Many local newspapers have trouble finding writers because the pay is lousy, the prestige is low, the assignments are dull, and the hours are inconvenient. But by taking on such an assignment, you can earn a few spare-time dollars—and, more important, get your byline in a real newspaper.

Save every article you write. You'll soon have a file full of clips that can help you secure writing assignments at larger daily, regional, or even national newspapers. Also, take a basic journalism course at your local adult education program or community college to learn proper newspaper style.

Comic Books

Suddenly, superheroes are undergoing a renaissance, thanks to the recent spate of comics-related blockbuster movies. You can get in on the action by writing for comic books. One thing comic book editors look for is a demonstrated ability to tell a story. So if you've written and published fiction, even for literary magazines that pay only in contributor's copies, say so.

What's the best way to break into writing for Superman and the Hulk? "Do it yourself," says freelance comic book writer Andrew Helfer. "By that I mean you should find an artist (lots of aspiring ones prowl the Internet), put together an original comic, and publish it yourself (it's pretty cheap to do). Before printing, however, send copies to Diamond Comic Distributors, Inc. (www.diamondcomics.com), to see if they'd be willing to distribute it.

"The point is to have a professional-looking comic that you can send to mainstream comic publishers. Comic editors don't want to read scripts, but they may be inclined to read a comic if it looks interesting enough."

Cartoons

Cartoons are a mixed bag. On the one hand, it's a difficult market to sell to, and your chances of making a sale to the *New Yorker* or other national publications are slim. On the other hand, vast experience and a large clip file of published works are not required; if a cartoon makes an editor chuckle and fits what he's looking for, you can make a sale.

"You never know what drawing will strike some editor as worthy of being published," says professional cartoonist Eric Allie. "Often the drawing you like least is the one the editor likes most. It is a maddening business. Monetary rewards may be few and far between. Cartooning must be personally rewarding before there is any chance of it becoming financially rewarding."

As with other kinds of creative writing, study the market: read magazines that publish cartoons and study the cartoons they publish. "One way to find out what kinds of work we're publishing, and also what kinds of illustrations and articles we publish, is to get a copy of our magazine," says Nick Jehlen, art director for *The Progressive*.

What if you are a writer who has ideas for cartoons, but not a professional artist? "I would suggest you at least try drawing your own cartoons," says Allie. "Drawing skills are not as important as having a sense and an ability to arrange visual elements in a clear, concise, and proper manner."

There are a few ways for you to get your cartoons published. Syndication through the big syndicates is one possibility. According to professional cartoonist Wally Littman, syndicates require 23 sample cartoons plus bios of the characters and the cartoonist. Also, they usually buy multi-panel cartoons like Dilbert and Blondie, not single-panel cartoons (see Fig. 6-1) like those published in the *New Yorker*. There are a few exceptions. Artizans and Cartoonstock operate like a syndicate, except they are willing to take single-panel cartoons.

The Lobster family reunion goes terribly wrong.

Fig. 6-1

Another way to sell cartoons is to mail them with an SASE (self-addressed stamped #10 envelope) to magazines and newspapers. Periodicals that publish cartoons include the *New Yorker, Playboy, Atlantic, Wall Street Journal, Harvard Business Review, Reader's Digest, Woman's World, Cosmopolitan, Glamour, Medical Economics, Boy's Life, Weekly Reader, Better Homes & Gardens,* and many others.

Nontraditional markets for cartoons include greeting card companies (e.g., American Greetings), corporations, and associations. Toyota, Sun Microsystems, Spring, Walgreens, the United States Postal Service, and Chicago Historical Society have all purchased cartoons.

"Even if you get rejected, try again," says Allie. "Continue to produce work; the more you do, the better you will get. Also, read as many cartoons as you can."

NONFICTION BOOKS

"Write what you know" is an oft-repeated piece of advice to rookie writers. Well, everybody knows something—and that something can be the topic for your first book.

How-to books are one of the most popular types of books, and one of the easiest to write and get published. An Amazon.com search found 63,703 books with the words "how to" in the title.

What do you know better than others? Your life experience usually yields the answer. If you had cancer, and you are alive, then you're an authority on surviving cancer. If you were a guest on *The Jerry Springer Show*, you know how to get on *The Jerry Springer Show*.

Your credentials—the work or life experience that prompted you to write the book—are what will sell an editor on you as the author. Many people might want to write a book about coping with children who have attention deficit disorder; but if your child actually has ADD, that adds a depth and authority other writers can't match.

If you're passionate about your topic, you may want to stay involved with it beyond writing a single book. Maybe you want to make it your writing specialty and even start a website on that topic.

Having an email list of 100,000 subscribers to your monthly online newsletter is mighty attractive to a publisher, because they can count on sales to that audience. Publishers call this a "platform"—a built-in readership who knows you and will buy your book—and editors look for that when they're signing new authors.

GHOSTWRITING

A ghostwriter is someone who writes books and materials for other people. The ghostwriter does the actual writing, but the material is published under your client's byline, and the client is credited as the author.

"All it takes to become a ghostwriter is the ability to put your ego aside while writing for a client, study his or her word patterns, have perfect communication with the client, and be an expert in people skills," writes Eva Shaw in her book *Ghostwriting: How to Get into the Business* (Paragon House Publishers).

Celebrities often work with ghostwriters to get their books (especially autobiographies) written, but those engagements usually go to experienced ghostwriters. As a novice, you're more likely to be hired by professionals, businesses, or individuals who want to write and publish a book but don't want to do the work themselves.

COPYWRITING

Writing promotional and educational materials for local and national businesses can be extremely lucrative. Business clients hire freelancers to produce a wide range of materials, from annual reports and radio commercials to websites and direct-mail letters. My copywriting assignments generate income for me of more than half a million dollars a year.

Your target prospect is the marketing director at a large business, or the president or owner of a small company. Pick up the phone or send a letter offering your services as a freelance business writer. Surprisingly, some of these clients are open to working with writers who have little or no previous experience.

TRAVEL WRITING

Almost all regional or state daily newspapers have travel sections, and this section is the easiest to break into for the beginning writer. The editors of these sections are always looking for articles on museums, amusement parks, gardens, historical houses, shopping malls, wineries, and other places to visit on the weekend, as well as pieces on vacation getaways.

The best way to get started: If you're going to an exotic destination for business or pleasure, contact the paper's travel editor and propose a story with an interesting hook (for example, diving for treasure in the Cayman Islands).

Travel writers don't make a fortune, but they get published and the travel is a nice perk, often worth as much or more than the fees they get for their articles. "In nearly two decades, I've written hundreds of stories about destinations as far-flung as Poland and Mexico," says freelance travel writer Steenie Harvey. "Editors actually pay my expenses as I travel the globe reporting on their behalf."

RESUME WRITING

Okay, resume writing won't lead to a gig writing articles for *The New York Times*, books for Random House, or annual reports for Coca-Cola, but it's an easy way to make a relatively high hourly wage doing what you love: writing.

Learning the craft isn't difficult. You can buy books that show you how to format and organize resumes and which method is best for your client. You can create resumes on your PC using either a word processing program such as Microsoft Word or a desktop publishing application such as Adobe InDesign. Most resume writing software does a lot of the formatting for you, so your job is to fill in the client's education and employment history, which you get from his old resume and by asking questions.

Clients aren't difficult to get: Run a small classified ad (with your phone number) in the Sunday business section of your local paper offering "resume preparation services." A small Yellow Pages ad will also get the phone ringing.

Once you become proficient, it might take you just an hour or two to prepare a resume, and you can charge anywhere from $100 to $300 each— the low end if your client is a student, the high end if she's a well-paid executive. On an hourly basis, expect to earn $50 to $150, not a bad wage for a novice writer.

How do you turn resume writing into a bigger opportunity? Let clients know you also do freelance business writing. So when they land a job, they can call you for reports, letters, proposals, and other corporate writing assignments their new employer needs.

TRADE PUBLICATIONS

Big consumer magazines can be tough for rookies to break into. However, thousands of business magazines, known as trade journals, are eager to hire rookie writers—as long as you can fill their pages with relevant, well-written material for their specialized audience. (For a complete listing of trade journals, see the *Writer's Market* from Writer's Digest Books.) Trade publications are such an ideal entry point into print for new writers, that this section gives you complete instructions for selling to the trades.

What stories would a trade editor assign to a freelancer like you? A popular format is the case history, where you tell how one company solved a particular problem—including what the problem was, the solutions they considered, the method or product they chose to solve the problem, how they implemented the solution, and the results achieved.

Another is the industry roundup, where you might do brief profiles of products or companies in a particular area (for example, in a construction magazine you might discuss the available types of building insulation). Many trade journals run articles on business skills or management topics such as how to be a better leader or reduce stress on the job.

Pay scales for trade publications are generally lower than for consumer publications. But the editors aren't as demanding, requiring fewer interviews and rewrites.

Writing for trade publications is a great way to break into magazines, get a byline, hone your skills, and build a portfolio of published articles. The best place to start: Look at the trade journals you get at work. Your familiarity with your industry and those publications will give you a better feel for how to talk to the magazine's readers.

If you're concentrating on trying to sell your manuscripts to *Redbook*, *Esquire*, *Reader's Digest*, *Travel & Leisure*, *Sports Illustrated*, and the other consumer magazines, you should know about a larger, less competitive, and potentially more lucrative other world of magazine markets: the trade journals.

I think you'll find breaking into these specialized magazines easier than breaking into the big-name, general interest publications, too. Be aware that per-article pay rates don't rival *Playboy*'s or *Family Circle*'s, but neither does the competition among freelancers.

Since trade journals accept a larger percentage of the articles proposed by writers, you might be able to make more money writing for the trades than for consumer magazines. Trade magazine editors often rely on "outsiders" for much of what goes into the magazine, sometimes as much as 60 percent of the copy. Because the trades have smaller staffs and a strong feeling of loyalty to their readers, they often welcome new ideas from those familiar with their field.

I've had many pleasant and rewarding experiences writing for the trades. For example, an editor at *Computer Decisions* obtained material from my seminar on technical writing. The editor asked me to turn it into a 1,200-word article on how to write user's manuals. Using the material already at hand, I wrote the piece and had it in the mail in under an hour. A week later, I received the magazine's check for $750.

Before you attempt to make your own profits in this market, it's essential to understand just what these magazines are about. Trade magazines serve the needs of a special interest market.

Trade journals exist in just about every field. Whether you're interested in aviation (*Aviation History, General Aviation News*), fertilizer (*Fertilizer Progress, Farm Chemicals*), or turkeys (*Turkey World*), there's at least one appropriate magazine for you to approach.

Trade journals exist to keep professionals up to date on developments, conferences, trends, and practices in their field. Readers need the information the journals provide to help them do their jobs better. As a result, trade articles are practical and specific, and depending on the magazine, can be in-depth or technical. All provide straightforward coverage of a specific industry.

Unlike their consumer cousins, these magazines don't strive to be flashy or singularly entertaining. They look different, too: generally less slick than the mass-market magazines. Visuals are used to communicate information, not to add glitz or lure readers.

Your first step to writing for the trades is to decide which journals interest you, and which match your background and writing capabilities. You don't need industry experience or an engineering degree to write about most subjects covered by the trades, but you will have to know how to research and interview.

Take me as an example. I have a bachelor's degree in chemical engineering, but I find that my background doesn't affect my ability to turn out clear, comprehensible trade articles on a wide variety of topics. My wife, Amy, has written about such diverse subjects as meatpacking, printing, health insurance, strategic planning, prefabricated metal buildings, and public relations. I've published numerous articles outside my chemical engineering specialty, including pieces on semiconductors, aerospace, defense, and computer software.

Since more than 6,000 trade journals are published, you must zero in on the publications that are appropriate markets for you.

First, list subjects you're interested in writing about. Then search *Bacon's Publicity Checker*, the Business Publications edition of SRDS (*Standard Rate and Data Service*), or *Writer's Market* for listings of trade journals that cover these topics. (These books are available at your local library.) *Bacon's* and SRDS contain the most listings, but *Writer's Market* provides a more detailed description of each journal's editorial requirements.

From that list, request sample copies of trade magazines that relate to the subjects you listed. In studying these issues, see what kinds of stories the editor uses and note their degree of technical difficulty.

Determine whether these pieces are written by staff writers, outside technical experts, or freelance writers. (Check article bylines against the masthead's list of staff writers or read the author bios printed with articles.) Most trade editors combine work from staff writers and freelancers.

If every contributed article carries the byline of a chemist or an engineer and you are neither, querying the editor is probably a waste of time. Likewise if the material seems hopelessly technical to you. On the other hand, if you have an interest in, say, computers, but terms like asynchronous and ASCII are unfamiliar to you, a dictionary of computer jargon might be all you need to write an acceptable article.

Types of trade articles you can write

In studying your sample issues, you'll notice that trade journals commonly use eight types of articles. Not all magazines may buy every type, but understanding how each is constructed and what each tells readers will help you create salable ideas.

- Features are lengthy and in-depth articles, addressing a specific problem, trend, or development of interest to readers. The feature is the issue's main attraction and is generally supported by considerable research and interviews. For example, *High Tech Marketing*'s feature story, "Are There Equal Rights in High-Tech?", included interviews with 10 executive women and quoted the results of three relevant career and salary surveys.

- Industry roundups focus on a specific type of product important to readers' businesses. The roundup examines in depth the advantages and disadvantages of the various versions of the product, often mentioning specific manufacturers. One such article in *Packaging* highlighted various foam packaging products on the market and their applications.

- Case histories examine one company's experience with a product, service, or new process or technology. They are shorter than features (usually one to two magazine pages with photos) and follow a problem-solution-results structure. One case history we wrote showed how super-absorbent meat pads increased sales and cut rewrapping time in a supermarket chain. Another told how a petrochemical company solved a costly underground oil leak problem using a management consultant's decision-making technique. The key factor that makes an article a case history is that the article tells how one company used another company's product or service.

- Tutorials, also known as how-to's, offer practical, specific tips on such topics as how to increase efficiency, control costs, maintain machinery, select equipment, save energy, or prevent pollution. "Plotting Your Course" in *Audiovisual Directions* told audiovisual producers about a new, more convenient format for writing, typing, and revising scripts.

- Interviews profile an industry leader, trendsetter, "rising star," or professional who has solved an on-the-job problem or achieved outstanding success in the field. For instance, *Computer Living* ran an interview with Stephen Wozniak, cofounder of Apple Computer, Inc. Such pieces may be written in either Q&A (question-and-answer) or story format.

- Company profiles describe how a particular company has become successful. Though these tend to focus on the management style and philosophy of the company's president or top executives as revealed in interviews, they also examine key decisions and how the company faced problems.

  In *Food in Canada* magazine, "Golden Valley Builds on Total Market Base" told how a food processing firm grew from a company with two products to one with 82 different items and sizes. Sprinkled with quotes from the president of the company, the piece included a brief history, descriptions of new market ventures and products, its future sales plans, and a discussion of the company's conservative marketing approach. Unlike a case history, which is the story of the successful use of a single product in one specific application, the company profile is more far-reaching, covering the progress, development, and growth of an entire firm.

- General management/business articles offer advice on general interest topics, such as time management, public speaking, writing, and performance appraisals. These can be ideal articles for lay authors because they require no specialized knowledge of the industry and are written from personal experience or library research. Amy and I wrote a series of nine articles for *CPI 100* on such topics as "Improving Interpersonal Relationships," "How to Improve Your Presentation Skills," and "Sharpening Your Listening Skills."

- Essays present the writer's personal opinion on an industry-related trend or issue. For example, I contributed a "Perspectives" column to *Business Marketing* magazine that said corporate marketing managers needed to be more sensitive and considerate in dealing with freelance writers and artists hired by their firms.

Not every magazine presents these common article types in the same fashion. Note in your sample issues the tone, style, and content favored by individual editors. To be able to pitch an idea effectively, you must familiarize yourself with the magazine by reading several issues to get a general feeling and to pinpoint their audience.

An additional tool available to writers is the editorial calendar. Many trade journals annually plot the major topics to be covered in each issue throughout the year. Proposing a piece that ties in with a topic planned for a future issue can work to your advantage.

"If people respond to our editorial calendar with ideas for specific issues, great," says trade journal editor Rick Dunn. "Or if they can provide background for a story we want to do, they'll have an edge in getting into the magazine." (Request a copy of a magazine's editorial calendar from the editor at the same time you send for sample issues.)

Your ability to develop salable ideas may depend on your familiarity with the industry. Personal experience in a given trade may point you to potential articles for the appropriate journal. But there are many sources for those writers without previous work experience in the industry.

Company marketing and public relations departments often will tip writers to newsworthy problems, technologies, and overall trends. If you can establish a rapport with a person who works in an industry you plan to cover, pick his or her brain about special problems, new products, or new techniques.

Contacts within companies also may direct you to their customers (who use their products) or to their public relations agency, if they have one. Since PR account executives live to promote their clients, they can be an excellent source, especially for case histories.

All of these sources also can supply literature and background information. *O'Dwyer's Directory of Corporate Communications* lists the names, addresses, and phone numbers of public relations directors at 4,000 of the biggest U.S. corporations and 1,000 of the top industry trade associations. *O'Dwyer's Directory of Public Relations Firms* can tell you the same information and the clients of more than 1,400 U.S. public relations agencies.

By asking these organizations to put you on their mailing lists, you can keep up with news in the field on a regular basis. Just write to the PR directors and explain that you're a journalist covering their industry. Inviting material from many sources will help you develop industry roundup articles.

Don't overlook newsletters, magazines, newspapers, and TV as additional sources of ideas. Short items about business, industry, and technology can serve as the starting points for full-length trade journal stories. For example, one of International Paper's well-known "Power of the

Printed Word" series of advertisements gave me the idea for an article I wrote on "Improving Your Presentation Skills."

Once editors know you and your work, they may come to you with article ideas. Many times, freelancers are asked to write monthly columns (with a guaranteed payment for each) for trade journals based on earlier work for the magazine. For example, based on a single article on how to write catalog copy, an editor asked me to contribute a regular column to a catalog marketing newsletter.

Don't sell trade journal writing short

Although trade journals may be a different world from consumer magazines, they are part of the same industry. Editors of trade publications treat writers exactly the same as consumer publication editors; similarly, the editors at *Packaging*, *Modern Material Handling* and *Turkey World* expect to be treated with the same respect you'd give the editor of *Ladies' Home Journal* or *TV Guide*.

In querying editors of trade journals, there are two points that you'll want to stress more than you might in a proposal to a consumer magazine:

Sources

If you're an expert in the field, fine. If not, you will need to interview qualified people and collect as much printed material as you can. Title, position, and experience of your sources can demonstrate your professionalism and get your idea approved.

For example, if you're writing a feature article on "How to Reduce Electrostatic Discharge Damage in the Manufacturing Plant," you probably would want to talk to production line supervisors, electrical engineers, and packaging engineers. Other sources of information could include manufacturers of electrostatic discharge control materials, university researchers, and industry trade association officials.

To find these individuals, consult the O'Dwyer directories or, for the academic research labs, the PR directors of local colleges and universities.

Photos

If you're writing about a product, the editor will probably want to run photos of it. If your article is a company profile, stating the availability of photos of the people you interview might help make the sale.

Check *Writer's Market* or sample issues to find out which magazines use photos with stories. You don't have to be a professional photographer—color photos taken with a digital camera are acceptable to many publications. Other sources for photos are trade associations, companies, and PR firms.

It's after you've won an editor's approval that you'll discover the major differences between the worlds of consumer and trade magazines. Writing trade journal articles requires a different approach than writing for popular magazines. The following tips will help you produce articles that sell.

Timelines and the informational value

Timelines and the informational value of a story are almost always more important than writing ability and style. Don't worry about catchy leads and clever phrases. Instead, ask yourself, "Will what I'm writing be interesting, helpful, and clear to the reader?"

Here's the lead of "Ten Ways to Stretch Your Advertising Budget," a general business article published in *Plastics Industry News*, a magazine for advertising managers in the plastics industry. Note that the paragraph is factual and functional, not fancy:

> Most business-to-business advertisers have smaller ad budgets than their counterparts in consumer marketing. Here are ten ways to get more out of your advertising dollars—without detracting from the quality and quantity of your ads and promotions. In some cases, these ideas can even enhance the effectiveness of your marketing efforts.

A clear, straightforward, logical presentation

A clear, straightforward, logical presentation of the story is best. Trade journal readers are busy people; they read them not for entertainment but for the information that can help them. So make your article concise and to the point, as in this lead from a piece on "A New Approach to Surge Suppression," from *Electronic Component News*.

> A new type of surge-suppression technology, recently introduced by RCA Solid State, has been developed to protect sophisticated electronic circuits from rapid, high-voltage power surges that conventional surge suppressors cannot handle.
>
> This new surge protector, called a Surgector, is really a two-in-one device combining two proven components—a zener diode and a thyristor—in a single unit.

Here the reader is given the whole story, in capsule form, in the first two sentences of the article.

Concentrate on getting all the facts

While entertainment-oriented magazines require a hook or angle to set apart their feature stories, the trades seek out articles that show readers how to save money, time, and labor, or improve on-the-job performance.

Be specific

Support claims and statements with statistics, examples, studies, and explanations. Jim Russo, former editor of *Packaging*, says, "If someone tells us something is more efficient than something else, we want to know how much more efficient."

Here's how I used a few choice statistics to beef up my article "How to Write Business Letters That Get Results":

> How many letters actually get their messages across and motivate the reader? Surprisingly few. In direct-mail marketing, for example, a 2 percent response rate is exceptionally high. So a manufacturer mailing 1,000 sales letters expects that fewer than 20 people will respond to the pitch.

Be objective

Your article should give useful, accurate, honest information and advice, not rewritten corporate bulletins and press releases. If you do a story on vacuum pumps, talk to many pump manufacturers, not just one.

If you are describing a new management technique, give the pros as well as the cons. "One-sidedness doesn't interest us," says Mark Rosensweig, editor-in-chief of *Chemical Engineering*. "We want all the disadvantages spelled out, as well as the advantages."

Write for the level of the magazine's audience

Write for the level of the magazine's audience, not for the editor and not for yourself. If you're just learning a subject, it may be difficult to refrain from explaining and defining basic terms or techniques. However, remember that readers may be more knowledgeable than you and may be bored or insulted if you offer them elementary material.

Here's an excerpt from an article I wrote to get design engineers to consider using magnesium in the products they are designing. The copy doesn't talk down to the reader, but it isn't overly technical or dull either:

> Magnesium has a strength-to-weight ratio equal to steel's, is lighter than aluminum, and can be extracted from sea-water in virtually unlimited quantities. It is rugged, fatigue resistant, and easier to machine than all other structural metals.
>
> Until recently, high cost, together with its alleged flammability and susceptibility to corrosion, limited the use of magnesium as an engineering material. Today the changing economics and availability of raw materials, coupled with new extraction processes, are closing the gap in cost between magnesium and its major competitor, aluminum ...

Follow an orderly, sensible progression

Introduce a particular problem, then describe its solution and the result. Or discuss the latest developments in an industry, the reasons for them, and their predicted impact on the bottom line. The article's organizational structure should make it easy for readers to understand and follow your story.

One organizational structure that works well for many types of trade articles is the list format. You just present your ideas of advice as a series of numbered points. I've written "Ten Tips for Better User Manuals" (*Computer Decisions*), "Practical Techniques for Producing Profitable Ideas" (*Chemical Engineering*), and "22 Rules for Successful Self-Promotion" (*Direct Marketing*).

Double-check your facts

If you have doubts about the technical accuracy of your article—especially if it's a complex, statistical piece—ask someone familiar with the subject to review it. This might be a neutral third party or someone you interviewed.

Be thorough

People reading your article may make decisions or procedural changes based on what you write. They require accurate and complete information.

Keep your notes and source material for at least six months

Keep your notes and source material for at least six months after the article is published. This documentation can be used to defend your article if readers question its accuracy.

What can you get paid?

Trade journals usually pay less than consumer magazines; in fact, some don't pay at all. And among those that do pay, rates are all over the lot. An experience I had tells the tale.

For a 1,500-word article on improving technical writing, published in *Chemical Engineering*, I received only $100. The next month, a corporate client asked me to ghostwrite a 1,000-word article on computers. The writing took only a few hours, and the client paid me $1,000. In general, rates paid by trade journals range from $50 to $400 per magazine page. But some pay more, others less.

The largest circulation daily newspaper in my county asked me to write a weekly 500-word column on marketing for small business. When I asked about payment, he seemed surprised: "This will give you great visibility in the New Jersey business community," the business editor told me.

On the other hand, I write a monthly column for *DM News,* a trade newspaper covering the direct marketing industry; they routinely pay their columnists a few hundred dollars per column.

The time to talk about money is after you've received an assignment letter from the editor. If the letter doesn't mention payment, write the editor, asking what fee he or she is offering.

Seasoned writers with a long list of credits—or writers with an exclusive story of particular interest to the editor—may be able to negotiate higher fees. But beginners may not be able to negotiate such treatment, and may have to settle for a byline that can lead to future sales.

Trade journals represent one of the easiest markets for novice writers to crack. They're also a reliable market for veteran writers. You probably won't get rich writing for the trades, but you can generate a steady income year after year.

Writing for Small-Press Magazines

While top magazines often have a subscription base of millions, editorial staff of 20 or more, and thousands of dollars to pay per article, a "little" is likely assembled by one person with a copier.

In other words, this isn't a glamorous market. Contributors have been paid in sample copies, subscriptions, even stickers. These contributors write for small presses to hone their craft. Not only are they gaining experience, but there's always hope that the magazine will grow and they'll be in on the ground floor. After all, *Rolling Stone* was once a "little."

Here are some things you should know about small-press magazines, whether they're literary journals or editorially driven:

- They're an easy way to break into print. Editors at small publications expect unsolicited materials; in fact, that may be all they get. Do you worry that only the intern reads the story you submitted to *The Atlantic Monthly?* At small presses, the editor reads everything.

- They're a good training ground. Yes, small presses are the minor leagues—but most ballplayers don't get drafted right out of high school. Like ballplayers, writers need training. Small presses are a great place to learn.

- There's less competition. With little or no pay, small presses are a good way to break into a competitive field. Since you don't need an agent or have to worry about massive competition from other writers, your work stands a greater chance of being published.

- There's a wide variety of subject matter. "My first sale was to *Cuadero Fayrdant*, a literary magazine dedicated to Ambrose Bierce," says Joyce Frohn. "I've also been published in *H.I.C.K.S.*, a magazine fighting the isolation of rural Wiccans. Then there's the fabled *Dog Hair Knitting Journal*. There's a small-press magazine covering every conceivable subject."

- They're a good way to establish a writer/editor relationship. The line between editor and magazine is very slight at small presses, since the editor is probably also the printer, publisher, and receptionist. The magazine may be assembled in her garage, basement, or attic. Get to know the editor, and you'll be getting to know a lot about the magazine. This can become an important relationship. The mentoring of a good editor can be a fundamental part of a writer's training.

To find small-press magazines that might be a good fit for your writing, start with *Writer's Market* (Writer's Digest Books) or *Gila Queen's Guide to Markets* (*gilaqueen.us*), which specifically lists small presses. Also look at the advertisements in small-press magazines, because editors often trade ads.

So start in the minors and hone your writing skills. Before long, you just might get your ticket to the big leagues.

THREE WAYS TO CRACK NEW MARKETS

If you're just starting out, or if you want to introduce your services to a new market, you need samples to show these new prospects—but you need to have clients first in order to create the samples, right? Writer Ilise Benun recommends the following three techniques to get around this catch-22:

- Offer to do work at a reduced rate for friends and/or networking buddies so that you can build your portfolio.

- Whenever you see marketing materials or other copy that you think you could do better, simply create that better example on your own nickel. Then reach out to the company, tell them what you've done, and offer to show it to them. That's something they'll want to see. They become an automatic prospect for whom you have customized your portfolio.

• Offer to do a free critique of a company's existing marketing materials or publications. That way, you can show what you know in a way that's directly related to your prospect, rather than show what you've done for others. By submitting an unsolicited critique to an editor, the late nonfiction book author John Jerome was given an opportunity to work for Harold Hayes at *Esquire.*

7

MAGAZINE ARTICLES: THE WRITER'S BREAD AND BUTTER

M ore than 8,000 magazines are published in the United States, and filling their pages with articles is the most common means of earning money for the average freelance writer. This chapter shows you how to come up with ideas for articles, present them to magazines, get hired to write the articles, and sell them for anywhere from $300 to $2,000 each.

KNOW YOUR MARKET

Magazine editors are often as style conscious as Paris fashion designers. Each piece of written "fabric" that falls between the pages of *Sports Illustrated*, *Southwest Art*, or *Cooking Light* is carefully tucked and tailored to fit specific standards. But contrary to popular belief, you don't have to read stacks of issues to nail a magazine's style—although it can't hurt.

"When I first sold to *Nation's Business* years ago, the editor commented that I was 'obviously extremely familiar' with his magazine," says writer Sandra Dark. "In fact, I'd studied just one issue, using five steps that have helped me crack dozens of markets."

Length matters

After determining the acceptable word count, you must also consider the length of the paragraphs and sentences in your target market. In the narrow-column format of *Woman's World*, even moderate-length sentences and paragraphs appear to run on forever, whereas *The New Yorker* isn't at all averse to large blocks of words. To learn where to set your article's hemlines, select a representative article. Count the sentences in the longest paragraphs and the words in the longest sentences.

While you're at it, match your word choices to the readership's education level by checking the advertising. If ads tout economy cars, buy-one-get-one-free optical shops, and vacations to Branson, Missouri, the audience is more likely to be low to middle-income with a high school education.

Ads for Mercedes cars, Prada handbags, and vacations to Majorca signify high-income, college-educated readers. Keep in mind, however, that most publications fall somewhere between these extremes. Also check the photos of people in ads and articles for age, gender, apparent occupation, and estimated income.

Pick an opening

Do articles in your target magazine tend to open with humorous anecdotes, dramatic scenes, telling statistics, eye-catching quotes, or bold statements? Go out of your way to fit that bill.

"For a Kiwanis piece on refugee children, I needed a dramatic opening showing a traumatized youth's arrival in his country of refuge," says Sandra. "I searched the world over (via email) before locating a young Congolese refugee in the U.K. Leading with his story helped to personalize a tragedy of worldwide proportions."

Choose your people

How many sources are featured in articles of a similar type and length as yours? Are they experts, everyday people, or a mix of both? Are they of a distinct age group or social niche?

"Pay special attention to the caliber of experts," advises Sandra. "*Nation's Business* is aimed at small-business owners, so for an article on company identity, I interviewed a graphics designer who specialized in logos for small businesses. But for a Kiwanis piece on hearing loss, I could settle for nothing less than a top dog at the National Institutes of Health."

Also note when people are introduced. How many quotes and anecdotes are used? The more story elements you can quantify, the easier it is to judge whether your own work is in style.

Spread the news

How is key information introduced? Are statistics thrown into one paragraph or scattered throughout an article? How many sidebars are used, and what types of material do they contain? Are anecdotes or facts emphasized more? Does the writer of an article on out-of-control children tell of a family in chaos, and then ask experts on child behaviors for advice?

Get in the mood

Hitting just the right tone can be the toughest part of nailing an individual magazine's style. When *Oklahoma Today* requested a "nuts-and-bolts article on gardening in Oklahoma—but with lots of mood," Sandra scanned the tables of contents of several issues. A feature on bald eagles contained a wealth of information from wildlife experts, woven through poetic prose about this magnificent national symbol. The combination showed her just the balance of information and fanciful language she needed to nail the tone of her gardening article. With the proper mood set, she went back and checked the other four points on her market analysis list and was able to write an article that perfectly satisfied the editor.

HOW TO WRITE WINNING QUERY LETTERS

Freelance writer Carolyn Campbell outlines a formula that helps make the words *query* and *quick* go together. This method has sold 600 nationally published articles and cuts your query letter writing time to half an hour per letter.

First paragraph: The actual lead

Make the actual first paragraph of your article the first page of your query letter. Make it a traditional lead paragraph that will draw the editor in and make him want to read the entire article.

Help the editor envision your work as a finished article by crafting this paragraph as professionally as possible. Make it colorful, engaging, and interesting.

For instance, here is the first paragraph of a query letter that sold an article on strokes in younger men to a major consumer health magazine:

> A few months ago, while I was on the telephone with a client, I became temporarily unable to speak or take notes with a pen. When these symptoms disappeared after a minute or so, I did the stupidest thing I ever did in my life: I ignored them and went back to work.

If you need to interview an expert or person who is the subject of your article for factual information, call and ask for a 10-minute interview, saying that you will call again if the article is accepted. You do not need to write any more of the actual article unless you receive the assignment.

Second paragraph: The "Why you should care" paragraph

This paragraph tells why the article should be written and which readers will be interested in reading it. For a medical article, it might say, "50 million women will be diagnosed with breast cancer this year" or "Increasing numbers of people suffer from latex allergy." Here's the second paragraph from the query letter for the early strokes article:

> What I had was a TIA, or Transient Ischemic Attack. A TIA, which is a temporary decrease of blood flow to the brain, is a warning sign of an impending stroke—and if more men knew about it and recognized it, thousands of needless strokes could be prevented.

Aside from telling how many readers might be interested, it could also explain why a particular topic is timely, possibly because it relates to a news event or current trend. A regional angle could be mentioned here, too.

Alternately, this section could describe why the article topic is unique and deserves publicity. If it is a profile of an individual, it could include one or more sentences relating why this person is noteworthy and famous—or unique and undiscovered.

This section can also include reasons why an article fits a particular publication. Use a sentence such as, "I believe this article will be right on target for *Redbook*'s 38 million women readers who are under 40." If you know a specific section of the magazine, such as "Real Life Drama" or

"Sequels," that your article will fit, mention it here.

Include a possible title to further help the editor envision your idea as a finished article. "I feel this article, possibly titled, "River Rescue," would be an excellent story for the "Real Life Drama" section of *Woman's World*. When you're creating this paragraph, think of the query letter as a mini-article, including as many elements of the complete article as possible, such as a possible title, to help the editor visualize it as an article in his magazine.

Third paragraph: Why you should be the writer

This paragraph gives reasons why the magazine should choose you to write the story.

You can mention your experience, such as, "As the author of 300 nationally published articles, I feel that..." or your connections, "I have personally interviewed Michael Jordan and feel that..." or your qualifications, "As the author of a finance column for 20 years..."

Or include any proximity to the subject or specialized materials that you have. "As a master gardener for 20 years, I have a collection of photographs." If you have published clips to submit, mention that at the end of this paragraph: "I appreciate your consideration, and would be happy to submit nationally published clips."

All-purpose ending sentences

Here's a standard closing you can use in all your query letters: "If you will send me a possible word length and deadline, I will be happy to begin writing this feature immediately. I appreciate your consideration and have enclosed a self-addressed stamped envelope (SASE)."

Three additional query letter tips

- For maximum sales potential try to keep queries to one page. Two-page queries sell sometimes; three-page queries almost never sell.

- Remember to include as many elements of the finished article or book as possible. After you write a query, send batches of it out to as many potential markets as possible.

- Always include an SASE the editor can use to reply to your query.

The following query letter resulted in an article assignment for the author.

> Dear Mr. Koten:
>
> My small company, Center for Technical Communication (CTC), has a marketing director, sales manager, office manager, controller, bookkeeper, shipping manager, and administrative assistant. Yet we don't have a single employee on the payroll.
>
> How is this possible? Outsourcing. All of these functions are performed by independent contractors. Once a strategy embraced mainly by a downsized corporate America, outsourcing is now being used by small businesses of all types—from accounting firms to petting zoos.
>
> I'd like to write an article for your magazine titled, "7 Smart Secrets of Savvy Small Business Outsourcing," on how small businesses can use outsourcing to increase their ability to serve customers without adding staff or overhead. Topics include:
>
> - types of services that can be outsourced (and what should not be)
>
> - how to determine whether to outsource a particular function or task
>
> - where to find—and how to select—reputable third-party service firms for outsourcing
>
> - negotiating contracts, fees, and payment arrangements
>
> - how outsourcing can improve business results while reducing capital investment and operating costs
>
> - equipment and technology that can make outsourcing more efficient
>
> - examples of small businesses that have successfully outsourced functions previously handled in-house

- moving toward the concept of a "virtual business"—
  90 percent outsourcing, with all business partners
  connected via the Internet

- a sidebar of major national outsourcing firms with
  contact information and services offered.

By way of introduction, I am the author of more than
100 magazine articles and 50 books including *101 Ways to
Make Every Second Count* (Career Press). My articles
have appeared in *Cosmopolitan*, *Amtrak Express*, and *New
Jersey Monthly*.

I can have this article on your desk in 3 to 4 weeks.
Shall I proceed as outlined?

Sincerely,

Bob Bly

SHOULD YOU ENCLOSE CLIPS WITH YOUR QUERY LETTER?

Query letters may open the door to publications, but your clips (samples
of your published work) can mean the difference between that door staying open and it slamming in your face. And while reams of resources exist
for professional and aspiring writers, surprisingly few books or articles
offer much information on presenting your clips properly.

Here's how to use your clips to your best advantage:

- Send your best work. Never send anything with typos. (Yes, these
  things do get into print.) Once you've narrowed it down to your best,
  go for the most recent, as well as those clips that show you can write
  the kind of story you're proposing (e.g., if you're querying about a
  profile, include a profile clip).

- If an editor accepts clips via email, follow submission instructions
  carefully, especially if she requests a certain format. If she asks for
  clips in an HTML file, but you send them as a Word document, your
  email will likely be deleted unread.

- Always include the name of the publication where your article appeared and the run date. If these facts aren't included on the page with your clip, improvise. It's fine to simply write the name of the publication and the date neatly on the top of your clip.

- Make sure your copies are clear and easy to read, and your paper is in first-rate condition. It's a good idea to have a file of clips ready. Keep the file in a place where the copies won't get damp or torn.

- Send copies of your clips instead of the originals. If an editor does want originals, she'll specifically request tear sheets or hard copies in the writers' guidelines.

MORE TIPS FOR SUCCEEDING AS A MAGAZINE WRITER

Writer Daria Bruno offers the following tips for maximizing your success and income as a freelance magazine writer:

- *Market every day.* Don't stop. Set marketing goals. Even when you're swamped with work, send resumes and aim to make new contacts. The response time from companies isn't always immediate, so you never know when something will come up. Ideally, it will be at a time when you need it.

- *Have business cards.* With a paper clip, attach a business card to completed assignments, especially for new clients. Business cards are easy to keep, fit nicely in a Rolodex, and give your new client an easy means to find your contact information. Have business cards with you at all times. You never know when you'll meet someone at the post office or a barbecue who says, "My friend's been looking for a good editor."

- *Have a website.* You can include your URL in the signature line of all your emails and on your business cards. People love to look at other people's websites, especially when they know them. They can bookmark your site or find out further information about your services. You can also use your URL as an online, easy-access promotional tool and resume.

- *Have updated resumes* (in absolutely perfect condition) along with cover letter templates on hand so you can send them off fairly easily. Check job postings regularly on sites that list freelance opportunities. Set daily or weekly goals for sending out resumes and making cold calls (or sending emails).

- *Keep excellent records.* Maintain a database of all your contacts. Note when you and the editor were last in touch. Keep files for each client. Log hours for projects you're working on each day.

  When you get checks, move invoices from an outstanding to a paid folder. You never know when you'll need to pull up an old file of an earlier revision of something you are working on or an invoice from several months ago.

  Keep an electronic file of correspondence with clients. Being organized, making time for administrative tasks, having an excellent filing system, and keeping on top of paperwork are essential to running your own business. These things also impress your clients.

- *Diversify.* Widening your net can bring in new projects. "I picked up new clients as I diversified my skill sets to developmental editing, web copy, copyediting, and proofreading," writes Daria. "I called everyone I knew, including old employers."

- *Join professional associations and LISTSERVs.* Participating in a community of other editorial freelancers is hugely important for both learning and networking. By reading the posts on those lists, you can discover the variety of ways people handle different situations in their writing businesses.

  Another important aspect of professional affiliations and participation in online writer's forums is the valuable support and encouragement from peers and colleagues who genuinely understand your ups and downs. It's one thing to tell a friend or partner when a client is frustrating, when we're overwhelmed, or when things are just slow enough to make you howl; but advice, support, and encouragement from those who have been there can be a lifesaver.

- *Make time for your business.* "I know a lot of people who freelance and keep their day jobs," says Daria. "I sympathize with them—it's a lot of work. I chose to 'wing it' and I hit some serious rough spots financially, but eventually I pulled through."

Everyone has his or her own comfort level, but once you finally decide to do it, you have to be willing to sacrifice a lot. Daria notes: "I gave up weekends for a very long time. I worked until the wee hours of the morning. It's tempting, when you work from home, to take the afternoon off and shop or meet a friend, but I kept at it—always available. My response time was fast, my turnaround time even faster, and I followed up with clients, too."

This may not be for everyone. Relationships can suffer when you're at your computer 12 hours a day. You may not get dressed for days at a time. You may think you're losing your social skills. Essentially, it's like giving birth to something—you have to nurture it, take good care of yourself in the process, and just be there for it all the time to witness every growth spurt, to be available for any problem that can arise.

MARKETING AND
SELF-PROMOTION FOR WRITERS

I n his book *How to Become a Successful Freelance Writer* (Moonstone Press, 1981), freelancer Jordan Young writes:

> One thing I've learned along the way is that a writer must be aggressive, even if shy by nature. I was shy and introverted, but I outgrew it. As I got older, I realized I was never going to make any money writing if I didn't learn to sell it. You can write the greatest novel ever written—it will never see the light of day if you can't sell it. Don't expect an agent to sell it for you. You have to sell an agent on YOU before he will take on your work.

I'll go a step further: In most instances, the writers who earn the most money are not necessarily the best writers; they are the best marketers. The highest-paid freelance writers in most areas—including magazine articles, book publishing, and copywriting—are typically those who do the most self-promotion, not those who write the finest prose.

As a freelance writer, your time will likely be divided as follows:

• Half of your time is spent doing billable work—work you get paid for.

This consists mainly of research, writing, and rewriting materials for editors and clients.

- A quarter of your time is spent running your office (e.g., paying bills, making photocopies, trips to FedEx and the post office) and self-education (reading books and articles, taking courses, surfing the Internet).

- A quarter of your time is spent on marketing, promoting, and selling your writing services.

Notice that only half your time is spent doing work you can bill the client for! Therefore, if you work a 40-hour week, you actually complete only 20 hours of billable work. If your goal is to earn $2,000 a week, which equates to $100,000 a year, you have to bill your writing services at a rate of $100 an hour.

Can't charge that much? Then you have several choices. You can put in more hours. I work 60 hours a week, not 40 hours. You can also work more efficiently. For instance, I never waste time going to the post office or FedEx, because I hire an assistant to do it for me. Therefore, the percentage of my workweek that is billable is closer to 60 or 70 percent, not 50 percent.

You can also take on jobs that generate passive income. For example, when you write a book that continues to sell thousands of copies for years, you get royalty checks long after the work is done. Last week I got a $2,000 check for a book I wrote in 1982.

Or, like an increasing number of writers today, you can write and sell information products on the Internet. The revenues from my Internet marketing sideline business are a respectable $4,000 a week, and others are making many times that amount. Keep in mind that $4,000 a week comes to about $200,000 a year, and to earn that, I spent only a couple of hours a week! (Details in chapter 12.)

In this chapter, I'll share tips for marketing and promoting yourself as a freelance writer more effectively. The result: more work, at higher fees, and increased income.

TWENTY TIPS FOR SUCCESSFUL SELF-PROMOTION

These self-promotion tips can work for writers in a wide range of special-ties, but were developed specifically for freelance copywriters and others handling business and corporate clients:

1. Never tell anyone that you are not busy and that you are looking for work. (Clients want to hire those who are successful, not those who are hungry.)

2. Always put your name, address, phone numbers, fax number, email address, and website URL on every piece of promotion you produce. This makes it easy for potential new business to reach you.

3. Write a book. It positions you as an expert. Another great way to establish your credibility as an expert in your field is to create a con-tent-rich website.

4. If you don't have the time to write a book, write an article, booklet, or special report.

5. When you write that article, try to sell it to more than one publication. (You can change the title and a few of the examples to tailor it to each publication's readers.)

6. Regularly mail reprints of your articles to your prospects and clients. Attach a note or short cover letter to personalize the mailing.

7. Advertise your services in magazines aimed at advertising profession-als. Try a variety of journals and different ads until you find out which ads give the best results. Also try both classified and display formats.

8. Use direct mail to generate new business leads. A successful mailing of only a hundred letters can often yield 2 to 5 highly qualified new prospects.

9. Create a package of literature describing your services, background, fees, methods, clients, and so forth. Mail the package to people who request more information in response to your ads and mailings. Such a package is extremely useful in prescreening leads.

10. Some copywriters, such as the late Paul Bringe, have had great success using self-published newsletters to promote their services. Newsletters help build recognition and establish credibility with a select audience (the people who receive the newsletter) over an extended period of time. Your newsletter can be print or electronic. The latter, also called an "e-zine," has many advantages, including low cost, no printing or postage, and instant delivery.

11. Don't skimp on letterhead, envelopes, and business cards. The letterhead design and paper quality can convey an image of class and success.

12. Offer to speak and give seminars before trade associations and professional groups. Make sure potential clients will be among those in attendance.

13. Teach a course in advertising, marketing, or writing at a local college or university—day school or adult education. This establishes you as an "instant expert" in the field.

14. Network. Don't be a recluse. Socialize. Attend meetings, seminars, and luncheons. Volunteer to work on a committee. Become visible in the advertising community.

15. Recycle your material. A lecture can become the basis for an article or series of articles. Allow others to reprint your articles in their newsletters and on their websites as long as they credit you as the author and include your website URL. The articles can be turned into a book. Using your basic material over and over makes it possible to get broad exposure and still have time to devote to your copywriting business.

16. Be selective. Not every opportunity to speak, lecture, write, or participate is worthwhile. Focus on those promotional activities that will give you the most return on your time and effort.

17. Keep your name in front of clients and prospects with a premium: a giveaway like a calendar, pen, golf balls, or other item imprinted with your logo, name, and contact information. Most will appreciate your thoughtfulness. And the right premium—one that is kept in the office

for years—serves as a daily reminder of you and your service.

18. Let people know about your recent successes. If your latest piece of copy was a rousing success, get extra copies and send them to prospects and clients in similar fields. Include a cover note that says, "Here's what I've done recently. Now let me do the same for *you!*"

19. Save any letters of praise you receive from clients and build a kudos file. Selected quotations from these letters, or even reprints of the letters themselves, can dramatically add to the selling power of your next ad or mailing. (Be sure to get permission first before you quote someone in print!)

20. Keep written records of past promotions and their results. Only by measuring the success or failure of promotional experiments can we learn which promotions work for us and which will bomb.

How to Network Effectively with Editors, Prospects, and Fellow Writers

Networking is a high-tech-sounding name for a simple activity that has been going on for a long time: doing business through personal contacts. Writer and self-promotion consultant Ilise Benun defines networking as "a timely exchange of selected bits of information about your business that you offer when someone is ready to hear it."

The purpose of networking is to meet as many people as possible who can in some way help advance your career. Networking expert Donna Fisher estimates that 70 percent of jobs, for example, are found through networking.

Writing in *Success*, Steve Fishman defines networking as "the single-minded pursuit of useful contacts at every convention, seminar, or neighborhood barbecue. To the networked, every stranger represents an opportunity, the chance to find prospects, reach targets, or meet friends."

Why network? There are several benefits. First, writing is a solitary activity, and loneliness can be a problem. One way to cope with isolation is to force yourself to get away from the keyboard every now and then. It can be mentally stimulating and refreshing to have lunch with a group of writers or attend an evening lecture sponsored by a local business club. You meet new people, make friends, and exchange ideas.

Forming a network—a group of people you know and who know you—can open up many new doors for you. For instance, at one luncheon I met a man who recently opened his own printing business. We established a good rapport, and he now does most of my printing for me, paying closer attention to my jobs than other printers I had found through local Yellow Pages ads.

Networking builds a base of people resources you can count on to help you with many situations. Now I can turn to my card file and find artists, writers, printers, photographers, lawyers, accountants, computer consultants, website designers, and many other professionals who can be of service to me or my clients. I know I'll get immediate attention from these people because we've already established a personal relationship, no matter how brief.

Often I will refer one person in my network to another person who can help. For example, an audiovisual producer called and asked if I knew someone who could direct a corporate video for her. I was able to give her the name of an independent director I had met. The referral ended the producer's search and put some money in the director's pocket. And although I've never asked for it, I'm sure both of these people would be glad to return the favor someday.

Networking can also lead to more business for you. Most often, someone you meet through networking may keep your card and someday give your name to a prospective client. Or sometimes you meet a potential client directly. In either case, the more people who know your name, the better. The advantage of networking over advertising is that people you meet through networking are more likely to remember you because of the face-to-face contact.

Are you, like me, a reluctant networker? One way to get started in networking is to join several clubs or associations. Paying the membership dues somehow makes you feel as if you should at least attend a meeting or two to get your money's worth. Another way to force yourself to network more is to call up a colleague and invite him or her to attend an upcoming event with you. Do it several weeks in advance. Making the commitment early helps to prevent you from backing out at the last minute.

Some additional networking tips:

- Determine the mode of attendance with which you're most comfortable. Some of us are most comfortable going to our first meeting of a group accompanied by a friend who is already a member. I am most comfortable networking at events where I am a speaker.

- Don't be a wallflower. Walk over to people and make conversation.

- Get a drink from the bar and hold onto it, even if you don't drink. Having a glass in hand can help shy people overcome nervousness.

- Do not sell while networking. Your purpose is to make contacts, not to get a client to sign a purchase order.

- Listen more than you speak. Focus on what others are interested in. "When you have your attention on something other than yourself, your self-consciousness will disappear and others will be more likely to remember and appreciate you," says Fisher.

- Dress in proper business attire. Your comfortable, well-worn writing clothes are not appropriate for a business gathering.

- Don't rush out the door as soon as the event is over. "The best contacts I've made have happened after an event—in the bathroom, elevator, lobby, or even on the street," notes Benun. "That's when people's minds are open to it. That's when their defenses are down."

- When you get home, follow up by sending people a short note that says, "It was a pleasure meeting you; let's keep in touch." You might also enclose another business card, a brochure about your services, or a reprint of a recent article you wrote.

CREATE A BAIT PIECE

When you are pursuing corporate assignments, your potential clients want to be assured that you know what you are doing.

For instance, if you are offering your services as a speechwriter, you are more likely to win assignments when the client is convinced that you are an expert on the subject of speeches.

One of the easiest, fastest, and most affordable ways to achieve this credibility is with a bait piece. A bait piece is a short booklet, special report, white paper, or other informational document that gives how-to advice on a specific topic.

A speechwriter might write and self-publish a small pamphlet with the title "10 Tips for Giving an Effective Speech." The content presents tips on how to give a good speech. The objective, though, is not to give away free advice; it is to convince potential speechwriting clients that you are an expert in public speaking.

Having a bait piece serves three important functions:

1. It helps you generate leads from potential writing clients.

2. It convinces these potential clients to choose you instead of your competitors.

3. It helps ensure client satisfaction.

Let's take a brief look at these three items:

*   *The bait piece helps you generate leads from potential writing clients.* Clients are bombarded with sales pitches from freelance writers seeking their business. As a result, they often don't respond—even when your writing services might be a good fit for them—because they simply don't have time.

    Offering a bait piece in your promotions (direct mail, ads, email marketing) induces potential clients who would not otherwise respond to call or write you and request the bait piece.

    For instance, if you are sending out sales letters to corporate communications managers to generate inquiries for your speechwriting services, add a P.S. as follows: "P.S. Be sure to ask for a *free* copy of our informative booklet, '10 Tips for Giving an Effective Speech,' which can help assure that the speech I write for you is met with a standing ovation."

    Result: the offer of a bait piece can easily double or triple the response to your letter. Reason why it works: The bait piece is perceived as useful how-to information, not just advertising. Therefore, the potential client feels he will benefit from replying whether he hires you or not.

- *It convinces these potential clients to choose you instead of your competitors.* When the client gets your booklet or pamphlet, reads it, and sees that your advice is useful and sensible, he becomes convinced that you are an expert in your field—and therefore is more likely to hire you.

- *It helps ensure client satisfaction.* In your booklet, you will be giving helpful advice on your topic—slanted, naturally, to reflect your point of view. Clients who read it and agree with it are therefore more likely to be satisfied with your work, because they share your opinion of what makes a good speech, website, or whatever you are writing for them.

Marketing by offering customers and prospects free, useful information—booklets, special reports, checklists, guides, manuals, newsletters, monographs, books, white papers—has been a proven, effective sales tool for decades. Why? Because they work! For instance, more than half of Information Technology (IT) professionals surveyed said that a white paper influenced a buying decision.

Earlier I introduced the idea of a bait piece—free information used to hook the reader into responding to your advertisement. Every commercial writer should use a bait piece in his or her marketing to maximize inquiries and leads.

During the recession in the early 1990s, I promoted my copywriting services by writing and printing a booklet, "Recession-Proof Business Strategies: 14 Ways to Sell Any Product or Service in a Down Economy." Because it tied into a timely topic, the press release I sent out to the media—mainly the business section editors of daily newspapers and managing editors of business and marketing magazines—was picked up in dozens of publications, including the front cover of *Nation's Business.*

To offset my printing costs, I charged $7 for the booklet (I don't recommend this; asking for money depresses response, reducing the number of leads).

Almost two dozen publications ran articles about my booklet ranging from a few paragraphs to a full page. I sold more than 3,500 copies, grossing almost $25,000 in sales. I also received numerous invitations to lecture about recession-proof marketing, generating thousands of additional dollars in speaking fees, as well as consulting and writing assignments from a number of companies.

Tips for marketing with bait pieces

- The easiest way to organize and write your bait piece is in a numbered list format; e.g., "Eight Ways to Help Search Engines Find your Website."

- Readers are attracted to titles that promise "Seven tips" or "Eight ways." They want to know what the seven tips or eight ways are.

- Keep the bait piece brief; 1,500 to 2,000 words are plenty. You can go longer if you need more room, but busy readers appreciate brevity and conciseness.

- The design of your bait piece need not be elaborate. Black ink on white 8 ½-by-11-inch paper is fine. No elaborate illustrations, graphics, or colors are required.

- The best format for offering your bait piece online is as a downloadable PDF file. To capture the lead, require the prospect to give you his information (name, phone number, email address) before permitting him to download the file.

- Bait pieces on electronic media—audios, videos, and CD-ROMs—really stand out. Audios are particularly effective because they are inexpensive to duplicate, and the potential client can listen while driving.

- How many bait pieces should you have? I recommend having separate bait pieces for each of your writing specialties.

- Narrow the topic and aim at a specific audience. A generic bait piece on "how to write effective copy" is good—but "10 tips for annual report writing" is more likely to pique the interest of the corporate communications manager looking for a writer to handle this year's report.

How to Get the Most Out of a Book Signing or Event

There are three main reasons for doing book events:

- It's a reason to contact your local media about your book; an opportunity to get on various calendars; and best of all, a way to get your book in stores.

- It's a chance to get to know a store's staff, a very good thing as staffers commonly make recommendations of books to customers. Taking cookies to the staff, writing thank-you notes, etc., are additional ways to enhance your position with the staff.

- It's an occasion to use your mailing list (you do have a mailing list?) to keep in touch with earlier buyers and prospective buyers of your book.

Don't try to do events on the same book at several stores in the same area. Don't dilute interest by appearing in too many places. This upsets the bookstore owners and event coordinators as it steals their thunder.

It's tremendously important that any author understand what marketing is all about. Enterprising authors have done very well in unexpected venues. For example, the author of a book about Harley-Davidson—the company, the machines, the mystique—regularly visits the Harley-Davidson shops and signs books.

Another author has a special map for cyclists along with his book on bicycling in his area. The printing crew got very interested in it when they were producing the maps and he wound up doing an impromptu signing at the printer's! Author Tom Hegg has a perennially popular book, *A Cup of Christmas Tea*, and is usually booked pretty solidly for talks, readings, and signings for church groups.

Other tips: The more buzz you can create about a book prior to seeking a book event the better. It doesn't hurt to have a box of books in the car at the time of the event in case the store has underordered or books have not arrived (it happens!).

Here are some additional ideas for promoting your book:

- Tell your friends about the book. Urge them to buy it and tell *their* friends.

- Post book fliers at places you frequent, and mail fliers to friends.

- Make sure your local bookstores are carrying it and that it is well displayed.

- Does your library have it? Talk with the librarian and offer to do a talk or other event focusing on the book.

- If you frequent a yoga center, art studio, acupuncture clinic, co-op, or any kind of related meeting places, would they perhaps sell copies or post a flyer?

- Ask friends to write a review on Amazon.com or BarnesandNoble.com, and post information on the book on related newsgroups and online bulletin boards.

- Write letters to any media people you know, or call them, and urge them to interview you or review the book.

- Write to Oprah and urge her to put you on the show. This is a long shot, but try contacting Oprah, Harpo Productions, 110 N. Carpenter Street, Chicago, IL 60607.

- Do you know teachers? Ask them to consider using the book in a class.

- Let people know you are available to do readings, talks, workshops, and conferences.

MORE PR TIPS FOR WRITERS

As an author, it is important for you to know certain publicity strategies that will help your book get noticed. Here is a brief guide to what you can do to help.

- Know yourself. What are your abilities and what are your limits? Will you be willing to speak in public often and to large audiences? Are you willing to travel?

- Do you have any personal connections your publisher might be able to use?

- Are you willing to seize all opportunities, including contests, special awards, and book signings?

- Do you have any interesting aspects to your personal history that might help the publisher sell the book?

- Know how to market yourself. Prepare for all speaking engagements, even the smaller ones, as you would for the larger opportunities.

- Are there any promotional items, logos, or trademarked phrases that can be marketed with your book? Visuals often help to stimulate purchases. It is a way for the book to stand out in the reader's mind. Many times, repetition is what allows an image or phrase to stick.

- Is your book specific to a certain demographic? Can it be used as a college textbook? If so, for what type of class or lecture? The numbers involved in textbook sales can be large. Hundreds of thousands of dollars are waiting to be spent on books by colleges and lecturers. Can your book be one of those?

- Realistically answer this question: Is your book really appropriate for television or radio? We all want to be in the limelight, but is your book and (more importantly) are you appropriate for the television and radio media?

- Arrange speaking dates in advance. You want plenty of time to prepare and research the target audience. You want the audience to understand you and your book, so you need to understand them. Know everything you can about the show, venue, station, etc., that you are planning to appear at. If you can relate to the audience, they can relate to your book.

- Plan some local publicity (i.e., bookstore readings, public access television appearances, newspaper ads and reviews) to tie in to the event and garner more response for your book.

- No radio or television program is willing to promote your book unless you give them a good show. Provide a program that will entertain but also inform—engage your audience while still providing the necessary information.

- Have a sense of humor about yourself and your book. People respond to humor in a positive way. Why not be the author who is approachable and easy to relate to? If you can have fun at the event, the host will promote you and your book more so than they might for an author who makes it seem like work.

- Expect to give out free copies of your book. Producers, hosts, venue owners, and meeting planners will usually request at least one copy of your book. Also have media packages available upon request. You will have to absorb the cost of the mailing, but the publicity benefits greatly make up for that.

- Be prepared to appear or speak at inconvenient times. Oftentimes, radio or television stations will ask you to arrive and be on the air at inconvenient times. This should not be a hindrance. All publicity is worthy of your time, even at 4:00 a.m.

- Appear at libraries. Libraries are great places to do signings, as they are actively seeking out authors to bring into their branch.

- Realize that publicity takes time and effort to show results.

- Set reasonable goals. For a small press, a successful book signing is one that pulls 30 to 40 people with book sales to at least half of those present.. And even if sales at the event are modest, the store has bought a good number of books that will be on the shelves for months after the event.

- Use the local angle. Connect the book with something that will interest a regional audience. Communities always want to support their own members. Larger cities are not necessarily the first place you want to go. Get a buzz going in a more modest-sized city. It's easier to manage.

- Get creative. Make yourself and your book stand out. It's just one more book in an already saturated market unless you can find that special angle. Of the $23 billion spent on books, roughly $10 billion is spent in bookstores. The rest is through specialty markets.

- Do not underestimate the power of reviews. People rely heavily on them before they invest their money and time in a book, so get reviewed wherever possible.

- Send review copies of your book to local papers, radio stations, and colleges. Place an ad locally and/or nationally to support the review.

- Participate in Internet discussion lists, but be tactful about it. You need to establish a presence on the list before mentioning your book. Some lists prohibit any kind of self-advertising, so be aware of list rules. Some allow a brief signature line on your postings that could mention your book.

- Online magazines and websites are a valuable resource. Send review copies to various online publications, both big and small. This is a relatively low-cost manner in which to seek reviews.

- Use the "letters to the editor" pages of newspapers. They are free to everyone and often overlooked when one determines a marketing strategy. It is an obvious, easy way to get into the news.

- As soon as you are published, you are an expert. Use this to your advantage. Lend advice or provide quotes to other authors or lecturers. They will then have to include your name and book information within their speech and text, on their back cover, and so on.

- Seek out all news columns. Constant exposure to the public will allow you to not only promote your book regularly, but also become familiar to your audience. If they trust you, they will seek your information.

- Acquire appropriate training and certification, so that you have the necessary information and an adequate background.

- Get newspapers and magazines to write articles about your subject matter, using you as an expert source. It can be much more valuable to have your name and your book mentioned in a news or feature article than in a review, as more people read articles than read reviews, and you are presented as an expert in an article.

VENUES FOR BOOK PROMOTION

If you are willing to spend money for your book promotion, here is a list of sites and other options authors have found extremely useful. However, they do require out-of-pocket expense on your part. Use these services to get interviews, PR, and publicity for a fee:

- GuestFinder (www.GuestFinder.com). GuestFinder is a web-based directory of people available for radio, TV, and newspaper interviews. Available speakers receive their own web page that includes a picture, bio, and suggested interview questions, which can easily be accessed by producers looking for interview guests for their shows. This service provides them with the necessary information to schedule you for an interview.

- IMedia Fax Service (www.IMediaFax.com). This service allows you to target specific media outlets for press release distribution by supplying the critical information necessary to market effectively.

- *Radio-TV Interview Report* (www.rtir.com). This is a magazine and website that bills itself as the magazine producers read to find guests. They are the world's largest database of authors and experts who are available for live and telephone interviews on a wide range of subjects.

HIRING YOUR OWN PUBLICIST

Your publisher will most likely promote your book, but there is no end to what can be done in the way of publicity. A wise investment might be to hire a publicist of your own to work on your campaign. A good publicist will have invaluable connections that may accomplish quite a bit.

When you're considering a publicist, ask:

- What is your experience in the publishing business?

- Can I pay you by the hour?

- Do you require a monthly retainer?

Thoroughly research a possible publicist. Many times you will be charged regardless of the results yielded. Know beforehand your publicist's limitations and abilities. Also consider which type of publicist you require.

When you hire a PR advisor on an hourly basis, you pay only for what you need. You can tap into the professional's experience for their contacts, affiliations, and knowledge, but do the grunt work (e.g., stuffing press releases into envelopes) yourself to save money.

By comparison, when you hire a PR firm for a monthly retainer, you are guaranteed more or less constant attention and publicist availability. These more highly paid publicists should have a significant contact base. Retainer publicists are more likely to find the market for your book and get you noticed. Make sure you research a publicist before you commit.

The disadvantage of monthly PR retainers is the high cost. Most publicists average between $2,000 and $10,000 a month with a 6-month contract. And often, you pay these high rates for manual labor that can easily be done by you for far less money (i.e., sending out press kits, mailings, etc.).

GAINING VISIBILITY IN THE MARKETPLACE

Writer Mandy Borgmeler offers these PR tips for getting your name out and generating demand for your writing services or your writings:

- *Circulate.* Attend networking events in your hometown and surrounding areas. Check with the chamber of commerce for a list of these. Become involved with community activities. Volunteer for communities and offer to write promotional materials for free. You're likely to meet others who will pay for your services later, or refer you to someone who will. Join professional or community organizations geared toward your interests and get to know people.

- *Continuing education.* Dedicate yourself to professional growth. Attend writers' conferences and take notes. Involve yourself with helping others. Writers' groups are one way to do this. Critiquing of another writer's work is good indirect writing practice and often affords learning opportunities for you as well. Another way to learn from experience is to judge a writing contest.

- *Know your market.* Stay on top of industry trends, news, and events. Subscribe to trade journals specific to your genre or specialization, but also read those geared to topics you write about. Why not schedule two or three afternoons each month for spending at the library looking through current issues? Most newspapers have complimentary online versions you can read each morning.

- *Write and then write some more.* You've heard it before—write every day no matter what. Write and maintain a blog. Since marketing materials are part of my basket of services, my blog is all about marketing for the nonmarketer. This approach achieves four things: It helps get my name out (circulation), it establishes me as an expert in my field (an obvious competitive advantage), it forces me to keep learning my field and staying on top of the market, and it develops my skills.

- *Render extraordinary service to your clients.* Beyond meeting deadlines and submitting quality work, build a bond or relationship with your clients. Remember their birthdays, anniversaries, and other key dates. Write down important tidbits about their personal lives when you talk to them and store these tidbits in a file folder or as notes on your organizer.

- *Be a go-getter.* Get your name out, keep your eyes open, practice your trade, and take care of your clients, and you'll find yourself a step ahead of the writers who don't. Circulation keeps you fresh in the minds of potential clients or publications. Continuing education makes room for expansion of services. Knowing your market gives you an added edge, and honing your skills eventually makes you an expert. Take care of your client and he or she will take care of you with referrals.

9

BIG BUCKS IN BUSINESS WRITING

You can earn a six-figure income as a freelance writer without producing a best seller or selling scripts to the movies or TV. That's a realistic and achievable income for freelancers who pursue commercial freelancing—writing for corporate and institutional clients instead of book and magazine publishers.

And you don't have to crack into big companies like GE or Ford to do it! Of the nearly 11 million businesses in the United States, only 500 of them are Fortune 500 companies! Most of the rest—millions in fact—are small local companies. These businesses routinely use freelance writers to churn out fliers and circulars, releases to the local press, Rotary Club speeches, employee bulletins, customer newsletters, and other materials to sell products, promote goodwill, and motivate their staff.

In commercial freelancing, you perform writing services for corporations, entrepreneurs, trade associations, professional societies, colleges, museums, hospitals, and other commercial enterprises and organizations instead of for the traditional editor at a magazine or book publishing house. The material you write may have as its goal any of the following: to educate, to motivate, to entertain, to inform, or to persuade. But most assignments involve writing documents designed to sell (or help sell) a product, service, organization, or idea.

What types of commercial assignments are there? In a given year I will produce for my clients ads, sales letters, annual reports, direct mail packages, email marketing campaigns, e-zines, sales brochures, capabilities brochures ("corporate" brochures), catalogs, press releases, feature articles, speeches, slide presentations, videotapes, films, newsletters, booklets, pamphlets, websites, and any other materials they need to sell their products, communicate with employees and customers, or describe their activities.

What to Charge Business Clients

The biggest advantage of commercial writing is that it pays well. Many freelancers working in this field earn $75,000 to $125,000 a year and more. Unlike the magazine and book marketplace, where authors prepare queries and proposals they hope to sell to editors, clients in the commercial sector approach you, the writer, with specific assignments. They also provide all necessary background information, eliminating the need to do outside research.

According to an *Adweek* survey, 75 percent of commercial freelance writers charge by the project, while 25 percent bill at an hourly or day rate. And as freelancer Sig Rosenblum points out, "Fees are all over the lot."

I know many freelancers who charge $100 for a one-page press release; my fee is $800. I charge $9,500 to write a direct mail package; my friend Clayton Makepeace gets $25,000 plus a bonus based on sales for the same assignment. Hourly rates for freelancers also vary widely according to experience and geography.

To get a feel for what to charge, remember: Your initial meetings with your first prospects will quickly give you an idea of what constitutes a reasonable fee. For instance, let's say you ghostwrite speeches for local businesspeople. You find that some want to pay only $500 per speech while others agree to your quoted fee of $2,000, but no one expects to get it for less than $500 and no one is willing to go to $3,000. The range, then, is $500–$2,000.

It also helps to find out what fellow freelancers are charging for similar services. Many publish fee schedules, which you can get by calling or writing. Some, surprisingly, are happy to advise novices on what and how to charge. Your own fees, of course, will probably fall somewhere in the range of what others in your area are billing clients.

Any organization in your area that produces promotional, educational, or informational materials is a potential client for your freelance writing services. But many freelancers find prospecting for clients easier when they focus on companies in a particular field or industry—an industry in which the freelancer has prior experience.

When I started, I knew I could write competently in many different fields. Clients saw it differently, however. Banks wouldn't hire me because I had no financial samples in my portfolio. Pharmaceutical companies said to me, "We need a medical writer." Chemical and industrial firms, on the other hand, were thrilled to find a writer who was a chemical engineer by training and had been the advertising manager of a major manufacturer of chemical equipment.

The lesson here is that we live in an age of specialization. Your best bet for breaking into commercial writing is with clients in industries in which you have inside knowledge or previous experience, either as a writer or from some other job. Clients are eager to hire writers knowledgeable in their industry, who can advise them on promotional and marketing strategies, not just write copy.

FINDING CLIENTS

How do you locate clients? The *Standard Directory of Advertisers*, available in most libraries, is a good place to start. It provides detailed information on more than 17,000 companies nationwide that actively market their products and services, and is indexed both alphabetically and by state.

Who do you want to reach in these companies? If you write advertising materials—print ads, TV and radio commercials, sales brochures, point-of-purchase displays—contact the advertising manager, marketing manager, sales promotion manager, or manager of marketing communications.

If you specialize in corporate communications—annual reports, speeches, capabilities brochures, material for in-house publications—contact the manager of corporate communications.

If you write public relations materials—press releases, feature articles, case histories, newsletters—contact the manager of public relations.

If you specialize in employee communications writing, contact personnel managers or managers of human resources.

At large corporations, each area may be handled by a separate person.

At smaller firms, one individual may be responsible for all these functions. In either case, call the company and ask the receptionist for the name of the person in charge of the department you want to reach (if it is not listed in the *Standard Directory of Advertisers*). Nine times out of 10, this information is given freely over the phone.

Some freelancers get most of their work directly from corporations, called clients in the ad business, while others work primarily for advertising agencies, public relations firms, graphic design studios, audiovisual production houses, and other vendors that supply communications services to corporate America.

Listings for such vendors may be found under the appropriate category in your local Yellow Pages. For more detailed information on each company, consult industry directories.

Ad agencies, for instance, are listed in *The Standard Directory of Advertising Agencies,* again available at your library. Your contact will be the creative director, copy supervisor, or, at very small agencies, the owner or president.

In magazine and book publishing, writers approach prospective clients (publishers) with ideas they hope to sell. In commercial freelancing, the opposite is done: You approach clients and try to sell them on using you and your writing services. You are selling yourself, not a specific idea.

If the client likes you and decides to hire you, the client gives you an assignment to write according to specified guidelines. For example, the client may tell you, "We need a one-page ad selling our chemical product, a degreaser, to firms in the pulp and paper field."

If a client instead says, "Here is our product; tell us how to sell it," answering this question would require considerable thought on your part and would be considered a separate consulting assignment for which you should get a contract before starting. Giving away ideas for free, which is accepted as standard practice by book and magazine writers, is not done by successful commercial freelancers.

How do you make the initial contact and sell yourself to clients? Use the same approach as any business trying to sell its product or service: Market yourself.

What are the marketing vehicles used by successful freelancers working primarily in the commercial field? They span the spectrum from hard-sell promotions (such as classified and display ads, sales letters, brochures, self-mailers, and telemarketing), to soft-sell publicity vehicles such as giving speeches, networking, giving seminars, writing articles for the trade press, and distributing a free e-newsletter to your prospects and clients.

Direct mail is especially effective in making the initial contact. You can send a straightforward letter describing your background and writing services, either preprinted or computer-personalized, to prospective clients, both on the ad agency and corporate side.

In my own such letter, I include a reply card the prospect can mail back to request additional information on my services and a package of writing samples. The response rate of people sending back my reply card is 7 percent, which means by mailing 200 letters I can produce responses from 14 potential clients who say, in effect: "Yes, I'm interested in the possibility of hiring you to write for our firm. Tell me more about you." This is the type of response you want to generate.

Another powerful marketing technique is to publish articles in the trade press. Such articles—written by you on some facet of advertising, marketing, or business communications—help position you as an expert in the field and increase your visibility among the target audience you want to reach. Reprints of articles, imprinted with your address and phone number, make excellent additions to direct mail packages and can be used as handouts at shows, conferences, and meetings.

The most important ingredient of success in commercial writing is attitude. A recent conversation with the president of a small public relations and advertising agency summed this up nicely for me. He comments: "I have been dissatisfied with most of the freelance writers I have used. The problem is, they don't understand what they're doing. They think they're just putting words on paper. I tell them the background on a story, and they hand it back to me exactly as I gave it to them and say, 'Here's the story you wanted.' What they fail to realize is that our words have a purpose—they must sell, educate, inform, and motivate ... or the client is not getting his money's worth."

Or as ad man David Ogilvy puts it: "When I write an advertisement, I don't want you to tell me that you find it 'creative.' I want you to find it so interesting that you buy the product."

Let me give you a few tips that can help you produce the kind of copy commercial clients desire.

Writing Copy that Sells

- Keep it simple. On an episode of *thirtysomething*, college professor Gary questioned Michael's simple-minded approach to advertising. Ad man Michael replied angrily, "Much of the public has a second-grade reading level; they're not big fans of Shakespeare."

  I don't know about the second-grade reading level, but I agree that commercial messages should be clear, simple, and understandable. Remember, you are writing not to dazzle the reader with your prose, but to get the client's message across.

- Be concise. Don't waste words. Get your point across, then move on.

- Put yourself in the reader's shoes. The reader could care less about your client's products, or sales goals, or corporate policies. The reader cares about himself: his needs, his goals, his fears, his hopes. Always try to start with the reader, then build a bridge that relates to your sales message. For example, instead of "Our new telephone system …," say, "Your telecommunications needs …" or "Tired of paying through the nose for sky-high telephone bills?" You get the idea.

- Stress benefits, not features. Tell how the product, service, or idea helps the reader save time, make money, or improve his life. Instead of saying, "The *Encyclopedia of Health* is 467 pages long with 44 charts and graphs," say, "Now all the information you need to live a healthier, happier life is available from one single, authoritative source."

- Be specific. Avoid superlatives. Good commercial writing is fact-filled, imparting information the reader can use to make an intelligent decision about using your client's products and services. Many commercial writers mistakenly believe that consumers are stupid and that puffery will somehow bluff them into making a bad buying decision. They are wrong.

How do you get started in commercial freelancing? Although you can use the marketing techniques outlined above, the best way is simply to grab the opportunity to do this work when an offer comes your way.

And chances are, it will. Most magazine and book writers receive occasional offers to do corporate or ghostwriting work for commercial clients, but they pass it by. Next time such an offer comes your way, take it. Then build on this foundation.

The first client is the hardest to get. Once you have one commercial assignment under your belt, you can approach prospective clients as an experienced writer with a portfolio and client list, and not as a rank beginner.

Ask friends if their companies have employee newsletters, in-house publications, or annual reports. Ask them to find out the names of the people in charge of those publications. Then see if they can arrange introductions for you.

Getting your first clients and serving them well is extremely important. Do everything in your power to satisfy these clients and get more work from them. They become an important part of your marketing effort, providing references, testimonials, and proof of your ability to serve clients successfully.

Don't worry too much about fees at this point. The important thing is to build a portfolio, a client list, and a reputation for quality. Once you expand your client base and have a comfortable amount of work coming in, you can think about raising fees and dropping difficult or unprofitable accounts.

Increasing your income beyond this $100,000 ceiling takes work, but it is far from impossible. One way is to raise your fees, and as your reputation grows, you may want to do this. Another option is to find ways of working more efficiently, thus increasing billable hours.

Example: I know a freelance proofreader who, believe it or not, runs to the corner stationery store every time he wants to send or receive a fax. With the nominal cost of a fax machine today, this is foolish penny-pinching and an absurd waste of his time.

Another option is to hire an assistant to handle the mundane tasks of typing, correspondence, bookkeeping, and other general administrative functions, thus freeing you to concentrate on writing and marketing.

Several writers I know subcontract work to other freelancers who write at lower rates, and keep the difference as profit. This sounds fine in theory, but in reality finding other writers who meet your own standards of excellence can be difficult. The work they produce for you often is not what you would find acceptable for submission to the client.

One writer I know of describes himself as a "freelance information packager," and this is a good description of the direction many self-employed commercial writers are going in these days. For instance, in addition to writing ads and brochures, I also consult, teach, and market my own seminars on direct mail and other communications topics. Recently, I professionally taped one of my seminars; I now market the cassettes as a separate product. (Go to www.bly.com and click on Audio Tapes.)

The idea here is to take your expertise and offer it to clients and buyers in many different ways, shapes, and forms. You are no longer subject to the whims of the publishing world, but can become a self-sufficient entrepreneur—a "mini-conglomerate," if you will—selling information, expertise, and writing ability in a variety of ways and formats.

If you can think, learn, and write, there's no limit to what you can accomplish. And commercial writing—putting your skills to work for corporate clients paying big money for writing services—is one of the best and easiest ways to expand your writing activities, and your income.

TIPS FOR BEGINNERS

Okay. Let's say you want to break into the corporate market, but you've never written for business clients before. How do you get started?

You may be thinking, *That's an impossible market for me; I'm a magazine writer. Business clients only want writers with business experience.* Logical. But not true. In every market and endeavor, from publishing to brain surgery, there is a segment of potential clients willing and eager to hire beginners—amazing as that may seem.

Think about it: Every brain surgeon performs one operation that's his first. There has to be a patient for that operation. Therefore, many patients have brain surgery performed by a surgeon who has never done such an operation before. If people are willing to hire a rookie brain surgeon, is it so inconceivable that they'll hire a rookie writer?

You can sell your freelance business writing services locally, nationally, or both.

Call up the marketing manager, corporate communications director, or, in a smaller company, the owner. Ask if they have writing needs you can fill. It may take several calls to get through. Be persistent. Don't take silence as rejection: They may be too busy to return your call, but keep trying until you can speak with them. If they're not interested, they'll tell you, and then you can move on.

Send letters offering your services as a business writer. If you have writing samples that are at all relevant, offer to send clips and a resume. Relevant samples could include business documents written for your current employer or articles on topics related to your potential client's products.

Where do you find your first client? Start with your network of family, friends, and relatives. Do any of them have a business you could write for?

Do some pro bono work to get your first assignment. Volunteer to write copy for a nonprofit whose cause you support.

Take a copywriting or advertising course at a local college. Print clean copies of your corrected assignments and put them into a portfolio. If you're currently employed, explore whether there's writing you can do for your company.

CHOOSING YOUR MARKET

Many freelance business writers prefer to write primarily for Fortune 500 clients. There are several reasons for this.

First, the person you are dealing with—typically a marketing or corporate communications manager—is a communications professional. She understands what goes into good writing and can recognize quality work when she sees it.

Second, large corporations are accustomed to hiring professional writers and paying the fees they charge.

Third, big corporations have an ongoing need for writing for a wide variety of projects, including company newsletters, annual reports, websites, email marketing messages, sales brochures, press releases, articles, and speeches. There's a lot of work to keep you busy.

Other business writers prefer to work for small businesses. These small businesses tend to need not just copy but also marketing advice, and some business writers enjoy playing the role of marketing consultant. They typically want copy that can generate immediate sales results: email marketing messages, websites, sales letters, brochures, and ads.

On the other hand, small businesses usually have a limited volume of work, and sometimes lack the budget to pay the fees you want to charge. Also, the person you are dealing with—a business owner or manager—may have no appreciation for writing or for your skill. They may ask for rewrites, for no reason that makes sense to you, on copy that doesn't need it—a source of frustration to many business writers.

When you're looking for potential clients, target industries in which you're knowledgeable. For example, if you've published articles on health care, approach your local hospital about doing PR writing. Or say you want to write for high-tech companies. Start publishing articles on computers, software, telecommunications, and other technology topics. Clips of these articles will gain the interest of a marketing manager who may want you to write an ad or website on his high-tech products.

MOVING UP FROM ROOKIE TO PRO

I tell freelance writers who are breaking into the corporate market for the first time to do anything that is required to get their first three clients. Be flexible. Agree to anything. Your fee is unimportant, because what you need from these first three clients are:

- A client list with the names of three businesses

- Three sample pieces for your portfolio

- Testimonials from three satisfied customers

- Three clients willing to serve as references

Once you've scored your first clients, you'll have the credentials to move from the rank of rookie to professional. Then when prospects ask, "Who are your clients?" you have names. When they ask, "Have you done this type of work?" you'll answer yes, with confidence. When they ask for samples of your work, you have solid business writing samples to send.

10

WORKING WITH AGENTS AND BOOK PROPOSALS

• •

Y ou want to write a book and get it published. So, do you need an agent? And when should you get one?

While it is possible to sell your book to a publishing house without the help of a literary agent, having an agent represent you will greatly increase the odds of success.

"Publishers decided years ago that it was uneconomical for them to read unsolicited manuscripts." That's the opinion of Arthur M. Klebanoff, president, Scott Meredith Literary Agency. "Publishers rely on agents for recommendations," he says.

That being the case, I recommend you initially concentrate on selling yourself and your book idea to an agent. If you can convince a good agent to take on the project, then the agent will have primary responsibility for selling the book, saving you time and increasing your chances of acceptance. If you cannot get an agent to represent you, then you can represent the book yourself and try to sell it on your own.

I've done it both ways, and based on both personal experience and the state of the publishing industry today, my advice is to get an agent if you can. The exception might be if you have a preexisting relationship with a book publisher (or know someone who does) and feel your book is exactly right for that particular publisher.

WHY HAVING AN AGENT GIVES YOU AN EDGE

Most editors today will not read your material unless it is submitted by an agent. Agents act as screening devices for editors. Although submission by an agent does not guarantee a sale (far from it), the editor will at least look at the material. The editor's logic in doing so is that if the agent thinks the book is good enough to represent, it is at least worth taking a look at.

As a rule of thumb, the larger the publishing house, the more vital it is to have an agent. The smaller the publishing house, the more likely they are to look at unsolicited proposals not represented by an agent. University presses can also be approached directly by potential authors without an agent.

Another area where agents help is in negotiating favorable book contracts for authors. A book contract has dozens of clauses in fine print, each of which is negotiable and can greatly affect your total income from the book.

The basic function of an agent is sales. A good agent is one who is able to sell your writing and get you the best deal in terms of advance, royalty, promotional budget, and quality of editor and publisher.

GETTING YOUR FIRST AGENT

The best place to start is with your own personal contacts. If you don't know someone who has published a book, chances are a friend of a friend, or a relative of a friend, may know someone. Ask that author for a referral. Does he have an agent he can recommend to you? Does he have any suggestions on which agents to contact?

Go to a bookstore or library and look at recent books on topics similar to that of the book you want to write. Now read the acknowledgments at the beginning of the book. Many authors will thank their literary agents by name in the acknowledgments. Write down the names of these agents, look them up in a directory such as *Literary Market Place*, and contact them.

This technique of looking for agents in book acknowledgments works well because agents, like other people, have their own particular interests, and an agent will be more receptive to your idea if it fits in with the type of books she likes to work with.

Send a brief letter of introduction. Explain where you got their name and who you are, and briefly describe the type of book you want to write. If you have writing credentials or are an established expert in the subject matter of your proposed book, say so.

THE AGENT'S PERCENTAGE

An agent collects a percentage of all advances, royalties, and other income (e.g., sale of serial rights, movie rights, etc.) generated by your book. Typically, this ranges from 10 to 15 percent.

My advice on royalties is this: If you get a royalty check, that's a nice bonus. But don't count on royalties when you forecast your annual income for the year.

Yes, some writers get huge royalties. According to a report in *The Week* (June 10, 2005, p. 42), Merv Griffin earned between $70 million and $80 million for writing the theme song for *Jeopardy*, which he composed in less than a minute. And the royalties to the song "Happy Birthday" generate annual income of more than $1 million for the composer's heirs. But the sad fact is that 8 out of 10 books do not earn out their advance—meaning they generate no royalties to the author. So the author makes no money beyond the initial advance.

You do not pay any fees to your agent until he or she makes a sale for you, at which time the agent receives a commission as was discussed above. Agents typically absorb phone expenses, postage, travel, lunches with editors, and other expenses involved in marketing your book and running their agency. However, it is traditional for the author to pay for the cost of photocopying book manuscripts and provide the agent with as many copies as required (usually three to five copies for simultaneous submissions to multiple publishers).

Some agents do charge to read and critique manuscripts, but such services are often worthless. Most legitimate agents, if interested in your idea, will review your material and immediately tell you whether they're interested in representing you, without charging an up-front fee. There are some legitimate agents who, if uncertain about your idea or your qualifications, will agree to review the proposal or manuscript for a fee.

Many will refund the fee if they go on to represent and sell the book for you.

If the agent is favorably impressed and agrees to represent the book, congratulations—you have a literary agent!

WRITING YOUR BOOK PROPOSAL

You have a great idea for a nonfiction book. Your wife thinks it's a great idea. Your parents think it's a great idea. Even your neighbor who hates to read thinks it's a great idea.

But will a publisher think it's a great idea—enough to pay you an advance, commission you to write it, and publish and sell it?

That will depend largely on your book proposal. Here's where you demonstrate persuasively that your idea has merit. Of course, even a solid idea and a great book proposal can't guarantee success, but they surely can tip the odds in your favor. But if either the idea or the proposal is weak, your chances of a sale are slim to none.

It's no secret what book editors look for when they review book ideas and proposals. And your agent will expect you to know how to write a book proposal. She may offer advice and critique, but she won't do it for you.

You'll improve your chances of helping your agent sell your book for you, and win a publisher's contract, by testing your book proposal against the five key questions editors ask. Let's look at those questions and the best ways to answer them.

1. Is there a large enough audience interested in this topic to justify publishing the book?

The major New York publishing houses aren't interested in highly specialized books written for small, narrow-interest audiences. If you want to write the definitive work on troubleshooting of mainframe TCP/IP networks, for example, seek out a publisher of technical books.

Big publishers are primarily interested in bookstore books—that is, books that appeal to a general audience or at least to a large segment of the general population. Examples of such audiences include parents, small business owners, corporate executives, fitness enthusiasts, movie buffs, users of personal computers, teenagers, and other large affinity groups.

A book aimed at a major publisher must appeal to an audience of hundreds of thousands of people, if not millions. To sell your idea to the editor, you must demonstrate that such an audience exists. In our proposal for *How to Promote Your Own Business* (accepted and published by New American Library), Gary Blake and I cited statistics showing that more than 10 million small businesses exist in the United States, and 250,000 new businesses are started each year.

One excellent source of market data is *Standard Rate and Data Service*, which lists U.S. magazines that accept advertising and their circulation. SRDS is available at your local library or online at www.srds.com. If you're proposing a book on freelance writing, for example, you could look up writers' magazines and find that the two largest publications in the field have a combined circulation of more than 300,000; this is the potential market for your book.

But only a small percentage of the intended audience will actually buy your book, and a major publisher hopes to sell at least 5,000 copies of it. So if you're writing a book that appeals to only the 44,171 branch managers working at banks nationwide (say, a book entitled *How to Manage Your Branch More Efficiently*), and 2 percent can be persuaded to buy the book, you've sold only 883 copies—not nearly enough to make the project worthwhile for either you or a publisher.

2. Is this a book or a magazine article?

At the onset of the 1991 recession, I came up with an idea for a book I thought would be a strong seller: *Recession Proof Business Strategies: Winning Methods to Sell Any Product or Service in a Down Economy*. It was timely. It had strong media appeal. And it contained vital information readers desperately needed.

But, as my agent pointed out, there were two problems with the book. First, its timely nature. From conception to bookstore, it can take 18 months to 2 years to write and publish a book. If the recession was over by the time *Recession Proof Business Strategies* came out, the book would bomb.

Second, my agent was concerned that there wasn't enough material to fill a book. And he was right. The average nonfiction book is about 200 pages in typeset, published form, with approximately 400 words a page.

That's 80,000 words—about 320 double-spaced typewritten manuscript pages. Your book might be longer or shorter, ranging from 35,000 words (a slim, 100-page volume) to 200,000 words or more. Trouble was, when I finished writing everything I knew about recession-proof business strategies, I had 5,000 words—too short for a book, too long for an article. The solution? I self-published *Recession Proof Business Strategies* as a $7 booklet and sold several thousand copies. So a booklet, not a book, was the right vehicle for this material.

Many book ideas seem strong initially, but wilt under close examination. For example, a (to me) wonderful book title popped into my head a while back: *How to Survive a Midlife Crisis at Any Age*. My coauthor loved it and wanted to do the book. But when we sat down, we couldn't think of anything to put in it! We soon abandoned the idea.

How do you know whether your idea is a book, an article, or a booklet—and how do you convince a publisher that your concept is a big one? Here are some guidelines:

First, see if other books on the topic have been published. The existence of a few similar titles indicates that this idea is big enough to deserve a book, since other publishers bought and published book-length manuscripts on the topic.

Second, go to the library and see what else is written on the topic. If you feel overwhelmed by all the magazine articles, newspaper stories, booklets, pamphlets, surveys, reports, and statistics on your topic, that's a good indication the topic is meaty enough to justify a full-length book.

For example, I heard a public service announcement describing a toll-free number you could call to get safety information about any car you were thinking of buying. I thought, *There seem to be a lot of these free consumer hotlines; why not organize them into a reference book?*

I researched the subject and discovered there were indeed hundreds of such hotlines. New American Library bought the book and published it as *Information Hotline USA*. If I'd uncovered only a few such hotlines, New American Library would have rejected my proposal.

The third step to convincing a publisher that your topic is broad enough to warrant a book is to organize your information into chapters. Think about how you would logically explain your topic or present your information, and organize it into major categories. These will become chapter headings.

A full-length nonfiction book typically has 8 to 15 chapters. If your outline has fewer, the publisher may think there's not enough information to fill a book on your topic. Shoot for an outline with at least 9 chapters.

On index cards, organize all your research material by chapter. Then add the most important or interesting items as bullet points in your chapter outline to create a complete table of contents for your proposed book. Here's how my coauthor and I described chapter 15 in our proposal for *How to Promote Your Own Business:*

> Chapter 15: On with the Show—Trade Shows and Displays
>
> Why do people attend trade shows?
>
> How to select the shows at which you will exhibit
>
> Creating effective trade show displays
>
> Five things you can do to attract more prospects to your exhibit: demonstrations, product samples, free gifts, contests, and entertainment
>
> Other uses for your display materials: retail point of purchase, malls, lobby displays

This type of detailed table of contents proves to the publisher that your topic is appropriate for a book, not just a magazine article.

3. What's different or better about your book?

The first page or two of your book proposal must contain an overview of your idea. This overview describes what the book is about: who it is written for and what's in it.

Your overview must also tell the editor why and how your book is unique, different, or better than other books already published on this topic. And you must do this within the first two paragraphs (if you don't, the editor probably won't read further).

The hook or angle that makes your book different can take many forms: It might be a slant toward a different audience, a better way of organizing the material, or inclusion of topics not covered in other books.

The key is to make your book seem both different and better.

For instance, if the other books aren't illustrated, say that your book will be—and explain why that's important. If the other books are lengthy, promise to write a more concise book. If the other books are incomplete, describe the topics they omit—and tell how you'll cover them in your book.

When we were planning *How to Promote Your Own Business*, my coauthor and I hoped to write a book on advertising that would appeal to small business owners rather than advertising agencies, PR firms, and other advertising professionals. We used this as our hook; our proposal began:

> *How to Promote Your Own Business* is not a book for the professional publicist, promoter, or advertising professional. Rather, it is a practical working promotion guide for the 10.8 million Americans who own their own businesses, and the 250,000 entrepreneurs who start new businesses each year.

We wrote a previous book, *Technical Writing: Structure, Standards and Style*, because we believed the existing technical writing books were too lengthy and dull to be suitable as references for working technical writers. We wanted to create a handbook for technical writers that emulated the concise, to-the-point style and format of *The Elements of Style*, William Strunk, Jr., and E.B. White's popular style guide for general writers.

Our proposal called our book "the Strunk and White of technical writing," which instantly communicated the key appeal of the concept. Our agent sold the book—within three weeks—to the first publisher who looked at it. Interestingly, McGraw-Hill also used the phrase "the Strunk and White of technical writing" in publicity and promotional materials describing the book.

Another section of your proposal that positions your book in relation to others on the same subject is the "Competition" section. Here you list and describe competing books; each listing should emphasize how your book is both different and better. Here is an example from our *How to Promote Your Own Business* proposal:

> 1. *How to Advertise and Promote Your Small Business,* by Gonnie McClung Siegel, John Wiley & Sons, 1978, 128 pages, $4.95 trade paperback.
>
> This book is part of John Wiley's "Small Business Series." The author neglects several vital areas of small business promotion, including mail order; sales literature; trade shows; and displays, contests, and newsletters. There are very few examples of actual promotions, and the author gives no indication of the costs involved or the results achieved. The book does not provide step-by-step instructions for selecting and implementing promotions.

Include in the "Competition" section those books that cover the same or very similar topics as your book, that are published by a major publishing house, and that are no more than five years old. Do not include self-published books or ebooks.

How many books you list in this section will be important. The presence of two to six competitive books shows there's a market for this type of book, while still room for one more. On the other hand, if there are seven or more books, a publisher may think the field is overcrowded, and you'll probably have a difficult time making the sale.

4. Will people pay $22.95 for this book?

The average hardcover nonfiction book sells for $22.95 or more, the average trade paperback for $12.95. Your book must be interesting or valuable enough to make readers part not only with their money (remember, they can always read your book for free at the library), but with their time as well (many people would rather watch TV, go to the movies, or nap than read a book).

When it comes to nonfiction, readers typically buy books to learn something, for reference, or to be entertained.

A how-to or reference book proposal should stress the benefits readers will get when they buy the book. Will it help them save time and money? Make money? Look beautiful? Feel young? Live longer? If your book will make readers' lives better and easier, say so. In our proposal for *How to Promote Your Own Business,* we said:

> *How to Promote Your Own Business* is unique because it
> goes right to the heart of the problem: How can the owner
> or manager of a small business—a person with little time,
> money, and promotion expertise—promote his business
> as effectively as his bigger, wealthier competitors?

If your book is biography, journalism, history, or any other form of
nonfiction written primarily to entertain, your proposal should highlight
some of the more fascinating details of the book. Your aim is to make the
editor want to read the whole story.

5. *Why should the publisher hire you to write it?*

Your proposal must show why you're uniquely qualified to write the
book. Such qualifications fall into two categories: writing credentials and
expert credentials.

Writing credentials establish your expertise as an author. In an "About
the Author" section of your book proposal, write a brief biographical
sketch of yourself, being sure to include such information as:

- Titles, publishers, and dates of publication for any books you've
  written.

- Total number of books and articles written (if the number is
  impressive).

- Names of major magazines and newspapers in which your work
  has appeared.

- Excerpts from favorable reviews about your work.

- Sales figures for your best-selling books (if they're impressive).

Expert credentials establish your position as an authority in the topic
of your proposed book.

Actually, you don't have to be much of an expert. The trick is to make
yourself seem like an expert to the publisher. For instance, author Wilbur
Perry wanted to write about mail order. To make himself more appealing
as a potential author for a book on the subject, he started and operated a
small part-time mail-order business from his home. This gave him the

credentials he needed to convince John Wiley & Sons to publish two books by him on the topic.

In my experience, your expert credentials don't need to be in-depth. Editors understand you can research the topic, and they don't require you to know everything about it before buying your book. They just want to convince their editorial board—and buyers—that you know what you're talking about.

Of course, having a published book to your credit is one credential that always impresses publishers. And that's a credential I'm sure you'll soon have if you follow the five key points covered in this chapter.

One other thing the publisher wants to know is whether you have a platform, which means, do you have a vehicle through which you can sell copies of your own book? For instance, I have a monthly online newsletter on marketing, "The Direct Response Letter," with more than 40,000 subscribers who spend a combined $4,000 a week buying my books, reports, and tapes from me online.

That gives me a platform for promoting any books I write on marketing or related topics. On the other hand, this same platform would not convince a publisher that I can sell copies of books on non-marketing topics. So my platform, and this is true of most authors, is limited to a narrow range of subject areas—in my case, marketing, sales, entrepreneurship, copywriting, and freelance writing, the topics I write most of my books about.

As for structuring your book proposal, make sure it contains the following sections:

- *A title page.* The book's title and the name of the author are centered in the middle of the page. In the upper left corner, type "Book Proposal." In the bottom right, type your name, address, and phone number (or, if you have one, your agent's).

- *Overview.* Summarize what your book is about: the topic, who will read it, why it's important or interesting to your intended audience, and what makes your book different from others in the field.

- *Format.* Specify the approximate length of the book in words, number of chapters, types of illustrations or graphics to be included, and any unique organizational schemes or formats (for example, is your book divided into major sections or do you use sidebars?)

- *Markets.* Tell the editor who will buy your book, how many of these people exist, and why they need it or will want to read it. Use statistics to dramatize the size of the market. For example, if your book is about infertility, mention that one in six couples in the United States is infertile.

- *Promotion.* Is your book a natural for talk radio or *Oprah* (be realistic)? Can it be promoted through seminars or speeches to associations and clubs? Give the publisher some of your ideas on how the book can be marketed. (Note: Phrase these as suggestions, not demands. The publisher will be interested in your ideas but probably won't use most of them.)

- *Competition.* List books that compare with yours. Include the title, author, publisher, year of publication, number of pages, price, and format (hardcover, trade paperback, or mass market paperback). Describe each book briefly, pointing out weaknesses and areas in which your book is different and superior.

- *Author's bio.* A brief biography listing your writing credentials (books and articles published), qualifications to write about the book's topic (for instance, for a book on popular psychology, it helps if you're a therapist), and your media experience (previous appearances on TV and radio).

- *Table of contents/outline.* A chapter-by-chapter outline showing the contents of your proposed book. Many editors tell me that a detailed, well-thought-out table of contents in a proposal helps sway them in favor of a book.

BUILDING YOUR WEBSITE
AND PUBLISHING YOUR EZINE

W hen the Internet first gained attention years ago, if you would have recommended to me that I put up my own website, I would have laughed in your face. Two author friends, Roger Parker and Jeffrey Lant, advised me to do so back then ... and yes, I laughed in their faces.

But today go to www.bly.com. Who's laughing now? Not me, as you can see!

Would I recommend to new freelance writers that they set up a website? For most, absolutely. Why? Several reasons.

First, time. Clients and editors are pressed for time. Many rely on the web to find new information and resources—including freelance writers. The easier and more convenient you make it for potential clients to find you and evaluate your services, the more you'll get hired. Your website does that for you.

We live in the age of now. People want instant information ... instant gratification ... instant fulfillment of their orders, inquiries, and wishes. The prospect who has to wait for your resume and clips in the mail may lose interest by the time they arrive. But if these documents are available on your website, he or she can instantly learn more about your background and writing style—enough to become comfortable that you're the one for the assignment.

The second major reason to have a website? Prestige. When clients ask to see samples, and you say, "Do you have access to the web? My portfolio is online at www.me.com," it impresses the heck out of them. Having your own website shows your technology savvy—a characteristic editors increasingly look for in freelancers in today's computerized publishing environment.

There's another advantage to putting up your own website: It teaches you the process of how to write for the web. Some writers see the web as the enemy of print. I see it as an additional, lucrative market for our services.

You can earn $500 to $1,000 a page writing web copy for clients. Some clients, however, may suspect writers who say they know how to write for the web but don't even have their own site; it's comparable to the shoemaker's children going barefoot.

CREATING YOUR WEBSITE

If you want to take the time to master FrontPage or another web tool, you can build your website yourself. I hired a local web designer to do it for me; rates range from $50 to $150 per hour; I paid a young and extremely competent techie $75 per hour and was well satisfied.

Increasingly, programming, HTML design, and other technical aspects of Internet marketing are being outsourced overseas, especially to India and now the Philippines. For example, I use a web designer in the Philippines who charges me a *total* of $75 for a simple website.

The key to saving money when you put up your website is to do the writing, organizing, and planning yourself, so the web designer only has to handle page design and programming. I told my web designer exactly how my website would be structured, and gave him all the copy via emailed Word files.

One thing he did do for me was to scan the samples I wanted posted on my online portfolio. You don't have to do this—you can simply post text files of your samples ... but scans of color book covers, annual reports, catalogs, and other finished pieces add a touch of credibility that text files alone do not provide. Some of the pages of samples posted on my website are slightly crinkled from the scanning (accidentally), and this turns out to have a surprisingly appealing look.

Get an idea of hourly rates and an estimate of the hours required before you authorize your web consultant to begin work. Don't overdesign the website. You can get competent website designers to bid on creating your site by going to www.elance.com.

Remember, you're a freelance writer, not Nike or Apple. You want attractive, clean design with strong content, good organization, and perhaps some animation or interactivity thrown in to add color and interest.

And remember, websites can always be altered and improved easily and affordably. Start basic. Then add bells and whistles later on if you feel like it. My total out-of-pocket cost to put up my first website was less than $800.

Once your site is up, friends will constantly ask you how many hits your site gets monthly. This number is irrelevant. Your website is primarily an online portfolio of samples and credentials potential clients and editors can look up conveniently and rapidly to make a decision about hiring you.

Promote your site, but target prospective buyers, not the mass of 100 million Internet users at large. A thousand hits from web surfers who don't identify themselves and aren't in a position to hire you aren't worth one inquiry from a qualified prospect who responds by email, phone, fax, or guest page.

A guest page, by the way, is an online reply form prospects browsing your site can fill out to request more information. You can find this page when you click "Contact" from the main menu at www.bly.com. Don't require visitors to go through the guest page to email you. At www.bly.com, visitors can simply click on my email address, which is displayed on every page of my site. Up comes the blank form for sending an email.

SEVEN STEPS TO CREATING AN EFFECTIVE FREELANCE WRITER'S WEBSITE

When it comes to websites for freelance writers, the first question to answer, of course, is, "Do I even need a website?"

Well, if you intend to freelance in the business world, the answer is, you can probably get away with not having one. But you're better off with than without. Reason: All other considerations aside, writing web copy is a major source of revenue for most freelance copywriters today. If clients ask, "What is the URL for your website?" and you say, "I don't have one," they will be reluctant to hire you for online copywriting assignments. After all, if you don't even have your own website, they will think, how much about online marketing can you really know?

And since online writing is becoming a larger and larger percentage of all copywriting work, cutting yourself off from these assignments will have a significantly negative effect on your revenues.

Many copywriting clients are looking for a writer who can handle both their online and offline work. So being perceived as a writer lacking web savvy may cost you print assignments!

Okay. So you're going to bite the bullet and put up a website for your freelance copywriting business. Here are 7 tips that can help you get more bang for your web buck:

1. Register a branded domain name. Avoid domain names that are plays on the word *writing* such as www.writeworks.com. As a writer your brand is your name, so build your domain name around it: my website is www.bly.com.

2. Design your website to cater to the interests and needs of potential clients, not casual web surfers. Don't post content just because it's fun or amusing. Everything on the website should work toward a single goal: convincing potential clients to hire you for a writing assignment.

3. Organize your site so your potential clients can find what they are looking for quickly and easily. Keep the layout simple. Go to www.bly.com and you can see that all the content is available from a menu of choices on the left side of the screen, clearly labeled (e.g., testimonials, books).

4. Think about what your potential clients ask you for when they are considering whether to hire you, and then provide that on your website. In my case as a freelance copywriter, the two most frequent questions I am asked are, "Who are your clients," and "Can I see some

samples of your work?" So I have a "Clients" page that lists clients in alphabetical order by category (e.g., banks, ad agencies).

5. I believe your online portfolio—samples of your work the prospect can view and read with a few mouse clicks—is the most important selling feature of your freelance writing website. On my portfolio, I show a wide selection of samples, organized by category (e.g., ads, direct mail).

    When you click on the category, you see a list of samples within that category, labeled according to the name of the client. Click on a sample label, and you see a screen filled with thumbnails of every page of the sample. You can then click on each page to blow it up to a size where you can read the text.

6. If you have written articles, allowing visitors to read, print out, or even download your articles adds tremendous value to your site and may prompt them to return periodically. Do not charge visitors for the privilege of reading your articles. The web is a medium where offering free content is an effective marketing strategy, and it costs you nothing to post your articles and offer them for viewing.

7. Have a page on your website with pictures and descriptions of any books you have written. Link these descriptions to www.amazon.com so the visitor can buy the book online with a mouse click. Join Amazon as an affiliate, and you will get a small commission on each sale.

One other point: By offering site visitors some free content in exchange for their email address—either a free subscription to an online newsletter or some free content, such as a special report available as a downloadable PDF file—you can quickly build an opt-in email list of visitors who have registered on your site.

The fastest way to get people to opt into your e-list—and give you both their email address as well as permission to send email messages to that address—is to offer both a free e-newsletter as well as an additional bonus. When I send traffic to www.bly.com/reports, visitors are told they get 4 free bonus reports worth more than $100. Visit the page online to see how it works.

By sending the people on your subscriber list your regular online newsletter—as well as solo email messages with special offers (e.g., an invitation to a speech you are giving or an announcement about the publication of your new book)—you can quickly convert web visitors into paying customers. For the freelance writer who wants to make money, this is the primary reason to have a website in the first place.

PROMOTING YOURSELF WITH AN ONLINE NEWSLETTER

Do you get any electronic newsletters emailed to you on a monthly, weekly, or daily basis? If so, then you are an ezine subscriber. But have you considered publishing your own online newsletter instead of just reading those produced by others? I do. And it has been my most successful self-promotion—generating thousands of dollars in extra income every month. Yours can, too.

In my case, I'm a freelance copywriter specializing in direct marketing. A couple of years ago, I started writing and publishing a free monthly ezine, "The Direct Response Letter."

In the ezine, I write about what interests me: direct marketing, copywriting, online marketing, small business, and related topics. My readers—I currently have more than 40,000 subscribers—include corporate marketing types, small business owners, budding entrepreneurs, marketing specialists, writers, and self-employed professionals.

Go to my website at www.bly.com and notice the ezine sign-up box on the home page. You can also click on "Archive" within that box to access an online archive of all past issues of my ezine—and see the design, format, style, length, and content of my ezine.

Now, here's the benefit: Since these 40,000 people read my ezine every month, they feel they know me. I am someone they trust, no longer a stranger. And so they will buy products and services I either produce myself or recommend.

For instance, if I have a new book coming out, mentioning its publication in my ezine causes a big jump up in the book's sales ranking on Amazon.com that day—the ezine helps sell copies.

Or say I want to drum up some corporate writing assignments. By making a special offer, I can quickly get work. For instance, in one issue,

I offered one-third off my regular rate for writing an email message. Within 24 hours, 12 companies wanted to take me up on the deal.

You can make these offers within the body of your regular ezine or in a solo email promotion sent to your ezine subscriber list. I send out my ezine once a month, and do approximately one additional solo email each week.

One of the solo emails is for one of my books or services; the other is to promote my information products—ebooks, audio albums, tele-seminars, and conferences. I also promote other people's information products to my elist, choosing only those products I think are good and my readers would like. For such promotions, I receive an affiliate commission ranging from 20 to 50 percent of the sales generated.

In fact, you can't really market yourself and your writings effectively online unless you have an ezine. Here's why: The Internet is a powerful new channel for marketing both your freelance writing services and your content (e.g., books, tapes, special reports). On the Internet, renting lists of email addresses and sending emails to sell products and services doesn't work—even for big corporations that can afford to do so. The lists are too expensive, and the response rates are too low to make them profitable.

Many have tried and failed. The reason online marketing to cold email lists doesn't work is that people are reluctant to buy online from strangers. And when you send email to those on a rented list, you are a stranger to them.

Instead, online marketing is a two-step process. In the first step, you offer a free subscription to your ezine to everyone who visits your website. While people won't generally buy from a stranger online, they can be induced to request freebies. Offer them a free ezine in exchange for their email address, and many will take the bait.

Offer everyone you meet—publishers, editors, clients, prospects, fans, readers, audiences at your lectures—a free subscription to your ezine in exchange for giving you their email address. With patience and effort, you can build your subscriber base until your ezine reaches thousands of readers on a regular basis.

By signing all these folks up as subscribers, you in essence convert them from casual readers and one-time buyers, to loyal fans, and eventually to paying customers who buy your writings or writing services when you offer them online.

Finally, a few more tips for creating and profiting from your own ezine follow:

- Use text instead of HTML. It is easier and faster to create, and requires no design work.

- Schedule publication for once or twice a month. To publish more frequently creates too much work; to publish less frequently is missing an opportunity to maintain awareness of you and your writing in the reader's mind.

- Keep your ezine brief. Mine has just five or six items per issue, with each article typically just two or three paragraphs.

- In my ezine, 80 percent of the content is useful how-to tips on my specialty, direct marketing, and the other 20 percent is plugs for products and services. This seems to be the ad ratio most readers will accept; more self-promotion than that, and you risk having people unsubscribe.

- Since you're already a writer, you'll have no trouble writing your own ezine. But what content should be in it?

- If you're a nonfiction writer, short articles about your specialty—e.g., gardening, fitness, or whatever it is you write about

- If you're a fiction writer, news about your books, signings, readings, and other literary activities

- If you're a freelance copywriter, tips relevant to your writing specialties—e.g., online marketing, public relations, speechwriting, direct mail, or whatever

- Ask for subscriber feedback; ezine readers love to be heard. I often tell my subscribers I am working on a new book, name the topic, and ask them to share their knowledge to help me research my book. They love to do it, and I get free research assistance out of the deal!

DO YOU NEED A BLOG?

Blogs, short for *web logs*, are being heralded by many as the next big thing in interactive online communication. "Blogging is a true revolution," raves technology writer Fang Xingdong. "One needs no training and there is no cost."

What exactly is a blog? "A blog is an online journal," explains blogging expert Deb Weil in her Business Blogging Starter Kit (www.wordbiz.com). "It's called a journal because every entry is time and date stamped, and always presented in reverse chronological order."

According to Deb, a blog is "a platform from which to lobby, network, and influence sales. It's a way to circumvent traditional media and analysts. And blogging can be done instantly, in real time, at a fraction of the cost of using traditional channels."

There are many subcategories of blogs. Political blogs came to national prominence during the Bush/Kerry presidential race; they remain active and popular. Blogs can focus on ideas, industries, technologies, products, companies, or social issues such as adoption.

Online marketing consultant Rick Bruner says that 20 percent of Internet users—approximately 35 million people—read blogs. The common denominator for a successful blog is a topic that people are: (a) interested in reading about online, (b) get enthusiastic or excited about, and (c) want to discuss with others.

If your blog is popular and draws heavy traffic, you may be able to sell advertising on it—theoretically. But in reality, I don't think many advertisers are interested in advertising on writers' blogs.

So how can a blog make you, the writer, money? By helping to increase your visibility on the Internet. The hope is that some of the people reading your blog will be potential clients (though the majority probably won't be) ... and what they read may impress them sufficiently to convince them to hire you for a writing project.

"I've found my blog "CONTENTIOUS" to be a fabulous marketing tool for my editorial, training, and consulting services," says writer and *WD* contributor Amy Gahran. "I've seen it work well for independent professionals who seek to establish a relationship with their potential audience."

Many writers have told me that their blogs serve a networking function; they help to build valuable contacts and relationships that can lead to paying gigs.

For instance, marketing writer Jennifer Rice won Microsoft as a client because an executive there had read her blog. She also got hired to do consulting for a restaurant concept out of Lubbock. "I didn't approach either company," says Jennifer. "I got inbound emails from these guys saying they had read my blog and liked how I think. They hired me on the spot."

Another marketing writer, Brian Carroll, told me he landed a book contract with McGraw-Hill largely on the strength of his blog. And writer/consultant Kirsten Osolind reports, "I've scored a column in a national magazine and four clients from my blog."

The bottom line: For the writer, a blog *can* generate a measurable ROI—not directly (readers don't pay to access your blog), but by enhancing your visibility and getting your name around to clients, publishers, and editors.

Blogs are relatively easy to set up. There are a number of blogging software packages—some free, others that you pay for—you can use to start your own blog. Simply visit their websites and follow the instructions. Blogging authority Deb Weil recommends www.typepad.com. My webmaster used WordPress (wordpress.org) to create my blog (www.bly.com/blog/blog.htm). I've seen a few others, and the blogs they create all look pretty similar to me.

Be sure to have a link to a "Real Simple Syndication" (RSS) feed on your blog. By registering with an RSS feed, visitors can actually subscribe to your blog—in that the RSS feed automatically notifies them whenever you add a new item or post to your site.

One benefit of having a blog is that it can increase both your search engine rankings and (as a result) the traffic to your website.

"The search engines, especially Google, love blogs," says blogger and online marketing consultant Paul Chaney. "You'd be amazed at how many of your posts will end up in the top 10 returns. If search engine optimization is a concern to you, blogs are the best way I know to move up the ladder as well as increase your page rank."

Now here's a warning: If you are a professional writer, the quality of the writing in your blog should be as good as it is in your essays, articles, books, and other conventionally published writings.

Some bloggers show a noticeable tendency to ramble and produce stream-of-consciousness musings for their blogs. Your random thoughts and insights may be of interest to you, but few other people care.

What type of content should you post on your blog if you want to attract and interest readers—and be taken seriously by potential clients, editors, and publishers in a position to buy your words?

Your blog content should consist of some or all of the following:

- Insightful analysis and carefully considered opinions

- How-to information—tips, strategies, methods, and ideas

- Inside information, interviews, and research presenting little-known facts and data

- Up-to-the-minute links to other blogs and websites of interest to your readers

Your blog should focus on a well-defined area, which of course should be the things you write about in other media: marketing, gardening, distance learning, politics, or what have you.

When I'm writing my blog, I write the entries in Word first, which makes it easy to edit and review each entry. I usually write several blog items at a time and store them in a Word file called "blog entries."

Keep your posts relatively brief. Messages longer than a few paragraphs or points are best suited to other formats, such as an article, ebook, or special report.

Finally, keep your blog active. Blogger Deb Weil suggests a minimum frequency of at least one new entry every week.

Remember, if you stop posting items to your blog, people will remove it from their RSS feed list—dropping you from the list of blogs they read on a regular basis. You'll be reducing your readership, which goes against the whole point of a blog: to get your ideas and thoughts read by as wide an audience as possible.

12

Writing for the
Internet and Multimedia

The Internet is new and exciting—the future of communication. Maybe. But right now, authors are struggling to overcome the culture of the Internet, which includes an orientation toward receiving free information (rather than paying for it) as well as less-than-rigid enforcement of copyright laws and protection.

As far as the freelance writer is concerned, the Internet is a mixed bag. On the one hand, some writers are making quite a bit of money writing for the Internet ... getting thousands of dollars per assignment (I am one of them). These assignments come mainly from companies that market their products and services on the web, and need strong online copy to support those marketing programs.

These can be a mix of small Internet entrepreneurs, midsize companies, and large corporations. Each of these marketers has different needs. The Internet entrepreneurs are typically selling information products—ebooks, boot camps, and other information products—online. They require emails to drive traffic, and "landing pages"—small websites dedicated to selling a single product—to convert that traffic to orders.

Midsize companies are often "brick and mortar" businesses. They have little knowledge or sophistication about the Internet, and only a vague notion that they need something more than a website to monetize their online presence. You can charge several hundred dollars per hour advising them on how to use the Internet to market their products and services, and thousands of dollars writing the web pages and other online copy they need.

Large corporations understand, or at least think they understand, how to use the Internet as a marketing medium. They need a variety of online marketing materials written: email campaigns, ezines, white papers, web pages, banner ads, pay-per-click ad campaigns, and blogs, to name just a few. Corporations are also big buyers of search engine optimization (SEO) copywriting services.

Despite the growing demand for online copy, the Internet has a long history as a medium for the open and free exchange and dissemination of information, which translates into thousands of people writing all kinds of things online—websites, blogs, e-newsletters, emails, short stories—and giving them away for free with no apparent remuneration. And when information is free and plentiful, and published as a vanity activity by amateurs, it unfortunately means little or no pay for professional writers.

In this chapter, we'll look first at the two worst writing opportunities on the Internet (as far as making a six-figure income is concerned), and then move on to the five best.

Two Worst Online Writing Opportunities

Writing for e-newsletters

Many freelance writers think they can make money writing articles for email newsletters. After all, there are thousands of such newsletters, and the publishers need content. A big opportunity for you, right?

Wrong. E-newsletter publishers are inundated with articles from contributors who will allow them to run these articles for free, in exchange for promoting the author's product or service to the e-newsletter's subscriber list. With more material than they could ever hope to publish offered to them for free, e-newsletter publishers have little need to pay writers to create original material for them.

Even if you can find a client who is willing to pay for content, the fees can be miniscule. One Internet entrepreneur I met at a conference told me he was able to get five short articles written to use in his online marketing efforts for $25 each.

Corporate clients may actually pay decent fees to have articles written for their e-newsletters. But the vast majority of Internet marketers will pay little or nothing, as they are offered more articles for free than they could ever hope to run.

Ghostwriting ebooks

Most ebook publishers are solo Internet entrepreneurs. While they do hire writers to ghostwrite the ebooks they sell, the pay is paltry, averaging $20 a page. For a 50-page ebook, that's only $1,000, and it's a work for hire: The publisher owns all rights and the author gets only the flat fee—no royalties.

I know this area well, not as a writer but as a client: I am an active publisher of ebooks, which I sell online at www.bly.com (click on Products), and I pay my writers an average of $1,000 per ebook. Keep in mind that they do not only the writing but the research as well. I generally provide just the topic and whatever content on the subject I already own and have the rights to—usually old writings of mine that they can update and recycle in the new ebook.

As a freelance writer, you have little or no leverage in getting clients like me—small Internet marketers—to pay you more for ebooks. Unbelievable as it sounds, there are many competent, smart writers out there who will write ebooks for $1,000 or less: on practically every ebook I assign out at $1,000, I can find another writer who can do it for $500. Amazingly, they will do a good job for $500.

I am a minority among Internet marketers in that I pay a 10 percent discretionary royalty on net sales; few other Internet marketers pay a royalty to their ebook authors. I buy the text from the writer on a work-for-hire basis, meaning I own the copyright and all other rights. This is not negotiable; if a writer insists on holding back rights, I hire someone else.

Five Most Lucrative Online Writing Assignments

So where can you make good money writing Internet copy? Five opportunities:

Websites

With almost 1.5 million domain names registered worldwide and more than 2 billion pages posted on the web, there are thousands of businesses that need to create, improve, or expand their websites—from small local businesses to Fortune 500 corporations. Depending on the client, you can get anywhere from $250 to $1,000 per page or more writing website copy.

The fee of $250 to $750 per page is for straight copy. Design is handled by the website designer or HTML programmer.

The fee does not include keyword search or SEO copywriting, for which many writers charge extra. Keyword search means the writer goes online to find the keywords that are searched most often on the major search engines, using online tools like inventory.overture.com, and presents this list to the client. SEO copywriting means that the copywriter deliberately uses these key words to increase each web page's search engine rankings.

SEO copywriting begins with your keyword list. Select, from those most frequently searched terms, two or three key phrases that are targeted for your web page and grammatically fit into your copy for that page.

Organize your website so that there are separate pages for each product and service you offer. You can then optimize each page for the specific key words and phrases related to the product or service featured on that page. When writing copy for a web page, make sure each of the two or three key phrases you selected appears at least three to four times within your copy—more if you can make it fit.

Read what you have written aloud. If your text sounds like spam, delete some of the key phrases until the copy is less stilted, and more natural and conversational. Remember, you are writing for human beings first, and computer algorithms second. The key phrases must flow smoothly within the writing.

Where do you drop these key phrases into your copy? Place them in each web page's headline and subheads, the main text (top to bottom), and the call to action links (hyperlinks). Use keywords as underlined hyperlinks. Write benefit statements near your main key phrases. When Google displays a brief excerpt of your page content in its search results, the benefit statement will appear along with the key word, enticing prospects to click through to the page.

Keyword phrases containing two to four words are better than single keywords, e.g., "Boston cosmetic dentists" is better than "dentists," because it is more descriptive and specific: A patient in the Boston area needing cosmetic dentistry can more easily find your site. Copywriters who not only write the web page but also optimize it for search engines can charge a higher rate: $500 to $2,000 a page or in some cases even more.

Another way to optimize your web pages for the search engines is with meta tags. These are key words or phrases embedded within the HTML code used to create each web page.

As far as the search engines are concerned, the most important meta tags are Title, Description, and Keywords. These tags control what surfers see when your site is listed in the search engines, which means they help people decide whether to visit your site.

"Title" is what your visitors see at the top of their browser window when visiting your site. Make sure each page has a title that makes sense to your visitors.

Be descriptive. Failure to put strategic key words and phrases in the page title is often why web pages are poorly ranked. Title meta tags should be 50 to 75 characters including spaces.

"Description" is the opening statement people see when your website comes up in search engine findings. The description should concisely answer the question, "What is your product or service and what does it do for the customer?" Recommended length: 50 to 175 characters, again including spaces.

"Keyword" meta tags, as the name implies, are the key words and phrases that Internet users search most often when looking for your product or service. In addition to strategically placing these key words and phrases in your web copy, they should also be listed in your meta tags.

Don't cram the keyword meta tag with every key word and phrase you find using the research tools; five to seven key words in the meta tag is ideal.

To look at the meta tags on a website, choose the "view" menu from your browser's tool bar. Then click on "source" to open a Window containing the HTML code for that page. If the meta tags aren't optimized according to the above guidelines, rewrite to improve.

Micro-sites and landing pages

While most business websites contain information on all of the company's products, a micro-site is a website dedicated to selling a single product (for example, see www.selling-yourself.com).

These micro-sites use long copy and are closer in tone and style to a multipage mail order sales letter than a home page. Ebooks and other information products are typically sold using such micro-sites (see www.golfersmind.com). Fees range from $2,000 for a novice to $7,500 for an experienced writer with a track record of writing successful money-making micro-sites. I use microsites to sell all of my information products online. For an example of how to write an effective landing page, visit www. bestkeptcopywritingsecrets.com. On this page, I sell a $39 ebook on copywriting techniques; and when I send an email to my list inviting them to visit the site, 9 percent of those who click through to the landing page place an order for the product.

A landing page is similar to a micro-site, though not as copy intensive. Landing pages are used to sell a wide range of products, including music CDs, appliances, clothing, cosmetics, beauty aids, computer hardware, and general consumer merchandise. Fees range from $750 to $3,000 and up.

Some marketers use the terms "microsite" and "landing page" interchangeably. Some call a long-copy online sales letter with no navigation—meaning your only options are to read, click to order the product, or click away—a "landing page." When you add some limited navigation to the landing page (e.g., buttons that allow you to view pages with testimonials and other copy), it becomes a "microsite."

Email marketing messages

Email marketing messages are the online equivalent of old-fashioned direct mail: unsolicited sales letters sent to prospects in the hopes that you can convince them to buy your product.

A solo email, also called an e-blast, is a single email marketing message sent to a list of prospects. Fees range from $500 to $1,000 for relatively short email messages, while for longer emails (some are two to three pages long) you could charge $1,500 to $2,000 or more.

Clients may also ask you for an email series—a sequence of three to six or more related email messages sent in series to prospects, often using an autoresponder (software that sends the emails out automatically to anyone who registers on a website). A reasonable copywriting fee would be $500 to $1,000 per effort in the series.

Ebooks

While there's very little money to be made in ghostwriting ebooks for others, many writers have found writing, publishing, and selling their own ebooks online to be enormously profitable. Many I know personally report earning $1,000 to $10,000 a month in sales from a single ebook title. And since there's no printing or shipping cost (the ebook is downloaded by the buyer as a PDF or other type of file), your profit margin is high. A little later on in this chapter, I will give you an overview of how you can make money writing and selling ebooks and other information products online.

White papers

A white paper is a hybrid marketing document, half sales brochure and half article. The idea of a white paper is to educate your prospect in a way that makes them more favorably inclined to buy your product.

Example: a software company is selling a content management system (CMS), software that makes it easy for them to update and add website content. The prospects knows what a CMS is and understands how they work. But he has not purchased because he does not see that the functionality it gives him justifies the high cost. Solution: the client offers a white paper called "Calculating ROI from a CMS" showing how quickly implementation of a CMS will pay back the cost of the software. To see examples of real-life white papers, visit www.bitpipe.com.

Although white papers can be printed and mailed via the U.S. Postal Service, the vast majority are available on company websites as downloadable PDF files. While length varies, the trend today is toward shorter white papers, typically 6 to 10 pages. For a white paper of that length, writers charge $3,000 to $5,000—more for complex topics in which the writer is also an expert or consultant in the subject the white paper covers.

The first step in writing a white paper is research: gather background material on the topic, from both the client and your own Internet searches. The second step is to ask the client, "What is the marketing objective of this white paper?"

Importantly, topic and marketing objective are often not the same thing. For a white paper titled "Administering COBRA," the topic is how to administer COBRA benefits. But if you are selling software to automate COBRA administration, your marketing objective might be something like: "Get human resources managers who need help in administering COBRA benefits to call us and ask for a demo of our system."

Once you have defined the marketing objective, then it's much easier to select the appropriate content from your vast library of source material for inclusion in your white paper. It will also be easier to ruthlessly prune research materials that sound interesting but do not help achieve the white paper's marketing objective.

There are three categories of content you should include in your white paper. The first is content that directly enhances the effectiveness of your white paper in achieving your marketing objective.

For instance, I recently wrote for a client a white paper on how to comply with a particular federal regulation concerning data privacy; let's call it "Regulation X." One of the white paper's marketing objectives is to convince readers that they should in fact make Regulation X compliance a priority (many do not).

So quite logically, I went on the Internet and researched whether any organization or their employees had suffered negative consequences from not achieving full Regulation X compliance. Many of them had, and I added some of that material to the white paper to drive home the point that you can't ignore Regulation X, and doing so would be harmful to both your company and your career.

The second type of information you can add to a white paper is useful tips or how-to information. On the Regulation X white paper, the client provided me with a list the federal government publishes on "9 simple steps to achieving Regulation X compliance."

The list is short and sweet, and so I included it in the white paper as a sidebar. The purpose of the white paper is not to serve as an actual how-to manual on Regulation X compliance; that's beyond the scope of any document limited to white paper length. But the reader feels he is getting some useful, actionable ideas from the sidebar, and so is more inclined to read and keep the white paper.

The third type of information your white paper should contain is content that compares the various options for solving the problem and steers the reader towards yours. In my Regulation X white paper, there were two types of options. Most software companies sold one specific tool to enable compliance in each of the different rules covered by Regulation X.

My client, by comparison, sold a single comprehensive tool that covered all areas. In the white paper, we gave a seemingly objective analysis of the two options, which of course indicated that the advantages of the single-source approach outweighed those of the rule-specific tool approach—a belief that would naturally lead the reader to pick our software over competitors.

Now, when you are writing a white paper and there is a ton of information readily available on that topic, the temptation is to take the attitude "the more content we can cram into our white paper, the better." But that's wrong. Why? Because your reader is busy. If your white paper has the heft of, say, *Moby Dick*, the reader will put it aside. The reader has limited time, and the writer's task is one of *selectivity:* knowing what to leave out is almost as important as knowing what to put in.

So what do you leave out? To begin with, leave out information that the reader could just as easily get elsewhere but does not help forward the white paper's marketing objective. In the Regulation X white paper, for instance, the client had initially wanted to put several pages outlining the various sections and subsections of Regulation X. I asked him where he had gotten this detailed write-up. He replied that he had lifted it from a government website almost word for word. I recommended just summarizing Regulation X, its purpose, and its importance in a paragraph or two, and then including a link to the site for readers who wanted the complete description.

Next, leave out extraneous detail. I also asked the client, "Does knowing the full Regulation X requirements line by line help the reader decide which tool to use?" No, the client admitted, it does not. Then it's extraneous detail, I replied, and should not be included because it adds length without adding value.

The third type of information you should leave out of your white paper is material that is interesting but irrelevant. I read a white paper on fuel cells that went into detail on the history of batteries, and included the invention of the voltaic cell and galvanic pile. It was fascinating but totally irrelevant to the auto maker deciding which fuel cell technology to put into his electric car.

GETTING ONLINE WRITING ASSIGNMENTS

I suppose you could position yourself as an online copywriting specialist and pursue only Internet writing assignments, but that makes sense only if (a) you come from the online world (e.g., you worked as a writer for a dot.com) or (b) you are crazy in love with the Internet and prefer it to the printed page.

For most freelance commercial writers, our bread and butter is still offline copywriting—ads, brochures, press kits, articles, speeches, and annual reports. So the fastest way for us to get online assignments is to let our regular clients know we also do online work.

For instance, if you are hired by a client to write a product data sheet, suggest that you can also turn it into a product page for their website. If a client hires you to write a sales brochure, ask whether they need a white paper to help market that product. Writing a sales letter? Suggest to the client that they can send the same message via email—and you can prepare the online copy for them as well.

When you do this, you can increase the volume and revenue from each client 25 to 100 percent by handling their online as well as their offline copywriting needs.

While I don't have space in this book to outline the similarities and differences between online and offline writing, let me say it this way: *Online and offline are much more alike than they are different. But although the differences are small, they are important and must be learned.*

To this end I immodestly recommend my book *The Online Copywriter's Handbook* (McGraw-Hill). But let me now tell you the two most important differences between online and offline writing.

When we write offline copy, we use words our instincts tell us are compelling to our readers. But when writing web pages, we must also strategically place the most frequently searched keywords within our copy, as discussed earlier in this chapter. Online writers must be aware of keywords, know how to do keyword research, ask clients for lists of relevant keywords, and use those keywords in their copy according to the SEO copywriting "best practices" we've discussed. Offline writers have no such concerns.

The second major difference between online and offline copy is hyperlinks. Online copy allows us to place hyperlinks within our copy. When the reader clicks on the hyperlink, he is immediately taken to another web page. This web page may provide more information on the topic, information on related topics, or a mechanisms for downloading free content or ordering a product.

What type of online writing assignments are freelance writers needed for? As already discussed, one of the most common and lucrative online writing assignments is the microsite or landing page, a long-copy web page dedicated to selling a single product online. Fees are all over the lot: some novices charge $1,000 or less, while experienced writers get $7,500 and up.

Email marketing messages can range from a few sentences and a link to a microsite to longer messages equivalent in length to a multi-page direct mail letter. Fees vary with length, from a low of $1,000 to as much as $2,500 or more.

Online ads are of two types: banner ads and short text ads to run in ezines. E-newsletter ads average 50 to 100 words, and a banner ad may literally have only half a dozen words. So fees are modest: a few hundred dollars per ad.

In my experience, the two biggest areas of demand for online copywriting that also pay the most money are landing pages (for Internet marketing entrepreneurs and direct marketing clients) and SEO copywriting (for corporate websites). Not only is there large demand and great pay, but also very few writers know how to do these tasks well or have a track record enabling them to command the top fees. So if you want to make a lot of money writing online copy for clients, I'd focus on one of these.

THE POT OF GOLD: SELLING YOUR OWN INFORMATION PRODUCTS ONLINE

The real gold for a freelance writer online is building a large list of prospects and readers, and then writing and selling to that list your own information products.

I've only been doing this for a year or so, but already, it has changed my life, generating thousands of dollars in additional income per week, with only a couple of hours of my time required, now that I have built my elist and created my product line, although I am always working on expanding both the list and the line.

The first step in making money with Internet marketing is to build an opt-in email list: a list of prospects who have given you their email address as well as permission to email marketing messages to them. The fastest and easiest way to build a large elist is to publish a free monthly ezine, as discussed in chapter 11. As people sign up to subscribe to your free e-newsletter, their names are automatically added to your opt-in subscriber list.

At minimum, you should have a prominent ezine sign-up box on the home page of your website; see www.bly.com as an example. However, there are so many free ezines published today, that the announcement of yet another one is unlikely to draw much interest on its own.

Therefore, you should offer an added incentive for people to subscribe to your free e-newsletter and join your list. This incentive is typically free content, such as a free ebook. For an example of this type of offer, go to www.bly.com/reports, where I offer a free "marketing library" with a retail value of more than $100. Offering valuable free content can double the amount of people who subscribe to your ezine.

Of course, to get subscribers, you have to drive traffic to your home page or wherever you have your ezine sign-up box. There are a variety of techniques for doing this. Many Internet marketers use pay-per-click advertising, primarily Google Adwords. The key is not to pay too much per click, and to do that, you have to know approximately how much money each new subscriber is worth to you.

For instance, I have 40,000 subscribers who generate net revenues for me online of about $200,000 a year, so each subscriber is worth $5 per year.

I have not been doing Internet marketing long enough to know how long those subscribers will stay with me, so I do not know their lifetime customer value. But based on $5 per year, I could afford to pay $2 to get a new subscriber through advertising, but certainly not $10.

Say my goal was to build my elist, the most I was willing to pay for a new subscriber was a dollar, and 50 percent of the clicks to www.bly.com/reports resulted in a sign-up. It would take two clicks to generate one subscriber, so I could pay $2 for the two clicks, or a dollar per click.

Once you have an elist, you send them not only the free ezine they subscribed to, but solo email marketing messages selling specific products. But don't bombard them with too many emails or they will unsubscribe. If you have a monthly ezine, you can probably send subscribers one solo email message a week, but no more than that.

You can sell other people's products by becoming an affiliate for Internet marketers who have products your subscribers would be interested in. As an affiliate, you send an email promoting that product. The publisher fulfills the order, and pays you a commission on each sale ranging from 15 to 50 percent of the product price. As an affiliate, you can make money selling information products online to your ezine subscribers even if you don't have any products of your own!

As a writer, you have the editorial and research skills to write and produce your own information products. These can include ebooks, special reports, DVDs, CDs, software, tele-seminars, webinars, workshops, coaching, and consulting. For an example of one Internet marketer's product line, go to www.bly.com and click on Products.

The money in Internet marketing, or any other kind of direct marketing, is not made on the first sale, known as the "front end," but on repeat orders from your customers, known as the "back end." Therefore, you need to have multiple products to sell to your elist to really make money online. These products can be a mix of your products and other people's products you sell through an affiliate arrangement.

You should ideally have a mix of products in terms of media (e.g., ebooks, audio CDs, DVDs, seminars, coaching) and price points. In my product line, the lower priced products are ebooks. They range from 40 to 150 pages, and sell for between $29 and $49.

The price point is important, because the people who join your subscriber list for the free bonus items and free e-newsletter don't really know you well when they first become subscribers, nor have they demonstrated a willingness to spend money. They are more likely to begin a relationship as a paying customer when you make them an offer with a lower price point, specifically, below $50.

The lower price range of your product line, then, can be ebooks selling nfor $29 to $49, or even traditional paperback books selling for $10 to $20. The ebooks are more profitable, since they command a higher price, and there are no printing or shipping costs: they are delivered electronically via an email giving the buyer a link where he can download the ebook as a PDF file.

In the middle of my price range are my audio albums, which are recording of speeches, seminars, and interviews in which I speak on a specific topic. My audio programs typically consist of 3 to 6 audio CDs in a vinyl album. My manufacturing cost, depending on the number of CDs, is $8 to $12 per unit, and the sale price is $97. The buyer pays for shipping and handling.

High-end products can include coaching, conferences, workshops, seminars, and eclasses. I don't produce these myself, but find appropriate products in this price range, which can be anywhere from $200 to $5,000, and sell them to my list on an affiliate basis.

My main sales tool is an email marketing message I send to my list on a weekly basis. To see what this looks like, go to www.bly.com/reports, sign up for my ezine, and then study the emails you get from me each week.

What kinds of results are typical? Last week, I sent an email blast offering a $39 ebook on copywriting. Approximately 1,000 out of my 40,000 subscribers (2.5 percent) clicked on a hyperlink in the email to learn more about the product. When you click on the link, you are taken to a long-copy landing page dedicated to selling that single product; it's really a sales letter posted on the web. Of the 1,000 people who visited my landing page, 89 (8.9 percent) ordered the product, generating $3,471 in sales.

You will get additional traffic to your websites and landing pages from a variety of other sources. Some people will search for information on your topic using Google or another search engine and find your site. They may also learn about you from references to you in articles or books. The same week I generated $3,471 in sales from my email, I got an additional $679 in orders from miscellaneous sources—I call them "over the transom" orders—for a total of $4,150 for the week.

There is no shortage of good information available on Internet marketing. You can Google the names Joel Christopher, Fred Gleeck, Terry Dean, Jim Edwards, Joe Vitale, Rich Scheffren, and Yanik Silver to begin with, and feel confident that you will learn what you need to know by ordering their courses and programs. I also recommend my book Start and *Run a Successful Internet Marketing Business* (Self Counsel Press, 2007).

13

Maximizing Your
Personal Productivity

I've published 100 articles and 70 books in the past 23 years. I have six more books on press or under contract. I don't write books or articles full time, however. I work a day job as a freelance copywriter, consultant, and seminar leader.

This doesn't make me the most prolific writer in the world, or the most successful. Far from it. But every week colleagues, clients, and other writers ask me, "How do you write so many books and articles?" Here's how…

Make Personal Productivity a
Business Priority

I'm looking at my watch. It's 8:38 on a Friday morning. By my calculations, I have only 204,400 waking hours of life left. And I intend to make the most of the time still available to me. How about you?

Today the demands on your time are tremendous. Everyone has too much to do—and not enough time to do it. "You may delay," said Benjamin Franklin, "but time will not."

We live in the nanosecond nineties—the age of now. Customers are more demanding than ever. They want everything yesterday. *Miami*

Herald columnist Leonard Pitts comments, "We move faster than ever, but never quite fast enough."

Downsizing has left organizations leaner and meaner. Thousands of workers have been fired, and those who remain must take up the slack and are working harder than ever. According to a Harris poll, the average workweek increased from 41 to 50 hours between 1973 and 1993.

Time is precious. Yet many writers I meet do not seem to place much value on their time. They seem unaware that time is a nonrenewable resource that's consumed at a constant and relentless rate. Once an hour is gone, you can never get it back.

Yet you can solve many of your time-related problems—not enough time, too much to do, deadlines too short, bosses too demanding—simply by using your time more efficiently and refusing to waste it. Writer Dan Kennedy once explained why he was so hard to reach on the phone: "My staff jealously guards my time." Dan's staff may be overzealous, but they have the right idea.

Okay. Here's my advice on how not to waste your time:

- *Don't do everything yourself.* Hire assistants or acquire equipment to eliminate repetitive and routine tasks. Going to the corner stationery store to make photocopies is a waste of your time. Buy a small photocopier and keep it near your desk or hire an assistant to make copies for you, so you never have to go out and do it yourself again. I haven't been to the post office in 7 years, because that's a task better done by my $20-an-hour assistant than by me, the $300+-an-hour writer.

  Despise inefficiency. I spent the extra money on a plain paper fax, because photocopying the curly thermal paper from the old fax machine was an utter waste of time and energy.

- *Don't shy away from the Internet.* Learn your way around the World Wide Web. It's the most fantastic research tool ever available to writers. Information that used to require hours of research at the library to uncover can now be accessed online in a fraction of the time. Why get into your car and drive to read an article when you can bring it up on your computer screen in seconds?

  I urge every writer to become web literate and learn how to search websites for information on the topics they write about. Not only will it save time, but the content (and therefore the quality) of your work will be improved too. Even better, find a good Internet researcher who works at reasonable rates—$10 to $25 an hour—and outsource your online research to him or her.

- *Don't become addicted to Internet chat.* The Internet has great potential for saving time, but also for wasting time—especially in online forums and chat rooms. Limit your web surfing and emailing to research and communication related to your business. Otherwise, aimless online chatting can eat away most of your morning or afternoon before you know it. Use the Internet as a tool; avoid Internet addiction.

- *Don't get up.* You're most productive when you stay in your chair. Arrange your office so that everything is within easy reach. Don't, for example, work in the basement but keep office supplies in the attic. Going up and down the steps is wasted motion and energy.

- *Don't go out.* Or at least be selective about where, when, and how often you go out. You can get so caught up in networking, lunches, and writers' groups that you spend the whole week schmoozing, and consequently get little or no productive work done. Novelist Chaim Potok once began a talk by saying, "I feel guilty standing here talking about writing, because I should be home doing it." Stop talking about writing and instead, write.

- *Don't undervalue your time.* Assign a dollar value to it. If you work 40 hours a week and earn $1,000 a week, each hour is worth $25. Measure other activities you can do during writing time against that $25, and then make a decision whether these activities are worth pursuing.

   A friend of ours, for example, will drive a 40-minute round trip to a distant store to redeem $5 in coupons the local store won't honor. That works out to a savings of $7.50 per hour of labor. My hourly billing rate is many times that, so for me it makes more sense to pay the extra $5 at a local store, save myself the long drive, and spend the 40 minutes working at my hourly rate instead.

"Time is the most precious currency of life, and how we spend it reflects what we truly value," writes Richard J. Leider in his book *The Power of Purpose*. "Once we have spent it, it is gone forever. It cannot be re-earned."

Samuel Butler called time "the only true purgatory" and Emerson said time is "the surest poison." But I disagree. How you use your time is up to you. Writers, who sell nothing but time, must use it wisely. The best time to start doing so? Right now.

One of the drawbacks about the writing business is that, with a few exceptions (royalties, product sales, subcontracting), you don't get paid unless you work.

Dentists have a saying: "Unless you're drilling and filling, you're not billing." As highly paid as they are, dentists' compensation is tied directly to their labor, so they have to keep working to make money.

It's the same with freelance writers. The only ways for you to make more money are (a) to get paid higher rates and (b) to write more. And writing more boils down to becoming more productive. Most writers I see are not terribly productive, which is why their earnings are relatively modest.

Do you want to make a lot of money as a freelance writer—say $100,000 a year or more? Then 9-to-5 probably won't cut it. You'll have to put in more time—45, 50, even 55 hours a week or more. And you'll have to work more efficiently, to boot.

SIX BIGGEST TIME WASTERS FOR WRITERS

1. *Not keeping regular hours.* Many writers talk about the freedom of spontaneously going to the movies or shopping in the middle of the day when the mood strikes them. But do you see people in regular jobs doing this? Of course not.

2. *Permitting distractions.* If your desk is next to the baby's crib and the baby is crying, who gets the attention-baby or the project on your desk?

3. *Sleeping in.* The early bird catches the worm, and the late riser doesn't. If I start at 7 a.m. and you start at noon, you are 5 hours behind me before you even get to your desk.

4. *Talking about writing instead of writing.* Having long lunches with other writers may make you feel "writerly," except that while you are having that 3-hour lunch, you are not actually writing.

5. *Volunteering too much.* When others see your flexible schedule, they want to talk you into doing more volunteer work than is good for you. Resist the temptation. Learn to say no.

6. *Allowing technology to steal your time.* Do not chat on the phone, watch TV, play videogames, or surf the Internet for pleasure during your workday.

NINE WAYS TO INCREASE YOUR PERSONAL PRODUCTIVITY

Here are some of the easiest ways to stop wasting time, enjoy greater productivity, and increase your writing output—and income—substantially:

1. *Get up an hour earlier.* This one simple trick—getting up and starting work an hour earlier every day—can put thousands of extra dollars in your pocket. If you normally start your day at 9 a.m., tomorrow start at 8 a.m. And then do it every day.

2. *Work more.* The main reason why I make hundreds of thousands of dollars every year from my writing is that I work 12 hours a day, 5 days a week, 50 weeks a year. If you put in 30 hours a week now, think about upping it to 40—unless you're content with a modest income and don't desire to earn more.

3. *Put your deadlines on a wall planner or calendar.* Having a calendar posted on the wall in front of you, with all your project deadlines written in, keeps you on track. It is a constant, visible reminder that editors and clients are waiting for your copy—and you had better get to work.

4. *Use a weekly planner or organizer system.* I keep my project deadlines written on the monthly calendar (created in Outlook). But my daily commitments—mostly phone conferences and meetings—are recorded in a weekly planner.

5. *Post a to-do list.* Each day, I print a to-do list of the projects I am working on and pin it to the bulletin board next to my desk. The tasks are prioritized in order of deadline, so that I write the projects due sooner

first. When I cannot go further on the top item on the list—either because I am missing some information or I am tired of working on it—I move on to item number 2. And so on, and so on.

6. *Become technically proficient.* Learn the basic computer skills you need to function efficiently as a freelance writer in today's high-tech society. If a client asks you to send your manuscript as an attached Word file via email, and you don't know how, you'll waste a lot of time figuring it out—and that's time you won't get paid for. Don't have great computer skills? Hire an assistant who does. Or take a course.

7. *Prevent computer downtime.* Identify a good local computer repair service. Get a contract to have them come quickly if you have a major computer problem. As a writer, you simply can't afford PC downtime: A crashed computer costs you money and you risk missing deadlines. I use and highly recommend www.rescuecom.com.

8. *Have backup resources.* A plumber doesn't have just one wrench. Why then do so many writers have just one computer? Always have a working spare. Ask your PC specialist to set up mirroring so that all the files from your primary PC are automatically duplicated on your secondary PC's hard drive every night. That way, if your main machine goes down, you can start working on the backup PC without missing a beat. My PC also backs up to a tape drive every night.

9. *Outsource.* If you follow the advice in this book, you will soon be earning $50 to $100 an hour or more from your freelance writing. At this level of compensation, you should hire others who earn less than you do to handle routine tasks that take up valuable writing time.

   For instance, I have a freelancer who does Internet research for me; she charges $25 an hour. I have a freelance bookkeeper pay bills for me and keep my books, and again it's around $20 an hour. I hire a lawn service to rake my leaves, so I can spend more time making money at my keyboard (which is what I love to do anyway).

Of course, it's your choice whether you want to become as productivity obsessed as I am. You may choose against it. But remember the simple economics of both dentistry and freelance writing: The more work you get done today, the more money will be in your pocket tomorrow.

ENERGY AND ENVIRONMENT

One proven way to increase the amount of work you produce is to write when you have the most energy and when conditions are best. If you're a morning person, take advantage of that energy by writing in the early hours, before the sun comes up. Poet Donald Hall and novelist Georges Simeon, both early risers, finished most of their pressing work each day by lunchtime.

My peak periods vary. Sometimes I follow Hall and Simeon and start early. More often, I work a normal day at my consulting business; then, once the phone stops ringing and the office becomes quiet at the end of the day, I settle in for a couple of productive hours of writing on one of my current books or articles.

I believe a comfortable writing environment increases productivity, but space and solitude also help. I have an outside office, so I write free of the distractions of children, the TV, and the refrigerator. The quiet of an office away from the crowds—I'm on the third floor of a three-story building, so there's minimal traffic and noise—allows me to work uninterrupted. Don't keep a TV in your office. Do have a stereo if background music helps you work, as it does me.

Plenty of desk space and file cabinet storage also boost productivity. When you have room to organize and store work materials, they're close at hand and easy to find. Having to search for a book or folder wastes time. It can also cause you to lose your pace when you're in a writing groove. Two desks and a large table sit in my office, allowing me plenty of surface space for my various writing projects.

SMART WRITING

Want to be prolific? My best advice: Write about subjects you already have some knowledge of. The most prolific authors write as experts, not journalists. Dan Poynter, for example, was able to write dozens of books on parachuting and hang gliding because he is an active participant in these sports.

Write what you know. Write what interests you. If you're fascinated, the work will go faster and be more pleasant. If you already know the topic, lack of understanding or data won't bog you down. But if every piece you write is on a new or unfamiliar topic, your research will be more time consuming and you won't be able to write as rapidly.

Develop your interest by becoming a specialist in one or more areas of knowledge, then write about those areas from many different angles. As your familiarity with the topic grows, the quality of your writing will improve and you'll get more done in less time. Entrepreneur? Become a financial writer. Hypochondriac? Specialize in medicine and health care.

When you write on related topics, research materials collected but not used for one article or book can find their way into the next piece. Subjects given only limited space in the current project can be expanded and made into a series of follow-up works.

Keep organized clipping files on all subject areas you write about. To fill those files, spend at least 30 minutes a day reading newspapers and magazines. Scan them by pertinent articles; clip and file information you can use in articles and books. (Stay in a scanning mode, though; avoid the trap of getting caught up in miscellaneous reading, which can cut into your productive hours.) Always jot the source—magazine or newspaper, issue date, and page number—on every article clipping you file. This saves time tracking sources later on.

Another route to efficient researching is the Internet. Going to the library is a time-consuming process. Research can be done much more rapidly using your personal computer and a high-speed Internet connection.

SELL SMART

How you market your writing also affects your productivity and income. Knowing how to market will help you make more sales, more quickly. And knowing what to sell, and who to sell it to, can bring you assignments that let you earn more per hour of work.

Learn the proven formulas for writing query letters and book proposals. Study the query letters and book proposals of successful authors, and copy their models. Once you familiarize yourself with these formats, you'll be able to quickly generate project ideas and present them professionally to the appropriate editors and publishers. Two books I highly recommend are Lisa Collier Cool's *How to Write Irresistible Query Letters* and Michael Larsen's *How to Write a Book Proposal*, both published by Writer's

Digest Books.

Write on assignment, not on speculation. Send queries and proposals first, get go-aheads, then write to fill the orders. My experience is that I write much faster and confidently when I know what I'm writing is already sold and will be published. With speculative projects, I dillydally, making little progress, because no deadline looms and no one is waiting for my manuscript.

Always have a deadline. Usually your editor will assign one to you. If not, set one yourself. Make the deadline a specific date, and not just "I'll have it in a week or two." To make it more real, share it with your editor (or someone else who will ask you about the project's status). Jobs without definite deadlines often go on indefinitely and at a snail's pace. Work expands to fill the time available. The most money I've ever made writing has been on projects where deadlines were tight and I had to work quickly.

Seek out multiple markets so you can sell all of the different types of materials you write. Traditional publishers aren't your only option. Many authors self-publish certain works they feel aren't appropriate for traditional outlets. This allows them to write more freely without apprehension about which publisher will accept the piece.

For example, Joe Vitale, a Texas-based author with many published books and articles, got the urge to write a short piece on how to write faster and more productively. In 4 hours on a Sunday afternoon, he wrote a 2,500-word essay, "Turbo Charge Your Writing." Published as a 22-page pamphlet priced at $5.95, "Turbo Charge" has sold more than 7,500 copies—a handsome profit for the author by any standard. Today, Joe sells dozens of information products on the Internet, which has made him a wealthy man.

Study *Writer's Market*, but don't be afraid to send queries as the impulse strikes or opportunities arise. I have made numerous sales by contacting magazine editors, book publishers, and corporate clients whose names I came across randomly rather than through deliberate research. If you see a new magazine that appeals to you, write a query to the editor. If you see a book you like, contact the publisher. If you get a promotion from a local business, contact the owner and ask if he needs additional materials written.

I once saw a series of science books for young children in a toy store.

I liked the books and wanted to write for the series. I jotted down the name of the publisher and series editor, then wrote a letter proposing additional titles in the series. The editor didn't need more books for that series, but invited me to write a volume for a new series. Ultimately, I turned it down because the terms were not acceptable, but a book contract would have been mine if I had wanted it.

Proposing an additional title for an ongoing series of books is an effective strategy for making a quick sale—if the series is successful and the publisher is looking to continue it, the editors will be receptive to new ideas that fit well into the series. Four of my published books were sold in this manner.

The most common route to publication is to come up with ideas and pitch them to editors and publishers. I've also had success with the opposite tactic: asking editors and publishers what they want and writing it for them. This strategy is especially effective when one of your own ideas is turned down. Instead of simply walking away, ask the editor, "Well, what are you looking for?" Many will answer with specifics, virtually handing you a writing assignment.

Another common writer's oversight is the relentless pursuit of new markets to the exclusion of current customers. New markets are fine, but don't neglect your best prospect: the editor who has already bought something from you.

It's easier to make repeat sales to established customers than to make first sales to new customers. Come up with ideas aimed at the magazines and book publishers for whom you've already written. If they like it, you get a quick sale, since they already know and feel comfortable with you and your work. A new publisher or editor, on the other hand, not only has to be sold on the idea, he or she has to be sold on you as well, which takes longer and delays the assignment.

Write for those magazines you actually read. You have a better grasp of their editorial requirements and also know what they've done recently. Your queries will sound more authoritative and hit the mark more often.

Make magazine reading a hobby, and you will gain more intimate knowledge of potential markets. This practice will enable you to write queries more quickly, and your acceptance rate will be greater.

If you can land one, use an agent. Agents do the marketing for you, saving you time and freeing you to write. In most cases, literary agents handle books only, not articles or stories. So as far as short stories, essays, poems, and articles go, you're on your own.

I use an agent to handle all book deals. Even when the publisher comes to me directly, I turn the project over to my agent for negotiation. He'll do a better job, and I don't have the time or inclination to do it myself.

While he is negotiating the contract I am writing the proposal for the next book. Use of a good agent frees you from having to negotiate advances, royalties, and deadlines, so you can do more work.

I also use several agents who market me as a writer to corporate and business clients. They get a commission on every sale. The main reason to use them is that they handle a task I dislike—fee negotiation—and leave me free to handle more assignments.

GO HIGH-TECH

Many writers resist technology, especially those of us who got started by pounding on IBM Selectrics. But technology can dramatically increase your productivity, and the more you embrace it, the more you'll get done.

As we discussed in chapter 2, get the best computer system and software money can buy.

Ask the computer salesperson to recommend a system configuration in terms of processor memory and hard disk storage. Then get twice that or at least as much above the recommendation as you can afford. Why? Whatever you buy today won't be the state of the art as soon as you learn to use it, so you can never have too much computer.

The big debate in desktop computers for home offices has always been IBM vs. Mac. The Mac owners swear by them. The problem is, your clients—publishers and businesses—are all IBM, and they require their writers to email copy as Word files that can be opened, read, and edited on a Windows desktop. So I strongly urge you to write on a PC running Microsoft Windows and Word.

THE QUALITY CURVE

My writing goal is to be good but not perfect. Clients don't have the time or budget for perfection, and for most projects, being 95 percent perfect is good enough.

Writing, like most other human activities, follows a curve like the one below (Fig. 13-1). You get the most improvement from the first hours you put into the task, and then diminishing returns as you keep at it.

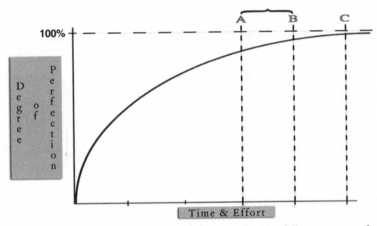

Fig. 13-1. Improvement in the quality of a written piece follows a curve: the greatest gains are in the earliest rewrites and edits.

Eventually, you reach the point where the improvement from additional hours does not justify the extra investment of your time, either for yourself, your reader, or your client. That's the point where it's time to stop, do a final read-through and proofing, and send your copy in.

That doesn't mean you deliberately leave in errors or make the piece incomplete. It means you stop polishing the piece when it looks good to you. Don't agonize over the fact you're not spending another hundred hours on it. Write it, check it, and then let it go.

Some writers spend years on a single piece or decades on a novel; Donald Hall said he revised one poem more than 600 times. But you reach a point where the changes you are making don't materially improve the work or its value to the reader. This is the point where I stop. To go on would not improve the result, and those writers who are perfectionists don't produce or sell much work—or make much money.

Prolific science fiction authors Robert Heinlein and Isaac Asimov wrote first drafts that were pretty close to the final copy. Heinlein sent out his first drafts unrevised, while Asimov read them once and made revisions affecting maybe 5 percent of the text. Asimov said that having a plain and simple style contributed to his being one of the most prolific writers of the twentieth century.

New writers can't expect to duplicate such efficiency. But you'll use your writing time most efficiently if you write in a natural, plain style. Your writing should sound like you and reflect your personality. Don't imitate or copy the styles of other writers, even those you admire. Imitation sounds easy but is in fact difficult, unnatural, and slow. When you write as if you're talking to the reader one on one, you write quickly and productively.

Aim for simple prose: short words, short sentences. Write to express, not to impress. Care about words and be a careful editor, but don't agonize over every comma to the nth degree. It's okay to be critical while you're editing, but don't be critical of your writing while you're writing it. Know that if you have something to say or you can say it in an amusing fashion, people will read and enjoy what you write.

Don't be held up by the false notion that you must uncover some great truth or present your reader with revolutionary ideas and concepts. Most readers read more for reinforcement than anything else, so if you tell them things they already know, they won't be disappointed; rather, they'll admire you for your insight and knowledge. (They'll also feel smug that what they believed to be true was validated in print.)

You can eliminate performance pressure by not worrying whether what you're writing is different or better than what others have written on the subject before you. Just write about the subject the best you can. Others will be interested and enthusiastic; remember they haven't read 99 percent of the material written on that topic.

Don't be afraid to write quickly. "Fast writing is good writing," insists Milt Pierce, a New York City freelance writer who has dozens of articles, books, and direct mail packages to his credit. Pierce says the pieces he writes quickly are usually the best; if he finds himself agonizing, he knows the writing isn't his best.

Actually, there is no direct correlation between writing speed and quality. It depends on the assignment and the author. If you're fortunate enough to be a fast writer, take advantage of your gift. Don't believe those who tell you that if you did it fast, it can't be good. I've read that Robert

James Waller wrote *The Bridges of Madison County* in 14 weeks. Critics panned the book, but millions of readers love it.

At the same time, don't tell editors and clients how quickly you write. Steve Manning, a Toronto-based freelancer who has written and sold as many as 132 articles in a year, says he never lets editors know how slowly or quickly he wrote a given piece. "It can take me anywhere from two hours to two days to do an article, but I never tell the editor," says Manning. "Editors assume that if the article was written quickly, it's inferior. If I let them think it took two to three weeks, they're delighted."

MORE PRODUCTIVITY TIPS

- *Write short articles and books instead of long ones.* The industry trend is toward shorter articles and books, so editors and publishers will be receptive to your manuscripts. You'll produce more articles and books in less time and your income will increase. You'll earn more advance money writing two short books than one long book. And in most instances you'll be paid more to write three 1,500-word articles than one 5,000-word article.

- *Recycle your articles.* Sell only first rights to your articles, retaining all others. Then resell these articles in other markets. Do variations. Most writers do an enormous amount of research for one article or book, and then drop that topic. If you can amortize the time spent on that research over four or five related projects, your writing business will be much more profitable.

- *Recycle your material.* One writer of paperback westerns writes many novels a year for different series. He keeps all his manuscripts on a hard disk and often pulls chapters from previous books to use in a new book, changing names, places, and some of the narrative to fit' the new story. In this way he can produce many more novels a year. You may think he's a hack. But his books sell, he enjoys his work, and he makes a nice living in a field where many struggle to pay the rent.

- *Don't let your out-of-print material stay out of print.* Get the rights back and resell them to other publishers for a new contract and advance. You can revise the manuscript and create a new version much faster than you can write a new book from scratch. Yet the advance you get for a revised book will be 25 to 50 percent of the advance you'd be paid for a brand-new book, so it's very profitable.

- *Work with a coauthor.* I've teamed up with several coauthors on various book and copywriting projects. One is a semi-celebrity. Another is a millionaire entrepreneur. They provided the source material; I wrote the book or copy.

  Without these coauthors on my team, I'd have a much harder time selling publishers on hiring me to handle the topics we are tackling together. Also, my coauthors' reputations add credibility and I hope will make readers want to buy our writing.

  A similar strategy is to coauthor with a fellow writer. Yes, you must split the income. But the benefit is that you also split the work. Again, you can write more in less time. And because you can divide the article sections or book chapters with your coauthor, you avoid writing on the aspects of the topic you're not as interested in. When I coauthored *Dream Jobs* (Wiley) with Gary Blake, we had chapters on various careers. I wrote about the industries that interested me (advertising, cable television, finance), while Gary handled topics I was disinterested in (fashion, food, travel).

- *Write for children.* Many people are negative about children's book publishing, citing the lower advances and the fact that royalties must be split with an illustrator. True enough—but most children's books run only a few hundred words compared to the 80,000 words or more in the average adult nonfiction book or novel. So while an advance on a children's book may be only a few thousand dollars, it's actually quite high when figured on a dollars-per-word basis—higher than for most adult books.

  A colleague recently published a children's book with Scholastic. It's a hardcover picture book selling for $14.95. The text portion runs approximately 500 words; every time someone buys those 500 words, my friend gets a royalty on $14.95.

  My books, typically adult nonfiction trade paperbacks, contain 100,000 words each—200 times the length of my friend's picture book. Yet I receive a smaller royalty payment for each copy sold, because my books' cover prices are lower and paperbacks earn lower royalties than hardcovers.

Fewer words don't necessarily equal less research, and compressing a topic into a few hundred words is a unique challenge in itself. Still, children's books can be a profitable outlet for your creativity.

- *Value your time and spend it productively.* Don't go to the library to look up a fact when you can call the research librarian and have her read it to you over the phone. Do interviews by phone instead of in person whenever possible to avoid travel and meeting time. My experience is that a 20-minute telephone interview can yield information equivalent to a 2-hour in-person meeting.

  Another advantage of phone interviews is that you can type notes directly into your computer. This eliminates the incredibly time-intensive activity of transcribing tape-recorded interviews, a task that can rapidly move a writing project from the black into the red. If you do tape record, have someone else transcribe the tape for you.

  Consider replacing your tape recorder and notepad with a laptop or notebook computer even when you do interview people in person. Denny Hatch, former publisher of *Target Marketing* magazine, says typing his interview notes directly into a laptop not only eliminates transcribing time but also results in more complete and accurate notes than scribbling in a notebook.

OVERCOMING WRITER'S BLOCK

In his book *Let Your Life Speak* (Jossey-Bass, 2000), Parker J. Palmer gives a pithy description of writer's block and its causes:

> It is easy to stare at the blank page and despair of ever having another idea, another image, another illustration. It is easy to look back at what one has written and say, "That's not very good, but I'd better keep it, because nothing better will come along." It is difficult to trust that the pool of possibilities is bottomless, that one can keep diving in and finding more.

My best advice for avoiding writer's block is to always keep busy and productive. Isaac Asimov said he could never be stopped by writer's block, because he had so many different projects he was working on simultaneously. If he got tired of writing an essay, he simply stopped and began work on a short story or novel instead. When he wound down on the novel, he'd move to a nonfiction book project or column.

When you're on a roll, don't stop. Keep going until the energy runs out. For example, I am typing this in my office at 8 on a Wednesday night. My wife called before and asked me to leave the office early to pick up dinner, but I begged off; I had momentum going with this piece and didn't want to lose it. In fact, I told her I didn't know when I'd be home. When I lose the momentum, I'll stop, turn off the computer, and go home.

Another effective technique for avoiding writer's block is to take on only those writing assignments you are enthusiastic about, and turn down the ones that bore you. By proactively marketing and promoting your freelance writing business on a consistent basis, you will generate enough potential assignments to give you this luxury of choice, and your productivity and satisfaction will soar as a result.

14

Awaken the Poet Inside You

Are you ready to get your poems published—finally ready to put your voice out into the world? If you've considered it even once, the time has come to share your experiences and observations of life on a broader scale, in a way only a published poem can accomplish.

It's a question that comes up for every poet who has dedicated countless hours to playing with verse until a deeper truth suddenly emerges with the subtle turn of a line. It often happens in such an amazing way that the poet suddenly sees the changes as inevitable—a poem now fit for submission.

But the question of getting published also comes up for anyone who has admired a poem, and in so doing, decides to write one; and in the pure, word-play pleasure of it, writes another, then another. In very little time, the poems multiply; some of them complete, ready for submission. Every poet starts this way, and it's not about the money.

Does Writing Poetry Pay?

Although well-known poets can command substantial speaking fees, most poets consider themselves fortunate if they receive a few copies of the publication in which their work appears. With the exception of winning top prize in a contest, most payments are small checks—enough to buy a latté, or if you're lucky—lunch. But for impassioned poets—those who know that poems feed the soul and not the bank account—the act of writing poetry is its own reward.

So is it luxury or necessity? If you love writing poems, it's always a necessity, something you find the time to do. Most likely you earn your money as most poets do, in more routine careers related or unrelated to writing. Even the most famous still teach, edit, write, speak, mentor and work at other jobs. David Tucker's praised collection, *Late for Work,* was compiled and written just this way, while he continued working his newspaper job as an assistant managing editor.

Ted Kooser, thirteenth United States Poet Laureate, worked as an insurance rep in his early years, writing and submitting along the way. Chances are you write your poems before the normal workday begins, or late at night when the hum of commerce has shut down. When you're done, you just squirrel them away in a desk drawer or maybe you've even gone to the trouble of making up a special file.

So why not leave it there? Why submit at all? Because there is an undeniable yearning in you that wants to go beyond the solitude of crafting a poem within your own familiar walls. Maybe the idea first struck when you found a dusty notebook. In it were some early poems, and to your surprise intense emotions arose, the words however old, seemed strangely fresh—what Ezra Pound once said of poetry, "News that stays news."

Although some poets get stalled at the submission stage, don't lose your nerve; just keep writing with your strongest intuition. If for no other reason, do it because it speaks to your unique experience of life. As the saying goes, you might as well be yourself; everyone else is taken.

GETTING READY TO WRITE A POEM

Before you actually submit, a few preliminary steps will serve you well; they're simple, daily sources of inspiration. The first is to make a habit of reading a new poem every day. If you're in a place where you can read it aloud, even better. Then examine what you like about it. *The Writer's Almanac with Garrison Keillor* is a great way to start.

Sponsored by the Poetry Foundation, the *Almanac* is a free email newsletter you can read online, print out, or listen to on the radio (NPR),

Real Audio, by podcast or web archive. It comes out every day and begins with a poem. One day you're likely to be mesmerized by the classics—Emily Dickinson or Robert Frost—and the next engrossed in contemporary poetry from W.S. Merwin, Charles Simic, or a newly published poet you've never heard of. The generous Literary and Historical Notes at the end of each newsletter will further inform and inspire you.

Pay attention to what appeals to you in a poem and what does not; and particularly why it does or doesn't. Whether it's traditional or free verse, whatever causes you to "feel" your senses and experience a poem in a richer way is, in some way, resonating with your own true voice and life experience. It doesn't mean you'll want to imitate what you've read—though you might—but it will help you reexamine your own work in light of a published poem. You'll likely find yourself asking, "What makes this poem work so well?" In asking, you may find that a poem of your own is begging for a different form, a change in line or thought that makes a deeper impact, putting you that much closer to submitting your work.

Once you've been doing your "poetry workout" for a while, if you skip a day here and there, you'll find yourself missing it, feeling the effects, much like what happens when you've dropped a day or two from your physical exercise routine.

Above all, don't waste a minute of your precious time reading mediocre poems; be selective. You don't want bad poetry floating around in your mind, or worse, unconsciously creeping into your own work like a sad song you can't get out of your head.

Pick the best and learn from them. How do you know? For example, you can start with one of the most easy-to-read and vibrant anthologies: *Poetry 180—A Turning Back to Poetry,* selected and assembled by Billy Collins. When Collins was first appointed Poet Laureate of the United States in 2001, he was inspired by a version of the Library of Congress "180" website (www.loc.gov/poetry/180/) to develop a program, "Poetry 180: A Poem a Day for American High Schools." This printed collection, however, suits poets and readers of any age. In 2005, he followed it with *180 More: Extraordinary Poems for Every Day.* And, you won't find duplication of what has become standard for poetry textbooks or other anthologies in either of his collections.

You can open the books to any page and get it—instant gratification—

enjoyment and delight in the diversity, and pure pleasure in the speaking of what you've read. Keep a pencil in hand though, because you'll probably find an idea for a poem of your own springing from the pages. As Collins writes in the introduction of his first anthology, "Flip through the book and pick a poem, any poem. I know every one is an ace, or at least a face card, because I personally rigged the deck."

ATTEND POETRY READINGS

Immerse yourself in what's available in your area. Just about every city has a poetry organization or literary guild, and every state has its own poetry association. Join at least one poets' group in your city, and become a member of your state poetry association. Membership benefits alone will put you on the mailing list and among the first to learn of any new publications that crop up—new submission sources that bridge the gap left by earlier printings of even the most comprehensive, standard marketing guides.

You'll also want to check regularly on events at your local library, community colleges and universities for schedules of workshops, special speakers, and poetry readings. While you're there, you can pore through poetry collections and journals; you're bound to find a few more submission possibilities. When you're in a bookstore, head straight for the poetry section and see what contemporary collections are being sold, as well as those hot off the press. On your way out, take the time to ask about any poets scheduled for book readings.

TOOLS YOU NEED

There are thousands of poetry websites replete with advice on how to write poems and how to submit them. But you don't have to bury yourself online for days at a time to get started. Even the most technophobic poets can begin by using some common sense guidelines—straight from published poets who have walked the same path you're about to follow.

But you'll be doing it with a road map that gives you shortcuts and essentials they discovered only after meandering too long on a less direct road to publication. You'll learn how to streamline the submission process to the point where marketing your work becomes less drudgery and more of a task you look forward to accomplishing.

Most poets subscribe to a number of poetry journals, magazines, and market guides, but you can narrow it down by choosing just those essential to your growth. When it comes to changing trends, submission deadlines, and availability of grants and awards, *Poets & Writers* magazine and *Poet's Market* top the list.

Poets & Writers is published six times a year, covers news and trends, in-depth features, submission calendars for contests, grants and awards, and much more (www.pw.org). All issues are well worth archiving for later reference.

Poet's Market, an annual *Writer's Digest* publication, is considered an indispensable marketing tool for most poets who want to get published. You'll find something for poets of all skill levels. It includes more than 1,800 listings for publishing opportunities and how-to-submit instructions specific to each publication. The guide is comprehensive, easy to use, and woven throughout are many helpful articles and interviews with poets and editors. It's worth the somewhat hefty cover price.

Both *Poets & Writers* magazine and *Poet's Market* can be found at just about any bookstore, and of course at your local library. For market access online, www.writersmarket.com is another way to go, with over 5,000 listings updated daily.

ARE POETRY CONTESTS A CROCK?

"It all depends" is the right answer, because if you win a contest, then the answer will be yes, but if you've spent a few hundred dollars in entry fees and have nothing to show for it other than lots of copies of last year's literary journals, the answer is probably no. If it's no, the opportunity to scrutinize your contest entry choices has definitely arrived.

Consider looking at www.winningwriters.com. It has a large database, described by *Writer's Digest* as one of the "101 Best Websites for Writers." Its email newsletter gives you instant access to *free* quality poetry contests, contest profiles—which contests to avoid and why—and a wide array of resources. The site also gives links to several award winning poems.

SUBMITTING YOUR POEMS

To start submitting, all you need is a batch of three to five poems—

ones you have decided are the very best that you can make them, and those that match the needs of the publication. Sounds easy, but selecting your poems is just the beginning.

When it comes to poetry, meticulous attention to detail is crucial: Carefully study publication submission guidelines; proof and double proof your cover letters; and always keep accurate submission records. Set up your work and submission files on computer and make sure you have hard copies of everything. Hard copies are imperative—not simply desired, because you'll eventually have several submissions and different batches out at one time. You need to know where they are at all times, and in what original or revised state you submitted them. Plus, if one publication accepts a poem, you need to inform all the other publications immediately. Contacting them is not a courtesy; it's a *must*.

Also, what if you've revised a poem and six months or even a year later you finally hear from an editor who wants to publish it? (Could it take that long? Yes, it can.) Unfortunately, you haven't saved the earlier drafts and have made substantial revisions since the first submission. Sure, you can send the revised draft, explain that the poem has undergone substantial revisions, but what if the earlier draft is what the editor prefers and you can't find a copy? Why risk looking like a disorganized amateur? Another tip: Keep all poetry revisions on file until after your poem has been published, then shred away.

As for rejection letters, get used to them; it's part of the process. Sometimes they're even valuable. A "good" rejection letter means an editor has taken time to handwrite a note, saying what he liked about your poem or what could be improved. This is encouraging news. Take the initiative and improve your poem. If the editor has asked you to resubmit, do it as soon as you can. Be sure to resubmit with a note of thanks for the feedback in your cover letter; keep it short, professional, and to the point. The editor is neither your buddy nor your colleague—at least not at this stage of your communication. If you have not been asked to resubmit, make the revisions anyway and send your poem off to another publication.

CHAPBOOKS

After you have publishing credits with several quality publications, you'll probably be tempted to consider a chapbook as your next step. A chapbook is a small volume—anywhere from 10-50 pages. Chapbook lengths vary quite a bit, and a good number of manuscripts are solicited through competitions. Buy winning chapbooks and study them carefully.

No matter if you're submitting directly to a publisher or through a contest, the number one rule is to request guidelines from each and every publisher that interests you. Read and reread the guidelines, follow them precisely, and take nothing for granted.

Chapbook publishers are just as selective and demanding when it comes to quality as full-length book publishers. You don't want your work disqualified or returned simply because you didn't follow basic format instructions. Ignoring a publisher's policies is the quickest way to get your manuscript back—unread.

Another big mistake is not giving enough time for review and revision before you send it out. While the first and last poems in any collection must be strong, every poem in between should support your theme in some way—whether emotional or narrative. Too little gestation time for your chapbook can undermine even the finest first effort.

Give yourself a few weeks for revisions, and then allow the manuscript to rest a few days. If need be, revise again. After that, ask a few fellow poets you respect and trust to read it. They can help you answer any questions you may still have about theme or sequence. Allow at least another week for them to respond. They're giving you their time and you want the most thoughtful feedback you can get.

Although it seems unnecessary to say, some advice bears repeating: Don't even consider sending your manuscript if you haven't read the publisher's existing chapbooks (a few poems available online is not sufficient). This is one big blunder that still gets made far too often. And finally, know that "acknowledgments" means a list of publishing credits, not an Oscar thank-you speech.

Once you've proofed, had others proof, and proofed again, congratulate yourself, and send it off.

Then, start writing more poems!

WRITING SHORT FICTION

BY HARLAN ELLISON®

There are no crafty techniques for marketing short stories. You send them to the appropriate magazines with a self-addressed stamped envelope (SASE). The "trick" to getting your short story published is to write a great short story, which is why in this chapter, I share with you some advice on writing short stories from Harlan Ellison, widely recognized as one of the great living short story writers.

One of the most common reasons for the rejection of a story has virtually nothing to do with the overall impact of that particular piece of writing. An otherwise excellent story can find itself being stuffed back into the SASE and being dropkicked into the mail chute because it had a slow, an obscure, a confusing, or redundant opening section. Though the characterizations are strong, the concepts imaginative, and the action sequences motor right along, if the story crawled on all fours from page one through, say page eight, before it got to its feet and started sprinting, chances are good that the editor grew impatient and decided the reading of one unsolicited manuscript should not become his or her life's work.

No sense railing at this seeming callousness. The editor is only human. And to be absolutely pragmatic about it, freed of the maudlin self-pity and justifications unpublished writers substitute for logic, the editor is only a reader, albeit a more trained reader than the casual magazine-buyer. If you can't grab the editor's interest, odds are heavily against your being able to grab Joe or Joan Reader with that slow opening.

To state that communication is the bottom line of all writing would be to jackhammer a truism into the tarmac. If the communication isn't there from the get-go, the reader has—it seems to me—an unconscious reluctance to trust the writer: That means the writer must work ever so much harder to get the reader into that mind-warp called the "willing suspension of disbelief." The longer it takes a writer to nudge, push or pull a reader into that state, the more chances the reader has of escaping the web of the fiction.

So it becomes clear that we must cherry-bomb the reader as quickly and as completely as possible, to the self-serving end of snaring the twisty beast. To that purpose, here are three devices I've found universally present in good writing. The first is the title, and we've already masticated that one. The second is the literary hook, the beguiling opening line, about which I'll discourse some other time. The third device is no device at all, but is one of the plimsoll-line measurements of craftsman like writing; it is knowing how and where to begin the story.

In editing the *Dangerous Visions* anthologies I read more than my share of stories that I eventually published, but often only after asking the writers for revisions that dealt with the opening pages of the work. And I've read many stories that made it into print even though they suffered from the same flaccid lack of muscle tone. In working Clarion, and other prestigious writing conferences, I've seen much the same thing. (And much less of that slow pacing at the beginning when I've bludgeoned my students into writing a story a day. When they have to write fast, they automatically understand that there is limited time available to them to grind out a complete story, so they instinctively reject superfluous or repetitious back story, compress rambling scenes, find side-roads that short-cut lumbering, dead patches of exposition and, in the words of the television industry, they "cut to the chase" immediately. In most cases it tightens the plot and drags the reader along.)

Understanding where to begin a story is a facility that comes with years of writing many stories. It's a mugg's game, trying to set down hard and fast rules, because it's different every time; and no set of rules really works. The best I can do, I guess, is try to give some examples and then examine them, and hope that I'm being clear enough so you can apply the lessons to specific stories on which you're working. But do please take this caveat into consideration as you read these comments: this is just a general rule of thumb, and you must take the Cortical-Thalamic Pause (as dear A.E van Vogt put it), noodle this information for individual assimilation. Not to put too fine a point on it, do as I suggest, not as I frequently don't do it myself.

All right, then, to it, with vigah!

Let's suppose a story. Um. Okay, how's this:

Bizarre story about a guy who has nothing but shitty relationships with women, who cannot cop to his own fractured persona. Argues with his lovers, brutalizes them, intimidates them. But though he's given to some low-level self-analysis—he's rather bright—he always manages to rationalize the encounters so he comes off looking good and the women always come off, in his mind, as immature or castrating or just plain fucked-up. So he sinks deeper and deeper into despondency, until he decides he'll never be able to find a woman who is good enough for him. Meaning, of course, a woman whom he can dominate while she manages to retain a sense of her own identity that doesn't threaten him. From this lightless perception of the world, skewed as it is, he comes across an advertisement for android companions, programmed to suit every need.

So he gets one, a beautiful woman who seems just right, because he has gone through extensive bio-medical brain-scanning that has pulled out of him and his needs a template that forms the basis of her identity. He marries her. Everything goes well for a "honeymoon" period of six months. And then he discovers that his android wife is having an affair with another man. He is so enraged by this, that he plans to kill her. But is it murder if you kill an android? Is it rational? Should he take her back into the shop to be re-programmed? Or will he finally understand that the flaws are in him, that he sows the seeds of interpersonal destruction because of his narrow view of other human beings?

(Yes, I know, I know, Bradbury did exactly this story, and then it was adapted for *The Twilight Zone,* but it's a place to start for a paradigm, so shut up and stop being such a pecksniff smartass.)

Now, that's the basic idea. It's not a story, friends. (That's something else to belabor at length in the future: knowing the difference between an "idea" and a "story," but not now, not now; stop pestering me.) But it's all we need to examine the point of entry into the story.

There is a kind of literary magic, the inarticulate power of certain auctorial magicians to transmute base metal ideas into the pure gold of a compelling story opening. Sheckley has the power, as did Phil Dicke; so do Kotzwinkle, and Ann Beattie, and Ron Goulart; so did Alice Sheldon before she killed herself, her ailing beloved husband, and James Tiptree; Jr., and Raccoona Sheldon, all on the same dark day. I could list dozens who lack that power, but I don't need to; you can do it for yourself. So where do we tap with that magic finger to start our story?

Well, here's one way:

> Walter Nesterman tried desperately not to hate women. He walked away from Francine's monad cursing her, cursing himself cursing his inability to have said what he wanted to say to her. The French called it l'esprit d'escalier, the spirit of the stairs, or as close to translation as could be managed in English, the mood of thinking retrospectively, as one walked down the stairs away from the argument, what one should have said. I should have told her, you stupid bitch, if you weren't having all these fights...I should have said, you're just flat out immature, that's your problem...
>
> But he hadn't. He had raged and fumfuh'd and gotten red in the face, and now another affair was over. It was the fifth lousy liaison he'd been involved in over the past year.
>
> And he felt at once furious and guilty.

Okay. Now there's nothing much wrong with that. I took pains to write it well, so I couldn't be accused of loading the gun in favor of an alternate method that I think is better.

Here's another way of doing it:

A snake uncoiled in Walter Nesterman's gut and the first thing he thought, a kind of inarticulate scream of rage within him, was I'll kill that android bitch!

Married less than six months and she was busily humping some other guy. His mind reeled across a surreal landscape of impossible possibilities. How could a pre-programmed android created specifically to his needs be unfaithful? Was it a human she was fucking, or another chemical construct? How was she slipping out to see him? Could it be a "her"? Was the flaw in himself, in the brain scan that had been pulled out of him to form her template?

But most of all, mournfully whistling like an autumn wind across his mind, was the cry Am I never to find a woman I can love?

And the certain knowledge: I gotta kill that android bitch!

Now that's closer to it. But even though we've eliminated all the back story of Nesterman's unhappy relationships and an examination of his personality in situ, it's still wrong. Or, more exactly, it ain't right. (Nothing, if written well and intriguingly, is wrong. See what I mean about how hard it is to pinpoint this problem? The rules simply don't hold.) Whoever Francine was, she's out of it as we open the story, so we don't need to lumber the reader with a reference to someone we're not going to see again. And both of these open on interior monologue of one sort or another. Granted (he said humbly), notwithstanding they're both moderately interesting, passionate interior monologues, they are, nonetheless, essentially passive. And we want to start at a dead run if we can. So I'd suggest something short and sharp like this:

Nesterman looked down at his wife asleep in the waterbed. Her eyes were closed, her breathing was shallow, and the recharger plugged into her right hip was glowing bright red. He held the laser knife tightly and warred within himself. Cut her lying android throat, or simply take her back to the shop and have them turn her into slag?

He couldn't escape the awful reality: not even an android, built to satisfy his every need, could be faithful to him. His beautiful chemical construct of a wife, beautiful charming Charlene was having an affair! And all he could think was: I've gotta kill this bitch!

Okay. Now, can you see the variations? In the first, we start six and more months before the nub of the story, with a lot of back plot and soul-searching that is pretty much dead time as far as plot progression is concerned. In the second, we bring the story six months into the present, but it's right at the moment when he's come to his decision to kill Charlene. And that might seem a pivot point in his life, which it is, but again we're dealing passively with a passionate, action-filled situation.

The third opening brings us to the moment that he's standing right over this sleeping, helpless woman, with murder in his heart. Now, if we want to have him back off because he's torn, because he's starting to realize the problem lies with him, not her, we have the basis for a subsequent series of scenes in which he has to disguise his feelings, in which he tries to draw out of her an admission of what's been going on, in which he seeks out the man or woman or artificial life-form she's having an affair with, in which he goes back to the company that made her and tries to find out what went wrong (nice idea: a psychologist who ministers to the fluxes and flows of both human and android principals)—an infinitude of possibilities for examination of the human condition. Not to mention an expansion of the basic plot situation.

Or if we want to have him kill her, right then and there, we can run it like Poe's "The Tell-Tale Heart" and have the miserable fucker going bananas because of what he's done.

Don't forget, what we're dealing with in this story is the moment of realization on the part of a complex and tormented human being that he is incapable of decent warmth and a lasting relationship. Therein lies the story, not the amusing conceit of what is entailed when one murders something that isn't really alive. That's the furniture. The theme is human travail.

I'm not sure if you get what I'm saying in these three examples, but I'll bat it around a little more and hope that one or more comments will concretize the rigor I'm suggesting you adopt as a religion.

Look: a novice would go with the question "Is it murder to kill an android?" Wrong. That's been done. Dozens of times, all the way back to Eando Binder's famous short story, "I, Robot" in the January 1939 issue of *Amazing Stories*. And it's a moot point at this stage of recombinant DNA research in our lives. It's no longer extrapolative when we're all reading a Time essay on the moral and philosophical conundrums inherent in such a real-life case. But right now all we have to work with is human beings, and this kind of story (it seems to me) is only valuable for us if it explores the labyrinthine byways of the human heart. It's an allegory, if you will. A paradigm. Using it as such, we can find out—if not for the entire world, then at least for ourselves as writers—what messes with human relationships. And to do that in a storytelling way, we have to get into the situation when it's already fully formed. Building to it can be interesting, but diving in while the action is transpiring around us makes it immediately arresting.

One way to do this sort of thing would be to start it at whatever point your own skill dictates, write on for a couple of thousand words, and then set it aside for a day, or even a few hours, whatever your work habits require.

When you go back, re-read it and ask yourself, How much of this tells itself through context? How much is revealed by the actions of the characters without telling the reader through static narration? How much can I show with scenes, rather than dropping in lumps of undigested exposition? How much of this is stuff I needed to know, as background, but is also stuff the reader need not see specifically?

Then cut. And once you've cut it, cut it again. And when it is clear that nothing else can be cut—cut it again. Go to the muscle and the bone. Strip away the rhetorical flab. And then...

Cut it again.

Boil down that first two thousand words of bibble and self revelation to a paragraph of hard, mean prose.

Take the writing of screenplays as a model. Never write a scene where someone sits alone in a room and there is a knock on the door, the person gets up and goes to the door, answers it, meets the visitor, invites the visitor in. they seat themselves and begin to have a long discussion that ends with a fist fight. Cut to the chase. Open the story with the first punch being thrown. Fredric Brown did that sitting alone in a room routine, and called it "Knock." Except his first line was a technical masterpiece. The last man on Earth—or in the universe, for that matter—sat alone in a room. There was a knock at the door...

So unless you can beat what a dead man did perfectly, you can forget it, chum.

I've digressed on that man-alone-in-a-room situation, because I know sure as the insensate Universe made little green apples, that some wiseass fan would take my using it as an example of dull writing and say, "Yeah, but what about the Fred Brown story?" And it's a perfect example, so I wanted to close up the rat hole.

What I'm suggesting is that any scene you use to launch a narrative can be cut in half, opened like a ripe orange, and the flesh in the middle has got to be tastier than the pith. So go to the middle of a situation, go past the back story material that got you interested in the first place, the stuff you can slide in as slivers of enlightenment throughout the first third of the story, the stuff that formed the original plot epiphany, when you said to yourself, "Hey, wouldn't it be interesting if..." It's what happens after that initial idea the world has come to call "a story."

Cut to the chase. Go to the first punch. Start at the instant the fire ignites. Disabuse yourself of the misconception that to write well, to write interestingly, to write with class and verve, one must try to emulate Proust or James. Those were storytellers of a different time, who worked in a medium that has changed enormously. We read faster now, we think more quickly, and clarity can be as complex as obtuseness. Now you must snare them immediately!

The job is to tell the story feelingly, and at a dead run if at all possible. To do that, you must consider the point of entry and make certain it is one edged with fishhooks. Once having impaled the reader, you'll find you're telling a story that has snagged you too.

And by the way, I may eventually wind up writing that story about Nesterman and Charlene, because if I call Ray and say, "Hey, kiddo, I've got an alternative take on 'Marionettes. Inc,', d'you mind if I go at it, if I drop a 'thank you' to you at the end?" my friend Bradbury will say, "It's an honor to be plagiarized by a talent as great as yours, Harlan!" So stay away from it, you geeks.

16

The Great American Novel

· ·

Have you always wanted to write and sell a novel but weren't sure where to start? The writing part is hard enough but how do you get your masterpiece published and sold?

This chapter will give you a basic blueprint for options you can pursue, like:

- *Agents.* How to find a reputable one and learn who to stay away from

- *Publishers.* The best route for you may not be a big publishing house in New York—a smaller house may be just the right fit for you

- *Marketing.* Here are some steps you can take to set up appearances and what you need to interest local TV and radio stations

Writing Your Novel

"The Great American Novel." It's a catchphrase writers have heard—and been saddled with—for a long time.

Writing a novel is organic; it comes from deep inside. While there are some tried-and-true formulas, the best teacher comes in two forms: writing and reading.

Why? Because to be a good writer you must be a good reader.

If you're interested in a particular area—or genre—of fiction like mysteries, romance, or science fiction, read as many books by different authors in those genres as you can. You'll quickly sort out the good from the not-so-good and learn to develop an eye for what works in a novel.

Reading novels teaches you structure, pacing and tone. It helps you learn how to develop characters and experiment with point of view and tension.

In fact imagery, tension and release are the three big factors in successful novels. Imagery is word painting. Richness of detail is what helps you connect with your audience and find a common ground the two of you can share. Tension keeps you turning the pages. And release ties it all together.

If you're into writing and want to learn the basics, there are several avenues to pursue. You can pick up some terrific how-to books like *On Writing* by Stephen King or *Bird by Bird* by Anne Lamott.

Magazines like *The Writer* and *Writers Digest* are chock full of articles to help hone your style and voice. And there are a slew of online courses to choose from. Try searching the Internet using keywords like "online writing classes" or just "writing classes" and you'll get loads of choices.

Investigate writing clubs in your area or find out how to join a critique group. And many writing ezines publish free newsletters each month with loads of information about writing how-to's and the business of being a successful novelist.

GETTING AN AGENT

Do you need a literary agent to sell your novel? There are as many opinions on this topic as there are bagel varieties in Manhattan. Before the competition to sell a novel became fierce, agents weren't as necessary as they are today. And agent's commission these days runs anywhere from 15 to 20 percent.

If your heart's desire is to be published with one of the "big seven" houses in New York—names like Random House; Little, Brown; or Doubleday—you'll probably need an agent to get your little toe in the front door. Many large houses refuse to look at unsolicited (read that unasked for and, many times, unwanted) manuscripts.

For the big houses, a good agent is like having a backstage pass to the hottest show in town. And it's because of the relationship the agent has developed with the editors.

Now, there are big publishers that will accept unsolicited manuscripts, but the chances of getting a book contract this way are less than winning Powerball.

Small to medium-sized publishing houses are easier to get into for an unknown writer and they're also places where you can develop a personal relationship with the publisher.

It's true that advances are small to not-at-all in these houses, but you'll have a greater chance of being published. And an agent isn't as critical—in fact it's sometimes less desirable—for small and medium-size houses.

If you decide that having an agent is the direction you'd like to go in, there are a few caveats to remember.

Anyone can call themselves a literary agent. There is no professional licensing that separates the good from the bad. There are, however, a few things you can do to protect yourself and your future reputation when selecting an agent:

- *Talk to other writers.* Word-of-mouth is one of the best ways to find an agent. Ask lots of questions about whether the writer is happy with his or her agent, if the agent is courteous and professional, and if the agent does what they say they'll do and on time.

- *Look for the AAR (Association of Authors Representatives) designation.* This isn't an ironclad guarantee that an agent is squeaky clean or will treat you the way you deserve to be treated. It does, however, add a layer of credibility to an agent's reputation because, by being members, agents must conduct themselves in a way that doesn't breach AAR's ethical code of conduct. AAR's website can be found at www.aar-online.org/mc/page.do, and contains a searchable database of agents.

- Never *pay a "reading fee"* to an agent. Reasonable fees for miscellaneous expenses like postage and copies are an expected part of working with an agent but paying someone hundreds—or even thousands—of dollars to read your manuscript is unconscionable. *That's* the kind of agent to avoid.

- *Read other author's acknowledgments.* Frequently, writers will thank their agents in the acknowledgement section of their books. If you're interested in or have written a novel in the same genre, make a note of the agent's name, gather the contact information, and submit a query letter.

You can find listings of agents both online at sites like AAR and Writers Market (www.writersmarket.com) as well as in books updated annually like *Jeff Herman's Guide to Book Publishers, Editors & Literary Agents: Who they are! What they want! How to win them over!* and *Writer's Digest's Guide to Literary Agents.*

The online version of Writers Market has a database of over 6,000 listings, updated daily, and contains a section where you can store information you've submitted to agents and publishers. There is an annual membership fee to join Writers Market online.

There's also a terrific website you can use as an agent and publisher research tool called "Preditors and Editors" at www.invirtuo.cc/prededitors/peala.htm. It has hundreds of listings and also gives warnings about shady agents as well as kudos for agents who are terrific. You can even find bulleted lists of do's and don'ts for spotting scam publishers and literary agents.

Above all, when you find someone who is interested in representing you, don't jump into a contract with them just yet. Interview them. Yes, you heard that right. Interview them.

Remember, your relationship with an agent is a partnership and the right one could last a lifetime. If your questions are answered to your satisfaction and you feel a rapport with this person, ask for the names and phone numbers of three other clients.

If the agent is reluctant to give out this information because of privacy concerns, ask if they would contact the writers and have them call you. You're looking for references here—just like ones you've provided when you've gone on job interviews.

Because that's what this is—you're interviewing for the position of *your* agent.

At a writer's conference a few years ago, best-selling author David Baldacci told the story of how he found his agent. He had just finished writing *Absolute Power* and had sent it, unsolicited and in full to five agents (usually you only send 1-3 chapters for the first go round). All five contacted him. He flew to New York and interviewed them all. He chose Aaron Priest of the Priest Agency because of the rapport he felt with him.

FINDING A PUBLISHER

Let's say you've decided to go the direct route to work on securing a book contract without an agent. Is it an impossible task?

No. Not at all.

We talked a little about the "big seven" houses in the writing section of this chapter. Most writers dream of snagging a large advance and a multi-book publishing contract with a big New York house. Visions of "New York Times best-selling author" dance in lights in your head.

Should you decide to do as David Baldacci did and send out unsolicited manuscripts, take a look at submission guidelines before sending in your work. You can find these guidelines both online and in guides like Writers Market and Jeff Herman's book.

Always send your letter to a specific person—never a generic "Dear Editor." Double check that the person you're writing to is still working for the publisher. A quick phone call will resolve this issue. Also, if the editor has a unisex name like "Pat," find out if it's a man or woman. That way you'll always address your letter properly.

Try to send the exact amount of material suggested by the submission guidelines. Some publishers want only a query letter to start with; some like a letter, synopsis and three chapters; and some want the whole enchilada.

An SASE, or self-addressed stamped envelope, is a must enclosure if you want to hear back from a publisher or agent. You'd be amazed at how many writers new to the art of novel submission forget to include the SASE. Including it will set you apart as a pro who knows the basics.

Frequently, small to medium houses are the best way to go to get published. No, the advances aren't those you'll see on Madison Avenue (sometimes the only advance you get are free copies of your book) but the royalties can be higher than the standard 10 percent and the relationship can be better.

Let's look at John Grisham as a perfect example. His first novel, *A Time to Kill,* which many critics feel is still his best book, was first published by a small press in Mississippi. Tom Clancy's first novel was also published by a small press.

So how do you find the right small to medium house for you? Turn again to writers, the Internet and bookstores.

Writers Market publishes a directory each year, which includes a section on book publishers, big and small. There's even a section on international and Canadian book publishers and each listing gives you contact information, how many books they publish a year, how much the royalty is, and what percentage of writers do not use agents.

Pay specific attention to what kinds of books publishers are looking for. For instance, you won't want to send your romance novel to a house that specializes in science fiction.

There are even guides to publishers in specific genres. A great guide for writers interested in juvenile fiction is *The Writers and Illustrators Guide to Children's Book Publishers and Agents.* This guide includes articles on how to break into the publishing business and examples of good and bad query letters.

Guides like these are stuffed with tons of useful information. You can order them online or go to bookstores like Barnes & Noble or Borders. These guides average about $25-$30 apiece.

There's also *The International Directory of Little Magazines and Small Presses.* It's about two and a half inches thick (literally!) and crammed with hundreds of listings. Unlike the other guides, though, there are no articles or samples. Just listings.

How do you begin to build a relationship with a book publisher? You may want to check with small or medium houses to see if they use freelance editors. That's one good way to establish a relationship that may give you an inside track to getting your work published.

Another way is to attend writers' conferences. Often, conferences will include sessions with agents and publishers. It's also a great way to meet fellow writers and find out more information about good publishers.

Print on demand (POD) publishing is rapidly becoming more widely used by novice and experienced writers alike. It's a version of self-publishing that does not require you to throw down thousands of dollars for a print run. You do pay a setup fee which could range from anywhere from $500–$1,000 depending on the POD publisher.

Books are printed as they are ordered and, so, printing costs are kept to a minimum. Many POD publishers offer book cover design assistance as well as securing your ISBN number and getting you listed in online databases like amazon.com and barnesandnoble.com.

This kind of publishing is a good option for a writer who would like to have a product to offer rather than just a raw manuscript.

Beware the vanity publisher

The vanity press is the kind of publisher you want to stay away from. A vanity press could charge as much as several thousand dollars to print your book. You may be locked into a specific print run (usually 2500 to 5,000 copies) and can't get your money back if those copies don't sell.

PROMOTING YOUR NOVEL

"Marketing" may be one of the most bittersweet words in publishing. Why? Because, quite often, a book isn't published because it's the Great American Novel but because it's something the publisher can market. You could have written prose that would make Hemingway weep. If you can't sell it with a great hook, you're toast.

Gone are the days of publishers—even the big dudes in New York—doing all the marketing and PR for your debut. Have dreams of that cool book tour and appearing on Oprah as the newest hit in her book club? Be prepared to put together your own media kit and start calling around to line up appearances.

For the most part, marketing will fall squarely on your shoulders. But that's a good thing. Because when you do this exercise once, you'll know who to contact, what works, and what doesn't. While there are general rules about marketing, you'll have to go through this phase to find what's comfortable for you.

Marketing and PR may seem like Mount Everest but you *can* schedule your own appearances and even a book tour.

Let's say you're going to be visiting friends or relatives in another state. Find out the names and phone numbers of local libraries, schools and bookstores to see if they'd like to have you do a reading or a book signing.

As far as travel expenses go, you've already planned the trip—throwing in a signing while you're there and having your friends and relatives help you out at the author's table is gravy. And you may be able to write off the trip on your taxes as a business expense—check this out with your accountant.

Don't forget local TV and radio stations. Producers are always on the lookout for local features and your book may just be what they're looking for. This is where a media kit will come in handy.

Use a glossy folder—you can get these in packs of 10 at office supply stores like Staples or Office Depot—and put things inside it like:

- *Pitch letter.* This is different from a query letter because, rather than trying to sell your book, it tells the producer how you see your segment fitting into their radio or TV show format.

- *Synopsis or excerpt of your book.* A synopsis is a one-page overall view of what happens in your book. It's a handy thing to have for every novel you write. You can also enclose the first chapter if it isn't too long.

- *Your bio and photo*

- *A freebie like a bookmark*

- *Business card*

The folder color itself shouldn't be loud or boisterous, unless that's exactly what your book is. Something professional-looking like navy or dark green is a good choice. On a 2" x 4" label, place all of your contact information (including the title of the book) and stick it on the front of the folder. That way, the producer won't have to search through it to find your phone number or email address.

Newspapers always have book reviews, especially on Sundays. Take note of who's in charge of that section and send your book with your media kit, asking if they'd review it. This goes for local and national papers.

Then there are book signings—the author's equivalent to being on

Broadway. It's a thrill to have a line of people stretching out the door, all waiting to meet you and get a signed copy of your book. The typical signing has an author's table, chairs, and stacks of your book. But you don't have to sit behind the table.

You can break out of that mold—and the psychological impediment of having a table between you and your fans—by either standing, sitting on the edge of the author's table, or having chairs where people can sit and chat with you while you're signing their books.

Doing a reading is another great PR tool, especially for kids' fiction. Children—and the adults who bring them—love to be read to, and this kind of word-of-mouth will help book sales.

Don't forget to put up a website. It's the best way to get the word out worldwide. Some web hosting plans cost less per month that a weekly mocha frappucino at Starbucks.

For instance, Yahoo offers a starter hosting program for $11.95 per month. You can build as many pages as you like and you don't have to know HTML code to do it. Post your bio and photo, a synopsis or an excerpt of your book, reviews and testimonials. And why not talk up your novel on YouTube and MySpace?

We've covered a lot of information in this chapter that outlines the basics of writing and selling your novel. It really is all about relationships—with writers, editors, publishers and the most important one of all: the relationship you have with your work.

Allow the passion you've poured into your novel spill over into selling and marketing yourself and your work.

17

WRITING AND SELLING THE
PERSONAL ESSAY

M ost people don't know that Kurt Vonnegut started his career as a technical writer for General Electric. Vonnegut said that technical writers are a rarity writers in that their writing does not allow for self-expression.

Having started my own writing career as a technical writer for Westinghouse, I can attest to this first-hand. Most technical writing is purely factual, and much of it, despite the best efforts of the writers, dry as dust. It is all about the subject matter, and little or none of it about the writer and his feelings. The lack of connection to human emotion is precisely what makes it so dull, even to readers who have the technical background to understand it and need to learn the topic.

Perhaps that's why I, along with so many writers, am drawn to the personal essay. If technical writing is the least personal of all nonfiction writing genres, the personal essay is on the opposite end of the scale.

It's human nature to want to communicate, especially our innermost thoughts, feelings, and opinions. Until recently, one of the only nonfiction forms to provide a forum for this self-expression was the essay. Today, blogs provide an online alternative to the personal essay for self-expression.

But while anyone can start his or her own blog, writing personal essays—and getting them published—is a challenge.

My success in this genre is mixed. For about a year, I wrote essays, about a dozen in all, and sent them to magazines that published such essays. All were rejected except one, which was published was in a small, regional paper aimed at parents, *The Parent Paper.* Yet it was satisfying to see my essay in print.

Despite my failure to sell my essays to other markets, the story has an upside. I mentioned my essays to one of my book editors, and he asked to see a few. The next week, he emailed saying that, if I could provide a few dozen more, he would publish a book of them—an unusual opportunity for an essayist who is not widely published in magazines. They sent me a contract, I wrote the additional essays, and the book, *Count Your Blessings,* was published a few years ago by Thomas Nelson.

ESSAY BASICS

Blogs are a fluid, flexible format. You can pretty much say anything you want on your blog—after all, it's yours; there's no editor to rein you in—at any length, although short blog entries are usually better.

Personal essays, on the other hand, are strictly limited in length: most magazines want your essay to fit on a single page, or at most, a page and a half. Length ranges from 500 to 1,000 words, with 700 to 800 words the target in most cases. With print media, there is very little flexibility in this length requirement.

Some writers find the short word count of essays confining, but really, it's a challenge specific to the essay format. In 700 words, you can never cover a topic comprehensively. So you must take a little slice of it—a pearl of wisdom, an anecdote, a dramatic story, a day in a life—and focus your concentration on this small thing, so that you illuminate it, making it meaningful and entertaining for the reader. And you must do so in just one page in a magazine.

QUALIFICATIONS

In many types of writing, especially nonfiction books, it is increasingly difficult to become published without credentials—both writing credentials (previous publications) as well as expert credentials (e.g., if you want to write a book on how to start and run a successful restaurant, your chances of finding a publisher are better if you are or have been a restaurant owner).

Personal essays, on the other hand, require only that you can write an essay engaging and compelling enough for an editor to want to publish it. Yes, if you have some credentials in the subject (e.g., you want to write an essay on saving the planet from global warming, and you are a climatologist) that may help you gain an editor's attention. So can previous writing experience, either published essays on any topic, or other published nonfiction works on the specific topic of the essay. But editors primarily make decisions on whether to publish your essay based primarily on the essay itself, not your name, reputation, or credentials. Exceptions? Of course, especially if you are a celebrity.

Is there a way to learn to write essays? As with virtually every other type of writing I can think of, there are only three ways to master essay writing: write essays, read essays, and study essay writing. For the latter, you can read articles and books on "how to write personal essays," or take a writing class and concentrate on essays rather than poems, stories, or novels.

Years ago, I signed up for a writing class with Barry Sheinkopf at the Writing Center in Englewood, NJ. My plan was to work on short stories, but the ideas that came to mind were for essays, not fiction. I wrote more than half a dozen essays during the 12-week class, which were much improved with Barry's editing; these eventually became the basis for my essay collection *Count Your Blessings* (Thomas Nelson).

COMING UP WITH ESSAY IDEAS

Theoretically, everything is grist for the writer's mill, and so ideas for personal essays can come from anywhere. The two basic sources for essay ideas are (a) things that happen to you and (b) other things.

"Things that happen to you" is obvious. As Ray Bradbury points out in his book *Zen in the Art of Writing* (Capra Press, 1990, p. 33), "it is in the totality of experience reckoned with, filed, and forgotten, that each man is truly different from all others in the world ... when a man talks from his heart, in his moment of truth, he speaks poetry."

All of us have dramatic events in our lives—loves, illness, deaths, loss, tragedy, failure, success—and one can easily argue that every human life is a never-ending drama, played out in a million little incidents that comprise the totality of that life experience. And, each of these dramas is unique: no human lives a life identical to any other human on the planet. It is this uniqueness and drama that form the core of a strong personal essay. "The most effective essay takes a small moment and lets it be a microcosm of a larger truth, a truth that resonates with all, even though this moment is personal just to you," writes Beth Levine in *The Writer* (2/02. p. 24).

But personal essays are not always based on personal experience; they can be based on something that doesn't happen to you but rather, something you observe that sparks a thought, idea, feeling, or mood. The reason it is personal is that *you* are writing about it subjectively, filtering the event, experience, or fact through your own life experiences and perceptions, which *are* unique. The result is that, while the subject you are writing about is not personal or unique to you, your thoughts, views, observations, and opinions on that subject are.

When I was actively writing essays, many more ideas for essays popped into my head than I had time or desire to write. Whenever a new essay idea pops into your head, write it down and place it into a file labeled "essay ideas." I carry with me at all times a pen and pad of paper in my front shirt pocket to make sure I never lose any ideas, whether for essays or anything else.

If the idea of writing essays catches fire with you, it will engage your mind in such a way that you never have to sit down and deliberately wrack your brain to come up with essay ideas. Instead, if you can shift into a mindset of "I am an essay writer," your brain will naturally home in on things that happen to you and things you read, sifting through this material until something resonates as a possible essay topic.

You'll know if you've found a subject that's viable for an essay, because you won't be able to get it out of your mind; and if it's really strong, you'll feel compelled to start writing it.

An example of an idea stimulated by observation rather than direct experience is my essay "In Praise of Orange Foods." I had often joked to people about the "orange food group" being Cheez Doodles, American cheese, orange soda, Tang, and Kraft Macaroni and Cheese—and usually, it got a nice laugh. One day I was simply struck by the futility of attempting to get people to eat nutritionally balanced meals according to the classic food groups of meat, dairy, vegetables, and grains, and started writing about it, using Cheez Doodles, which are a guilty pleasure of mine, and the "orange food group" as a starting point.

Another essay idea, "The Prisoner of Zelda," grew out of my dislike of the loud video games my kids were increasingly playing. Published in the *Parent Paper,* it began:

> "I'm a prison of Zelda," I said aloud the other day, mostly to myself, while sitting in our family room. It's a statement a successful dominatrix might hear with bliss, but my mistress is far crueler: Zelda's a video game my kids are addicted to.
>
> How does this affect me? You can ask only if you are not the parent of a video-game-addicted child. Parents like me, who have made the mistake of allowing a video game system into their home, know all too well the terrors this addictive activity can release.

Another essay, "Life After Monty," was inspired by a gift I received: the first luxury item of any kind I ever owned, a Mont Blanc pen. About halfway through the essay, I tell the reader how the pen, an expensive material possession, began to possess me as I worried endlessly about losing it.

> I began to obsess about Monty, patting my shirt pocket about three times an hour to make sure he was still there. I even started referring to him by name, which amused my wife and children to no end.
>
> If I put him down and forgot to pick him up again, I would panic when I found he was missing—and rest only when he was safely back in my pocket again. On a flight, I almost tore up a row of coach seats when Monty rolled under the cushions after I inadvertently left him on the empty seat next to mine.

WRITING THE ESSAY

"When you write a personal essay, you write on a topic of your choice, because you want to find the truth in your experience," writes Sheila Bender in her book *Writing and Publishing Personal Essays* (Silver Threads, 2005, p. 23). "If you find it, your essay will be interesting to someone else."

As with most short nonfiction, an essay has three parts: the beginning, the middle, and the end. Woven throughout that, the essay also has a theme: an opinion, conclusion, observation, idea, or point of view it seeks to communicate—and at least get the reader to understand or even empathize with, if not believe outright.

The beginning is the attention grabber. Consisting of the first few paragraphs, the lead quickly determines whether a reader will read your essay and turn the page. It also determines whether the editor will read and ultimately buy your essay. If the lead is not compelling and well written, rejection is virtually assured.

One way to write an effective essay lead is to describe, in an entertaining, nostalgic, or poignant fashion, a universal experience the reader can relate to. In my essay about my awful experiences with a mail-order nose hair clipper I purchased, this experience was unsightly growth of hair in places it shouldn't be as one gets older:

> The other day we were driving with the kids in our mini-van when my wife shrieked in horrified disgust, "You've got a giant hair coming out of your nostril!"
>
> I can't help it. As a man ages, hair becomes a problem. I'm simply at the stage where the hair in my nose and ears is growing much faster than the rest.

The beginning also either states explicitly or hints at the theme of the essay. In my "Prisoner of Zelda" essay, my theme was fairly explicit: if you give in and let your kids play video games at home, it will inevitably be a major headache and expense for the parents. In "Life After Monty," I addressed a familiar theme—the foolishness of becoming obsessed with acquiring material possessions, especially luxuries—demonstrated by my sad experience owning a Mont Blanc pen.

The middle expands on the ideas and premises laid out in the beginning, while also building toward the conclusions and premises that will be stated in the closing. For "The Nose Hair Chronicles," I used a lot of straightforward facts to engage the reader in the link between hair growth in inappropriate places and aging:

> You and I each start out with between 100,000 and 200,000 hair follicles on our scalps. Of course, you have more hairs on other parts of your body—about 3 to 5 million total. Hair grows on almost every part of the body except your palms, soles, and for men, the tip of the penis.

The end can summarize the discussion, draw a conclusion based on the evidence presented, reinforce and restate a theme already stated in the lead, or simply end on a wry, emotional, instructive, humorous, or even absurd note.

Here is the final paragraph from "The Nose Hair Chronicles":

> Since I can't control this unsightly growth, and conventional hair grooming seems not to offer a solution (should I perhaps braid my nose hair, or tie a bow around it!), I wonder if they can be harvested for more productive use. Possibilities include high-strength tensile wire, or transplant material for scalps with receding hairlines. "Hi," you may hear me say some day on a late-night TV commercial. "I'm not only the president of the Nose Hair Club for Men … I'm also a client."

Here's some of the narrative from the last few paragraphs of "Life After Monty," my rant against modern-day materialism:

> I learned that materialism never was and never will be for me. The less junk I have, the better. Purging myself of possessions is like purging my soul....

ESSAY MARKETS

Writer's Market, published by Writer's Digest Books, is the reference guide to magazine and newspaper markets for freelance writers, and by spending some time with the book, you can find magazines and papers that buy essays.

I suggest you also visit a local bookstore with a large magazine section, and spend time going through the magazines. Find magazines that cover the topic you want to write about, or reach the audience you want to write for. Flip through issues on the racks to see whether they publish essays. Many magazines publish one essay per issue, usually appearing on the last page of the magazine, opposite the inside back cover.

When you find magazines that publish essays similar to those you want to write, buy the issues, take them home, and read them carefully. Go on the magazine's website to see if back issues are posted, and if so, read the essays published within the last 12 months or so. Pay particular attention to style, tone, and length, but also to topic: if the magazine published an essay on how the writer overcame fear of the dentist three issues ago, they are not likely to want another on that same topic. On the other hand, they might be open to how you overcame another common fear or phobia, such as air travel or spiders—especially if you did it by getting a pilot's license or becoming a poisonous spider handler at the local zoo.

When you find a few magazines that you consider ideal outlets for your essays, subscribe to each for a year. This way, you will see all new essays as they appear, and will not embarrass yourself by suggesting a topic that was done last month (editors are sustained by the delusion that all writers who want to write for them read their magazines regularly, and though they know deep down this is not the case, they believe, perhaps rightfully so, that it should be).

Some magazines that run (or have run) regular essay pages: *Weight Watchers Magazine* ("Savvy" column), *New York Times Magazine*, *Los Angeles Times Magazine*, *Newsweek* ("My Turn" column), *Time* ("Essay), *The Atlantic Monthly*, *American West Airlines Magazine*, *American Way Magazine*, *CIO Magazine*, *Family Circle*, *The Front Porch*, *Smithsonian*, and *Hemispheres*. All have sent me nice rejection letters for my essays. Other essay markets include women's, inflight, religious, and parenting magazines.

MARKETING YOUR ESSAYS

Unlike the process of selling magazine articles, essays are not sold using query letters. Because of the short length, personal nature, and the importance of style, editors do not want to see query letters for essays; they want to read and review the entire essay.

To sell your essay, first write the best essay you can. Then target publications that are a logical fit with the subject matter. A business magazine isn't the logical outlet for an essay on the joys of parenting, unless it's a women's business magazine and the essay focuses on balancing motherhood and career.

Send your essay mailed flat in a 9-by-12-inch envelope to the appropriate editor at the magazine, either the managing editor or (if there is one) the editor in charge of the essay page. I mail it with a cardboard backing so it doesn't get folded or mutilated. Include a #10 self-addressed stamped envelope (SASE) for return of the essay and any letter of acceptance or rejection.

You can, in a brief cover letter, let the editor know the enclosed manuscript is an essay you hope she will consider for publication; if the magazine publishes more than one regular monthly essay, tell the editor which section your essay is intended for (e.g., coping with tragedy vs. humor in the workplace). If you have credentials that convince the editor you have something worthwhile to say on the subject or your essay—you are a published writer or have had an experience or accomplishment relevant to the essay topic—include these facts in your cover letter. The last paragraph should thank the editor for taking a look at your essay and let her know an SASE is enclosed.

Editor response to essay submissions is sporadic and spotty. Some editors send timely responses—a letter and your essay returned in the SASE you provided. Others may take months to respond, while some never get back to you. You can make a polite follow-up inquiry via mail, but do not pester the editor: unless you are a best-selling author or famous person, the editor feels little urgency to publish your essay or even respond to its submission, and that's a fact of life the essayist must live with.

Keep good records on the magazines where you submit essays, the editors whom you send them to, the date of submission, which essay went to which magazine, and the status (submitted, awaiting response, accepted, rejected). After every rejection, read the essay again, rewrite to make any possible improvements, and then print a fresh copy and send it out to a new publication. Avoid sending the rejected essay to any editors who are currently looking at your other essays and have not yet responded to those submissions yet. You want to create the appearance that you think the essays you send them are perfect for their publication; and you do not want to create the image that you are writing and mailing essays willy nilly, as fast as you can lick the envelopes, without considering whether it's really right for that particular magazine.

Is writing and trying to get essays published worth the trouble? Financially, almost never. For every essay you sell—payment ranges from free copies of the magazine to, at the high end, $1,000—you most likely will have to write and market ten essays that never sell.

The rewards are artistic, literary, and psychological. Writing essays is an intensely personal means of communication and self expression. For many writers, it is cathartic; for others, just plain fun! From first-hand experience, I can tell you that there are few events in the writer's life as satisfying as seeing your essay in print in a magazine, newspaper, or book. Even if your essays are never published, the personal satisfaction you get from writing them will be worth the time spent.

18

Growing Your Business

T here are only two methods of making six figures as a freelance writer, and only one that can do so reliably and consistently (the other is a crapshoot).

In this chapter, I'm going to describe these two methods and show you why you should concentrate mainly on just one of them.

The two methods of making $100,000 a year writing are:

- The Lottery Method

- The Business Method

The Lottery Method

The lottery method entails writing for many years, usually on speculation, in the hopes of hitting it big. These writers typically concentrate on film scripts, popular novels, and occasionally nonfiction books and TV scripts. The lottery method, if you in fact hit the lottery, offers the highest financial rewards a writer can earn.

By now almost everyone knows the story of how Stephen King wrote his stories and novels while living in poverty in a trailer on a hill in Maine, with a typewriter propped up on his knees as he sat in the space next to the boiler. *Parade* magazine reports that King earned $52.4 million last year.

Similarly, J.K. Rowling, an unpublished writer, scribbled tales of a school for young wizards on napkins while sipping tea in cafes. Her first four Harry Potter books sold 200 million copies in 55 languages. A British citizen, Rowling, with a net worth approaching half a billion dollars, is wealthier than the Queen of England.

King and Rowling have, in a sense, hit the lottery. For every Robert B. Parker getting rich from best-selling suspense novels, however, there are thousands of frustrated wannabe Spencer writers not earning a dime.

That's why going the route of "best seller or bust" is a crapshoot. Yes, you can get rich, but the odds are against hitting it big. The alternative, achieved by most writers, is hitting it a little or not at all.

THE BUSINESS METHOD

The business method entails treating your freelance writing as a home-based business, working at it steadily, providing writing services for clients who need them, and building up a steady base of clients who give you repeat business and lucrative assignments.

For example, a couple of writers I know specialize in writing annual reports. Their average paycheck: $10,000 per assignment. Do one annual report a month at this rate, and you will gross $120,000 a year.

Now writers following the business method can make good money, and they can do so with regularity, year after year. It's not hit or miss as is the case with writing best sellers or blockbuster movies for Hollywood.

CONVENTIONAL WRITING USUALLY DOES NOT PAY

The one way you're unlikely to make a lot of money writing is by doing books and articles, which unfortunately is what 99 percent of the writers who read writers' magazines, attend conferences, and join writers' groups want to do.

Therefore, you must pursue another type of writing, or at least supplement your fiction, scriptwriting, or article writing habit with it.

As discussed in chapter 5, to make $100,000 a year as a freelance writer, you have to bill $400 a day. The surest way to earn this amount of money is to pursue some type of commercial writing. Advertising copy-writing, technical writing, website writing, fund-raising, direct marketing, and public relations all fall into this category. It can be anything from writing catalog copy for a mail order company, to writing web pages for an e-commerce business, to writing speeches for CEOs, to writing travel brochures for resorts and cruise lines. The nice thing about it is that you can choose to write about subjects that interest you, for organizations that pay you extremely well.

Another key advantage of using the business method to grow your writing business is that clients come to you with assignments they want written, rather than you having to pitch ideas to them. This eliminates the enormous amount of time the conventional freelance writer wastes in formulating ideas with no compensation, making the freelance commercial or business writer twice as productive and three times more profitable.

Six Steps to Getting Clients

My colleague Will Newman recommends the following steps to finding writing clients; these are reprinted courtesy of the American Writers & Artists Institute.

1. *Brainstorm your passions.* What topics stir your passions? Politics, animal care, coin collecting? What are your areas of expertise? Music, the stock market, parenting? What do you love to do in your free time? What would you do if you had time? Which sections do you gravitate to in bookstores?

   Write down 10 subjects that you feel passionate about. Put the list aside for a day, then add 5 more. Don't censor yourself by saying, "There's no copywriting work in this area." Just write.

2. *Turn your list of passions into a list of local and regional businesses, agencies, and products.* Start with the Yellow Pages of metropolitan areas near you. Find businesses or organizations that reflect your passions. Use your imagination.

   For example, if you subscribe to *Prevention* magazine, talk with friends about your supplementation regimen, and eagerly seek out the health section of the newspaper; one obvious choice for you is alternative health.

Here's a brief list of possible business listings in the Yellow Pages that reflect your interest: health food markets, chiropractors, spas, massage therapists, alternative health newspapers and magazines, physicians, dentists, and other health practitioners.

3. *Talk to friends.* Tell friends what you're doing and ask for ideas. Don't try to limit their suggestions. Listen. And make notes.

4. *Arrange a personal meeting with potential prospects to discuss your writing services.* Prepare a 5-minute chat about how you could benefit each prospect's business. Then call or visit each establishment and ask for a 5-minute appointment with the owner or director.

    Be prepared to give your spiel right then and there. Briefly explain how you can benefit him or her. Consider making a one-time free offer. You're trying to develop your portfolio, so a few freebies won't hurt. They'll help build your portfolio fast.

5. *Do your best work,* regardless of what you're paid. Do not give substandard service or short shrift to freebie clients. If you do, why do you think they will become good referral sources and references for you?

6. *Get exposure.* While you're contacting potential clients, get some exposure to local businesspeople. Contact service clubs like the Rotary or Kiwanis and chambers of commerce. Offer to do a program for one of their meetings.

    Your program should be something of general business interest, and should last between 5 and 15 minutes. It should not be about your copywriting business per se, but about how your topic will benefit them (e.g., "10 Ways to Build Lasting Relationships with Your Customers").

    Have something of perceived value to pass out at the end of the meeting—something like a one-page summary of the 10 customer service tips, for instance. Attach your business card.

How to Handle Dissatisfied Clients

Recently the head of a large public relations agency said to me, "Boy, I don't envy you being a freelance copywriter. That's got to be a tough job, writing copy and then having clients make all those changes and revisions."

To a degree, he's right. H.G. Wells once observed there is no greater human urge than the desire to rewrite someone else's copy. And certainly, if you've been a writer for any length of time, you know that for many writing projects the most tedious part is routing the drafts, making changes, generating revisions, and getting approvals.

Why is there so much revising and rewriting of copy by clients and editors? Aside from the possibility that the copy being submitted is simply bad copy, I think there are two major reasons.

The first is that writing is one of the few activities in the business world where there is no RFP (request for proposal)—no predefined and agreed-upon specification to which the work must conform.

If I order a computer system, part of the vendor's selling process is to precisely define my needs and requirements. In their proposal to me, the vendor will spell out exactly what is to be delivered—down to the dimensions of the computer screen, the size of the hard drive, even the brand and type of modem. As a result, it's rather simple to determine whether the vendor has fulfilled my requirements.

But in the writing business, it's different. It would be absurd for the client to request, in advance, an article with so many subheads, so many commas, so many sentences beginning with the words *and* or *the*, so many paragraphs of such and such length.

And here's the root of the problem: If we cannot define a specification or requirement for the work before it is ordered, how can the professional writer be absolutely sure he or she is precisely meeting the client's preferences and expectations? We can't, of course—hence, the tendency to edit and rewrite any piece of submitted copy.

The second reason why copy is rewritten is best summed up by an ad agency executive from the television show *thirtysomething*, who, when asked to defend a campaign, replied, "Nobody knows anything." To some degree, he is right. There is no formula that guarantees a successful ad or best-selling novel. All creative efforts are educated guesses; all published materials are tests that determine the validity of our approach to the market.

A roofer can guarantee that the roof he installs for you won't leak. In fact, roofers have to make such guarantees, or they will not get hired. But an unknown novelist cannot guarantee that her first book will be a best seller, any more than a copywriter can guarantee that the direct mail package he writes for a client will sell a certain number of insurance policies or book club memberships.

Because writing is an art or a craft, and not an exact science, the professional writer's opinion is always subject to question and debate, in part because she cannot with certainty say she is right.

Few people constantly and boldly challenge the opinions of their neurosurgeons, accountants, attorneys, mechanics, or electricians, because these professions are viewed as scientific, and the practitioners are seen as technical experts with arcane knowledge beyond the understanding of ordinary mortals.

But in fields where decisions are more subjective—copywriting, graphic design, interior decorating, landscape architecture—clients frequently question the practitioner, because the client believes his opinion to be equally valid. As writer Hugo Williams observes, "The tricky thing about the writing industry is the more or less accepted notion that everyone's opinion, even on matters of grammar, carries equal weight."

Even if the client gives the professional carte blanche at the beginning of the project, the instant he sees something that is not exactly the way he would have done it, a revision or change is demanded.

Can anything be done to correct this situation and enable professional writers to make their clients happier faster?

- Writers and their clients may want to establish a set of specifications or guidelines for certain projects. Should product sheets be promotional or technical? Benefit or feature oriented? Deciding in advance can prevent disagreements later on.

- Think about presenting your ideas in memo or outline form before you go to first draft. Get your client to comment on and approve the proposed direction before proceeding.

- Writers should pay closer attention to the tone, style, and length of the client's existing published materials. If your style and theirs mesh, fine. If not, ask if they're looking to create more of the same, or if they want new materials done with your special flair and touch.

For instance, if I observe that all the sample pieces a new copywriting client has sent me are done in a certain style, I may ask, "Are you open to a different approach, or do you basically want another ad along these lines?" And what if they are inflexible? If I don't like their approach or cannot duplicate it, I walk away from the job.

Hiring an Assistant: Can It Work for You?

You probably think that hiring an assistant means hiring someone full time. We traditionally view a secretary or assistant as working a 40-hour week. But it doesn't have to be that way. More and more people today are looking for temp jobs, part-time work, and flex time.

An article in the New Jersey newspaper *The Record* reports that the use of part-time workers is growing. The Bureau of Labor Statistics says almost one in five American workers—approximately 22 million—are part-timers. The world's largest employer is no longer AT&T or General Motors; it's Manpower, a temp agency.

For the freelance writer, hiring a traditional 9-to-5 secretary as a full-time employee, with salary and benefits, is just one of several options, and it is the one most writers who hire help choose not to take.

The secretary, administrative person, or clerical person you hire to help around the office need not be on staff or work full time. Plenty of people want part-time jobs and will work at affordable rates in exchange for flexible hours.

Many word processing and typing services advertising in your local paper are really small one- or two-person businesses, and will be happy to sell you 10, 15, 20, or however many hours of their service you need per week.

There are freelancers and independent contractors who can handle anything you need done: editing, writing, proofreading, research, book-keeping, webmasters, even marketing and sales (e.g., literary agents). For editorial and administrative services, you can usually find bright, educated adults to do anything you need done for $10 to $25 an hour. Literary agents work on commission: you pay nothing up front, and they get 15 percent of your advance and royalties when they make a sale for you.

So why would a writer want to hire help? Well, why not? As writers, the only thing we have to sell is our time. We're like dentists who have to "drill and fill" before they can bill. Writers earn money only when we write. We don't get paid to make photocopies, go to the post office, file papers, send faxes, prepare taxes, lick envelopes, or take our laser printers to be repaired. Every minute we spend doing these administrative—and nonbillable—tasks represents a minute taken away from our paid writing.

Hiring other people to do these mundane tasks frees you to spend more of your time writing. Dr. Rob Gilbert, editor of *Bits & Pieces*, comments, "For maximum effectiveness, do only what you do best and let others do the rest."

When is it time to consider hiring a helper? When you're working as many hours a week as you want to be, yet are not getting everything done you want to get done.

There's no need to make a major commitment to see if having a part-time assistant suits your business and personality. Start small. Have someone come in two or three days a week, three or four hours a day. As you get even busier and more profitable, you can increase your helper's hours, and offload more of your drudge work to him or her.

What about money? Some writers tell me they can't afford help, and they may be right. A poet may want a secretary, but in today's business world, most secretaries earn more per hour than most poets.

To affordably retain an assistant, your hourly income should be at least two or three times what the assistant charges. If you pay $10 an hour, you should be making at least $20 an hour.

WHERE TO FIND AFFORDABLE HELP

When my longtime staff secretary quit because of a personal situation, I wondered where I would find another assistant. A colleague suggested that instead of hiring a full-time secretary, I find a typing/word processing/secretarial service to handle my needs.

I looked in the local paper and Yellow Pages and called several services. I explained to each service—most of whom were individuals working from their homes—that I was a writer looking for regular secretarial support.

Every word processing and secretarial service I talked to became excited by the prospect of having me as a client. Apparently, the word processing and typing business is sporadic and project oriented; having a regular client on retainer was unusual and a welcome change.

I interviewed several services and chose one person. I offered to buy 30 hours of her time a week, by the week, and pay for a month's worth of service in advance at the beginning of each month. In return, I wanted the best rate she could offer me and a high level of service.

This person, who is now my assistant, works from her home in a town eight miles away. It's close enough that she can come over to do some work here if required, but mostly we work by fax and email. In fact, her small word processing business has a part-time messenger to serve me and her other clients, and I see her only a few times a year.

This virtual assistant (VA) approach has some advantages. I like being able to work in privacy without having an assistant physically present (privacy and solitude are, to me, productivity boosters). And I have no overhead for my VA—she provides her own office space. I even benefit from her computer system, which is more fully loaded than mine, but is used to process a lot of my work.

The value of an assistant increases as they learn your procedures and business over time; this advantage does not exist when you hire college students and other transients who don't stick around.

One caveat: Since most of your fellow writers in your area don't use subcontractors, you may not be able to find someone through referral. Call people who advertise in the local town paper and Yellow Pages. Meet with them face-to-face for an interview before hiring them. Start on a trial basis, and don't promise anything more regular until both of you are satisfied the relationship is working well.

According to Dun & Bradstreet Information Services, 4 out of 10 small businesses outsource at least one function. Perhaps your small free-lance writing and editorial business can profit from a similar strategy.

How to Get Out of a Business Slump

Getting out of a slump is not difficult, though it often requires persistence. The problem is that most people either don't realize what they have to do to reverse a slump, or they are not willing to do it.

I have developed a three-part strategy for overcoming a slump that works for both business and personal setbacks. The problem is that the formula is so simple—it contains a total of seven words—that you may be tempted to dismiss it, even though it has worked for me and hundreds of other individuals.

Here is the formula for getting out of a slump:

1. Do something.

2. Do more.

3. Keep doing it.

Let's examine the three parts in more detail:

1. *Do something.* Do I mean do anything, no matter how random? Well, no. But almost. Here's what I mean…

    Most people in a slump spend most of their time worrying, ruminating, and planning. They suffer from analysis paralysis. They become so obsessed with making their next step perfect, they never take it.

    You can reverse a slump only through action, so you've got to act—now! Not sure if Idea A makes sense? Do it anyway. Not sure whether to take Path X or Path Y? Pick one and go forward. The very fact that you are taking action—instead of getting stuck in inaction—will automatically start you on the road to recovery.

2. *Do more.* There are two common reasons why people fail. One is that they don't do the work required to get the results they want. Putting into action just one or two ideas may help, but it's probably not enough to totally solve your problem. Getting out of a slump requires that you take what motivational speaker Anthony Robbins calls "massive action." How do you implement this strategy? Decide how much activity you think you really need to get fully out of your slump. Then do at least twice that amount.

3. *Keep doing it.* The second reason people fail is that they give up too early.

    Not everything you try will work. If you try one thing, then a second, then a third, and they all fail, do you give up? No. You try something else. Eventually one thing works okay. Another works better. And before you know it, you're well on the road to turning your situation around. But don't just forge ahead blindly. Evaluate the results of each effort. A corollary to Step 3 is: Do more of what's working, less of what's not working.

There you have it: three steps—seven words. Simple? Yes. Do they work? Try it and see for yourself!

More Advice on Getting Out of Your Writing Slump

Writer Susan Miles offers the following tips for getting out of a writing slump:

- *Increase your market research time.* Use your writing time to really research markets. Don't just skim your guideline database and directories—a practice we can easily fall into, particularly when we are on a writing roll. But hit your libraries and bookstores, and study the content/layout of the publications you wish to write for. Hint: Keep a list handy of those articles you've already written and sold during this exercise.

- *Prepare for the slow periods during your highs.* When motivation is high and the creative juices are flowing, make the time to stockpile a number of outlines, preferably in bullet point, of short, straightforward articles. By having these outlines on reserve for the times when you are feeling unmotivated, you have an easy starting point that will keep you writing and restore your confidence.

- *Give yourself a writing break.* Go walking, go for a swim, or hit the gym. Anything healthy will be time well invested in your writing. A fit and healthy writer will definitely be a more productive and creative one.

- *Pull out back copies of writing magazines.* This is a good time to catch up on advice articles, market updates, and structure tutorials that you missed or skimmed on your first read. Study them as you would a textbook at school, taking notes and highlighting points relevant to your own writing.

- *Change your writing habits.* If you write in the evenings, try writing first thing in the morning. If you always work on a laptop or a PC, switch to paper or a notebook. Change your pen or your paper, or work outside—anything that adds newness to your writing environment.

- *Forget the epics and work on list articles.* Forget the marathons and focus on some writing sprints. Write quick, short, sharp advice pieces with headings that start "The 10 Best ..." Later, when you are back in the groove, these can always be developed into longer features or essays.

- *Repackage and resell.* Take your previous articles that have been successful and edit and repackage them to sell to those markets you unearthed in your market research exercise.

- *Remove distractions.* During a writing high, distractions seem to filter themselves out, but during a lull they come through loud and clear. Be disciplined and shut off the Internet, the television, the radio, and the CD player, and give yourself room in your head for ideas and sentences to evolve.

- *Revisit your ideas notebook.* This process can unearth gems that you haven't yet polished—ideas and themes that may not have made your earlier pieces, but can help spark a new article or story.

- *Don't aim for perfection.* It may only be half an idea, two suggestions for your "The 10 Best ..." list—it doesn't matter, just get it down on paper. It's amazing how the rest follows just by your getting the first couple of ideas on paper.

MAKING YOUR WRITING
DREAMS COME TRUE

This chapter provides further advice on making two of your writing dreams come true: getting published and making money.

GETTING PUBLISHED: THE SELF-PUBLISHING OPTION

What if, despite following the advice I've laid out, you cannot attract a literary agent and sell your book to a publishing house? The obvious alternative is to publish it yourself.

Many writers I've met swear by self-publishing. The problem is, an equal amount swear at it.

In self-publishing, you are the publisher as well as the author. You pay to have the book typeset, designed, and printed. You are responsible for storing the inventory, shipping, distribution, sales, marketing, and promotion.

As publisher/author, you get to keep all of the revenues generated from sales (less expenses) versus the 6 to 15 percent of sales a mainstream publisher would pay you.

If your goal is to hold in your hands a nicely designed, printed book with your name on the cover, self-publishing is relatively easy. Anyone can have a manuscript typeset, take it to a book printer, and pay them to print the books.

If you want to sell a lot of copies of your book, self-publishing requires a long-term commitment on your part. You are your own warehouse, shipping department, accounting department, sales force, publicity department, marketing director, distributor, collections agency, and secretary.

To write a book and have it published by a traditional publisher means you can concentrate on writing, which for many of us is the part we like best. Self-publishing your book requires that you fulfill all the functions of author as well as publisher. In essence, it means you have to form and run a mini-publishing company.

How do you make the choice between self-publishing and regular publishing? Unless you are dead set in favor of one particular option—traditional publishing or self-publishing—here are some guidelines to follow.

Go to a mainstream publishing house when:

- You feel your idea would have wide appeal to a mass audience.

- Yours is the type of book that would sell well in bookstores.

- You want the prestige and status that come with selling a book to a "real" publisher.

- You do not have the time or inclination to be in business as a small publishing house and would prefer instead to concentrate on writing.

- You want to establish your reputation as a professional writer.

- You do not have the skills and expertise to self-publish (e.g., book design, marketing, distribution, desktop publishing) and do not have the desire to acquire them.

Self-publish when:

- Your idea appeals to a specialized, narrow target market; e.g., parachutists, chiropractors, car wash owners.

- Yours is the type of book that would sell well through direct response advertising (magazine ads, direct mail, catalogs, the Internet).

- The idea of self-publishing appeals to you.

- You have the time, talent, and inclination to handle all aspects of the publishing business—distribution, promotion, administration—in addition to researching and writing the book.

- Your book is not a one-shot idea, but rather you plan a whole line of books and related information products (seminars, audiocassettes, videos, special reports, etc.) to educate your chosen target market on various aspects of your topic.

- The "snob appeal" and status of being published in the conventional method is not important to you, and you won't be bothered by comments from those people who look down on self-publishing.

- You have been turned down by the major publishing houses, yet believe in the book so strongly that you are willing to act as publisher to see the book get into print.

- You are impatient and want to get the book out right away, rather than wait the 9 to 18 months it normally takes to write a book and get it published through a conventional publisher.

Many proponents of self-publishing (and some are valued colleagues and personal friends of mine) are highly critical of mainstream publishing. They like to promote self-publishing by being negative about big publishing houses.

You've heard it before, of course: Big publishing houses are book factories; they are more concerned with making products than marketing; they destroy your work in the editing process; they don't do a proper job of promoting or publicizing your book; most books don't sell and most authors don't make money.

But what they don't tell you is the flip side, which gives you a more balanced picture: Namely, that many authors who publish through traditional publishing houses are happy and satisfied with their publishers—at least some of the time. Their books bring them fame, prestige, and visibility, as well as enhance their careers. Many have become rich (even millionaires) from royalty payments when their books hit the best-seller lists.

Mainstream publisher or self-publishing? It's your choice. Let me know what you decide.

SEVEN STEPS TO BECOMING RICH AND SUCCESSFUL AS A FREELANCE WRITER

These tips come from my friend Burt Dubin, a coach for professional and aspiring speakers. While he wrote these tips for speakers, I feel they apply equally well to freelance writers:

1. *Have a mission.* You must have a strategic, intensive focus. Root this in your mission. Your mission energizes and enlivens all you do. It stimulates your purpose and your passion. It engages your courage and your commitment. Your mission is your primordial prerequisite, your personal key to the pantheon of champions. You discover the principals of identifying your true mission, a mission that comes from your heart, from your gut, a mission right for you and only you.

2. *Be a businessperson first.* Remember this principle: You are first a businessperson. Then you are an expert at something. Then you are a writer. Have regular business hours. When you are not on the road, be in your home office ready to receive calls (unless you are engaged in a writing project and do not want to accept calls).

3. *Position yourself strategically.* Identify your niche. Then position your uniqueness within your niche. Make yourself one of a kind. Be so unique that there is no available substitute for you. Consider these potential aspects of your uniqueness: Your educational credentials, your experience, your research, and your published articles and books, plus the brilliance and originality of your content.

    Did you say, "But I don't have any of that"? Well, start to create these elements. We all have to start somewhere. You can begin with nothing other than your pervasive desire to make a difference, your enthusiasm, and your passion. All the rest will be developed naturally, building block by building block.

4. *Control your expenses.* Keep a tight lid on office expenses. Create a home office. Hire family members to help you. Minimize all recurring bills such as rent and salaries.

    Some of the finest authors and speakers in the world, million-dollar earners, do this with just a half-time person and several computers to handle the details.

5. *Be a bulldog.* That is right. Be a bulldog when you're going after what you want. Persistence—resolute, absolute, incorrigible bit-in-the-teeth persistence—is the golden thread that runs through the life of every person of accomplishment. It is the prerequisite, the essential foundation of achievement.

    Calvin Coolidge said these words: "Press on! Nothing in the world can take the place of persistence. Talent will not. Nothing is more common than unsuccessful people with talent. Genius will not. Unrewarded genius is almost a proverb. Education will not. The world is full of educated derelicts. Persistence and determination alone are omnipotent."

    George Bernard Shaw wrote these words: "People are always blaming their circumstances for what they are. I do not believe in circumstances. The people who get on in this world are the people who get up and look for the circumstances they want, and if they cannot find them, make them!"

    Benjamin Disraeli said: "A human being with a settled purpose must accomplish it. Nothing can resist a will that stakes even existence for its fulfillment."

6. *Tune in to the trends.* Trends are the tides of the times. Engage them to advance your career. The one sure constant is change. The trends that are current today may be, almost definitely will be, different in a year or two.

    Your readers and clients are more sophisticated today. They want substance and value. They want to see their desired objectives attained as a result of your work. These objectives might include, as of now, improved market share, improved market penetration, increased net profit, increased sales, improved communications, improved behavior, and enhanced performance—as an outcome of your program.

    Decision makers want unique experts. Make yourself the authority on a vital topic or issue as quickly as you can. You are safer specializing in a topic than specializing in an industry.

They want long-term relationships. Make yourself worthy of commitment and repeat assignments as fast as you can.

Are you entertaining? Here is good news for you. Despite other trends, entertaining communicators will always be required.

Are you a nuts-and-bolts writer? You will always be needed. When you can promise and deliver measurable improvements in some aspect of productivity, you will always be in demand.

7. *Avoid the pitfalls.* These pitfalls include too many outside activities—such as memberships in community organizations, church, and clubs; a social life; and non-leveragable writing activities like writing your coin club newsletter. The paid writing business is a voracious consumer of your time and energy. Launching your career into orbit takes tremendous quantities of your time and energy.

You must push virtually everything else aside for the first few years until you are consistently generating a comfortable income. Do not, however, neglect your spouse and your children. They are your most precious assets, far more dear than any career.

Here is another pitfall: substandard management of your time; e.g., misplaced priorities, using $50-an-hour time to do $10-an-hour work, doing errands you can delegate to your spouse or children or gofers.

Do not reinvent the wheel. Remember the timeless words of top speaker Joe Charbonneau: "If you want to be a master, study what the masters have done before you. Learn to do what they have done and have the guts to do it and you will be a master too."

The next pitfall is failing to target market. Instead, do this: Focus on markets you enjoy serving, markets that need your help and your guidance, markets that can pay your fee, markets that can be identified and contacted, and markets that recognize and welcome your value.

The final pitfall is this: allowing anyone or anything to drain your energy. Joe Charbonneau put it this way: "People are either the wind in your sails or the anchor on your tails." Fire those people and conditions out of your life. Shun everything and every person that drains your energy and soaks up your time with no reciprocal value. Be relentlessly disciplined—a benevolent dictator.

PARTING THOUGHTS: 19 TIPS FOR A SUCCESSFUL FREELANCE CAREER

Here are 19 sound strategies for succeeding as a freelance writer, reprinted courtesy of the American Writers & Artists Institute:

1. Do more research than everyone else.

2. Understand the product and the prospect.

3. Write intelligently with well-organized, well-integrated themes.

4. Ask insightful questions of your clients and potential prospects.

5. Study what your client's competition is doing.

6. Remain open and flexible to comments.

7. If you have a strong belief about your copy, articulate it at both the concept stage and draft stage.

8. Be an advocate for the prospect. Push the client to find out what more you can give the prospect to make them buy. Try to increase the average sale.

9. Don't write with any preconceived notions.

10. Build up a network.

11. Make no enemies.

12. Always go out of your way to help people out.

13. Start by getting an in-house job for a crazy and creative company (a marketing company, not an ad agency)—somewhere where you are learning from the experts and where you can become part of a marketing team to learn the big picture.

14. Foster your contacts with quick notes of thanks. Or if you see an article or something that might be of interest to them, send it with a brief note.

15. Treat every project with equal weight. Doing good work and being consistent creates momentum.

16. Tell everyone you meet you're a writer.

17. Do more than what's asked of you.

18. Document all facts, claims, and statistics in your copy.

19. Never miss a deadline.

Notes

Chapter 1. Do You Really Want to Be a Writer?

Angell, Roger, "Andy," *The New Yorker*, February 24, 2005, p. 142.

Collins, Billy, *Nine Horses* (Random House, 2002), p. 6.

Heller, Joseph, *Portrait of an Artist, as an Old Man* (Simon & Schuster, 2000), p. 160.

James-Enger, Kelly, *Six-Figure Freelancing* (Random House, 2005), p. 3.

Matlack, Jennifer, "Healing Power of Writing," *Reader's Digest*, undated, p. 204.

Chapter 3. The Self-Confident Writer

Ray Bradbury quote from www.raybradbury.com, August 29, 2002.

"Writing Skills Matter on the Job," *Record*, September 22, 2004.

Chapter 4. Money and the Freelance Writer

Young, Jordan, *How to Become a Successful Freelance Writer* (Anaheim, California: Moonstone Press, 1981).

Chapter 5. The Freelance Writer's Business Plan

Brzozowski, Carol, "Freelancing and Raising Kids," *Freelance Writer's Report*, February 2005, p. 3. Reprinted with permission.

Chapter 6. Entry-Level Assignments to Get You Started

Frohn, Joyce, "Making It in the Minors," *Writer's Digest*, March 2005, p. 61.

Chapter 7. Magazine Articles: The Writer's Bread and Butter

Bruno, Darla, "Editorial Freelancing," *Freelance Writer's Report*, July 2005, p. 2. Reprinted with permission.

Campbell, Carolyn, "Queries on the Quick," reprinted with permission.

Cossens, Laura, "Put Your Best Clips Forward," *Writer's Digest*, August 2005, p. 13. Reprinted with permission.

Dark, Sandra, "Fit Like a Glove," *Writer's Digest*, August 2005, p. 52. Reprinted with permission.

Chapter 8. Marketing and Self-Promotion for Writers

Huff, Dianna, "How to Syndicate Your White Papers," Marketing Sherpa.

Sentient Publications, "What an Author's Friends Can Do" and "Publicity Strategies You Need to Know."

Chapter 13. Maximizing Your Personal Productivity

Brzozowski, Carol, "Freelancing and Raising Kids, *Freelance Writer's Report*, February 2005, p. 2.

Chapter 15: Writing Short Fiction

Ellison, Harlan, series of columns, reprinted with permission of the author.

Chapter 17: Writing and Selling the Personal Essay

Levine, Beth, "Take Your Experience and Give It a Universal Twist," *The Writer*, February 2002, p. 24.

Chapter 18. Growing Your Business

Miles, Susan, "How to Weather Those Writing Slumps," *Freelance Writer's Report*, May 2005, p. 1.

Newman, Will, "8 Steps to Finding Your First Clients," *The Golden Thread*, July 5, 2005.

Palmer, Parker, *Let Your Life Speak* (Jossey-Bass, 2000), p. 107.

Chapter 19. Making Your Writing Dreams Come True

"20 Tips for a Successful Freelance Career," American Writers & Artists Institute, "Getting Clients Workshop," 2004.

Dubin, Burt, "7 Keys to Getting Started in the Speaking Business," email newsletter, July 5, 2005.

Appendices

Appendix A: Books

Asimov, Janet, and Asimov, Isaac, *How to Enjoy Writing* (Walker and Company, 1987).

Barzun, Jacques, *Simple and Direct* (Quill, 2001).

Bly, Robert, *The Copywriter's Handbook*, Third Edition (Henry Holt, 2006).

Bly, Robert, *The White Paper Marketing Handbook* (Thomson, 2005).

Brennan, Thomas, *Writings on Writing* (Barnes & Noble Books, 1994).

Bunnin, Brad, and Beren, Peter, *The Writer's Legal Companion: The Complete Handbook for the Working Writer* (Perseus Books, 1998).

Camenson, Blythe, and Cook, Marshall, *Your Novel Proposal from Creation to Contract: The Complete Guide to Writing Query Letters, Synopses, and Proposals for Agents and Editors* (Writer's Digest Books, 1999).

Flynn, Nancy, *The $100,000 Writer: How to Make a Six-Figure Income as a Freelance Business Writer* (Adams Media, 2000).

Glatzer, Jenna, *Make a Real Living as a Freelance Writer: How to Win Top Writing Assignments* (Nomad Press, 2004).

Kopelman, Alice, *National Writer's Union Guide to Freelance Rates & Standard Practice* (Writer's Digest Books, 1995).

Layton, Marcia, *The Complete Idiot's Guide to Terrific Business Writing* (Alpha Books, 1996).

Poynter, Dan, *The Self-Publishing Manual: How to Write, Print, and Sell Your Own Book* (Para Publishing, 1999).

Shaw, Eva, *Ghostwriting* (Paragon House, 1991).

Van Laan, Krista, and Julian, Catherine, *The Complete Idiot's Guide to Technical Writing* (Alpha Books, 2001).

Venolia, Jan, *Write Right!* (Periwinkle Press, 1980).

Vos Savant, Marilyn, *The Art of Spelling* (W.W. Norton, 2000).

Writer's Digest Handbook of Making Money Freelance Writing (Writer's Digest Books, 1997).

Young, Jordan, *How to Become a Successful Freelance Writer* (Moonstone Press, 1981).

Zinsser, William, *On Writing Well* (Quill, 2001).

Appendix B: Websites

www.bitpipe.com

Online syndicator of white papers; if you write white papers; you can check for and download competitor white papers on your topic here.

www.writingformoney.com

Online newsletter on how to succeed as a freelance writer.

www.aar-online.org

If you are looking for an agent who doesn't charge fees, check out the list of member agents and their areas of specialty.

www.yudkin.com

Marcia has a great site on how to make more money as a writer and sell more of what you write.

www.awoc.com

Besides the free newsletter, freelance writers will find moneymaking tips.

www.freelancewrite.about.com

Links to resources relating to jobs, business writing, contracts, and grant writing.

www.parapublishing.com

Maintained by Dan Poynter, the king of self-publishing. Provides extensive information on self-publishing and promotion.

www.writerswrite.com

Comprehensive site offering *The Internet Writing Journal* magazine; research tools; and links to writing seminars, organizations, and contests. Offers 562 paying markets.

www.writers.net

Links to writers, editors, and writing resources.

www.coffeehouseforwriters.com

Provides community forum for critiques, online workshops, and resources.

www.asja.org

American Society of Journalists and Authors. A professional association for freelance writers.

www.writersweekly.com

The largest-circulation freelance writing ezine on the Internet. *Writers Weekly* is a free ezine packed with paying writing opportunities, writers' warnings, and ebooks that will make you a successful writer.

filbertpublishing.com

Writing, Etc. is the free ezine that will make your writing sparkle, help you write killer queries, and get you on the road to publication.

writersmarket.com

Writer's Market is a database giving you access to thousands of magazines that can purchase your writing.

groups.yahoo.com/group/workforwriters

A list (forum) for writers to find leads for jobs and assignments.

www.writingfordollars.com

Writing for Dollars, a bimonthly ezine, has writing tips and information on paying markets that will purchase your writing.

www.worldwidefreelance.com

This monthly email newsletter focuses on non-U.S. markets. A brief summary is provided for each listing.

www.journalistusa.com

Online directory of editorial and production staff, used by publishers and editors looking to hire new freelance talent.

www.thewriterslife.com/bobrecommends

Accelerated Program for Six-Figure Copywriting—course on writing direct response copy.

www.theromancewriterslife.com/bobrecommends

Writing for Love & Money—course on how to write and sell your romance novel.

www.makepeacetotalpackage.com/products/3150554_EasyWriters Club.html

EasyWriters Marketing Club—Clayton Makepeace's membership program on how to make money as a freelance direct response copywriter.

www.thetravelwriterslife.com/bobrecommends

The Ultimate Travel Writer's Course—course on freelance travel writing.

Appendix C: Software

Writing Software at a Glance

Title	Platform	Price	Website
Character Pro	Win	$70	www.characterpro.com
Dramatica® Pro	Win, Mac	$269	www.write-bros.com
Enfish	Win	$50	www.enfish.com
Final Draft	Win, Mac	$229	www.finaldraft.com
Final Draft AV	Win, Mac	$129	www.finaldraft.com
LifeJournal	Win	$40	www.lifejournal.com
Microsoft Word	Win, Mac	$229	www.microsoft.com
Movie Magic® Screenwriter	Win, Mac	$249	www.write-bros.com
enLighter	Win	Free	www.n-liter.com
Personal Knowbase	Win, Mac	$179	www.bitsmithsoft.com
Power Tracker™	Win	$129	www.write-brain.com
Power Writer™	Win	$99	www.write-brain.com
Storybase	Win	$80	www.storybase.net
StoryCraft Pro	Win	$200	www.writerspages.com
StoryView™	Win	$30	www.write-bros.com
TextAloud MP3	Win, Mac	$295	www.textalound.com
Truby's Blockbuster	Win	$33	www.truby.com
What's the Rule?	Win, Mac	$35	www.whatstherule.com
Word Menu	Win, Mac	$149	www.wordmenu.com
Writer's DreamKit™	Win, Mac	$38	www.write-bros.com
WriteItNow	Win, Mac	$10-$40	www.ravensheadservices.com

Appendix D: Organizations

American Medical Writers Association
160 Fifth Avenue, Suite 625
New York, NY 10010
(212) 645-2368

American Writers & Artists Institute
245 NE 4th Avenue, #102
Delray Beach, FL 33483
(561) 278-5789
www.awaionline.com

Direct Marketing Club of New York
224 Seventh Street
Garden City, NY 11530
(516) 746-6700

Education Writers Association
2122 P Street NW, #201
Washington, DC 20037
(202) 452-9830
www.ewa.org

Florida Freelance Writers Association
CNW Publishing, Editing & Promotion, Inc.
PO Box A
North Stratford, NH 03590
(603) 922-8338

International Association of Business Communicators
One Hallidie Plaza, Suite 600
San Francisco, CA 94102
(415) 544-4700
www.iabc.com

National Association of Science Writers
PO Box 890
Hedgesville, WV 25427
(304) 754-5077
nasw.org

National Mail Order Association
2807 Polk St. NE
Minneapolis, MN 55418-2954
(612) 788-1673
www.nmoa.org

National Writers Union
113 University Place, 6th Floor
New York, NY 10003
(212) 254-0279
www.nwu.org

Outdoor Writers Association of America, Inc.
121 Hickory Street, #1
Missoula, MT 59801
(800) 692-2477

Self-Employed Writers and Artists Network
PO Box 175
Towaco, NJ 07082

Society for Technical Communication
901 N. Stuart St., Suite 904
Arlington, VA 22203
(703) 522-4114
www.stc.org

Society of American Travel Writers
1500 Sunday Drive, #102
Raleigh, NC 27607
(919) 861-5586

About the Author

Bob Bly, age 49, has been a professional writer since 1979 and a full-time freelance writer since 1982. His annual gross income from freelance writing is more than $600,000, and he became a self-made multimillionaire while still in his 30s—solely from freelance writing (he has no trust fund and his wife is a full-time homemaker).

Bob is the author of more than 100 articles and 70 books, including *The "I Hate Kathie Lee Gifford" Book* (Kensington), *The Ultimate Unauthorized Star Trek Quiz Book* (HarperCollins), and *Make Every Second Count* (Thomas Nelson), a collection of his essays.

Mr. Bly's articles have appeared in such publications as *Amtrak Express*, *Computer Decisions*, *Cosmopolitan*, *City Paper*, *Science Books & Films*, *The Money Paper*, *The Parent Paper*, *Successful Meetings*, *Bits & Pieces for Salespeople*, *New Jersey Monthly*, and *Writer's Digest*. Bob writes regular columns in *Early to Rise*, *DM News*, *Writer's Digest*, *Internet Marketing Review*, and *Subscription Marketing*. His monthly ezine, *The Direct Response Letter*, reaches over 70,000 subscribers. Bob has been a featured speaker at writers' conferences nationwide.

Mr. Bly has held a number of writing-related jobs. He was a technical writer for Westinghouse Electric Corporation and a marketing communications manager for Koch Engineering. As a freelance copywriter, he has handled writing assignments for dozens of corporations, including AT&T, IBM, ITT, Value Line, Medical Economics, and Chemical Bank.

Questions and comments on *Getting Started as a Freelance Writer* may be sent to:

Bob Bly
Copywriter
22 E. Quackenbush Avenue
Dumont, NJ 07628
Phone: (201) 385-1220
Fax: (201) 385-1138
Email: *rwbly@bly.com*
Website: *www.bly.com*

Sentient Publications, LLC publishes books on cultural creativity, experimental education, transformative spirituality, holistic health, new science, and ecology, approached from an integral viewpoint. Our authors are intensely interested in exploring the nature of life from fresh perspectives, addressing life's great questions, and fostering the full expression of the human potential. Sentient Publications' books arise from the spirit of inquiry and the richness of the inherent dialogue between writer and reader.

We are very interested in hearing from our readers. To direct suggestions or comments to us, or to be added to our mailing list, please contact:

SENTIENT PUBLICATIONS, LLC

1113 Spruce Street
Boulder, CO 80302
303.443.2188
contact@sentientpublications.com
www.sentientpublications.com